Stage Fright, Animals, and Other Theatrical Problems

D1423960

Why do actors get stage fright? What is so embarrassing about joining in? Why not work with animals and children, and why is it so hard not to collapse into helpless laughter when things go wrong? In trying to answer these questions – usually ignored by theatre scholarship but of enduring interest to theatre professionals and audiences alike – Nicholas Ridout attempts to explain the relationship between these apparently unwanted and anomalous phenomena and the wider social and political meanings of the modern theatre. The book focuses on the theatrical encounter – those events in which actor and audience come face to face in a strangely compromised and alienated intimacy – arguing that the modern theatre has become a place where we entertain ourselves by experimenting with our feelings about work, social relations and about feelings themselves.

NICHOLAS RIDOUT is Lecturer in Performance at the School of English and Drama, Queen Mary, University of London.

Theatre and Performance Theory

Series Editor

Tracy C. Davis, *Northwestern University*

Each volume in the Theatre and Performance Theory series introduces a key issue about theatre's role in culture. Specially written for students and a wide readership, each book uses case studies to guide readers into today's pressing debates in theatre and performance studies. Topics include contemporary theatrical practices; historiography; interdisciplinary approaches to making theatre; and the choices and consequences of how theatre is studied; among other areas of investigation.

Stage Fright, Animals, and Other Theatrical Problems

Nicholas Ridout

CAMBRIDGE
UNIVERSITY PRESS

CAMBRIDGE UNIVERSITY PRESS
Cambridge, New York, Melbourne, Madrid, Cape Town,
Singapore, São Paulo, Delhi, Tokyo, Mexico City

Cambridge University Press
The Edinburgh Building, Cambridge CB2 8RU, UK

Published in the United States of America by
Cambridge University Press, New York

www.cambridge.org
Information on this title: www.cambridge.org/9780521617567

First published 2006

A catalogue record for this publication is available from the British Library

ISBN 978-0-521-85208-1 Hardback
ISBN 978-0-521-61756-7 Paperback

Contents

Acknowledgements

Colleagues in the Research Seminar of the Department of History of Art and Contextual Studies at Wimbledon School of Art created a space of genuine intellectual conversation and investigation in which elements of this project were conceived. Fred Orton and Gail Day, in particular, challenged and encouraged me to get serious.

The School of English and Drama at Queen Mary, University of London has been a congenial and supportive environment for the kind of work that I enjoy. Colleagues in Drama have all contributed in individual ways to making this work a pleasure to do. Maria Delgado's personal and practical support, in particular, has been invaluable.

The work of Societas Raffaello Sanzio has encouraged me to rethink the meaning and the nature of theatre in ways that continue to astonish me. For their work, their friendship and their hospitality I am particularly grateful to Gilda Biasini, Claudia Castellucci, Romeo Castellucci and Chiara Guidi.

I am especially grateful to Tracy Davis for giving this book a home in her series, and for the clarity and wisdom of her editorial advice. I am indebted, too, to Victoria Cooper and Rebecca Jones at Cambridge University Press for their expert guidance at every stage in its preparation.

Steve Connor read and responded with characteristic generosity to each successive development of this project. Alan Read offered enthusiasm, provocation and dialogue on some of its central concerns. Sophie Nield offered her critical judgement at a crucial stage and has been a constant source of intellectual solidarity. Nicholas Till – who bears some initial responsibility for getting me into the profession of thinking, teaching and writing – has contributed far more than he imagines. Shelley

Trower has read, heard and talked through this work and has been sensitive and steadfast in her support and encouragement. Bridget Escolme has been an inspiration from the beginning and our conversations over many years are part of the foundations of this work. In Joe Kelleher I found, during the course of this work, a friend and collaborator who has made going to the theatre, as well as thinking and talking about theatre, seriously pleasurable.

Introduction

Alas! That first matinée was to prove a bitter disappointment.[1]

The boy Marcel, narrator of Proust's *Remembrance of Things Past*, goes to the theatre for the first time. He is to see a performance of Racine's *Phèdre*, given by Berma, the greatest actress of the day.[2] He is attending the theatre against the advice of his doctor, who predicts that his illness will be exacerbated, and therefore that he will 'in the long run derive more pain than pleasure from the experience'.[3] His parents, who had previously forbidden him to attend, have relented, his mother saying "'Very well, we don't want to make you unhappy – if you think you will enjoy it so very much, you must go"'.[4] This situation causes him great anxiety: he does not wish to distress his mother by going to the theatre when she would rather he didn't. Even as it becomes clear that he is to go, and that his mother genuinely wants him to enjoy himself, his anxiety barely abates, since 'this sort of obligation to find pleasure in the performance seemed to me very burdensome'.[5]

But as the day of the performance dawns his joyful excitement at the prospect ahead of him overwhelms his anxiety, and he is full of pleasurable sensations. His pleasure increases once he has taken his seat. The theatre itself, the fact that he enjoys an unobscured view, the sounds of last minute preparations behind the lowered curtains all contribute to this pleasure. Even once the curtain has risen to reveal 'a writing desk and a fireplace' he continues to enjoy the experience. But what happens next induces a feeling of 'momentary uneasiness'. Two men appear on stage and start arguing loudly, and only gradually does Marcel realise that 'these insolent fellows were the actors'.[6] After what turns out to have been the curtain-raiser, there is an interval, during which the audience displays impatience and people start to stamp their feet, provoking in Marcel the terrible fear that this bad behaviour will be rewarded by a bad performance by the actress Berma, in whom he has placed great hopes of a transcendent artistic experience, beyond pleasure, of truth. As the performance of *Phèdre* begins, Marcel enjoys 'the last moments of my pleasure'. The opening scenes of the play do not involve Phèdre herself, so the entrance of the great Berma will be delayed a while. Yet, the first woman to step on stage bears a remarkable resemblance to Berma, as, indeed, does the second. While dealing with his confusion, Marcel appreciates their performances, until the entry of a third woman. This really is Berma. Attuned to hang on her every word, breath and gesture, Marcel is confounded by the reality of her performance. Her famous declaration of her love for Hippolyte – the speech for which he has mentally prepared himself – is delivered in a 'uniform chant', the great actress failing to find in the speech the contrasts which 'even the pupils of an academy'[7] would not have failed to discover and communicate. As he becomes aware of the 'deliberate monotony' with which she has delivered the speech, he is suddenly caught up in the audience's 'frenzied applause' and starts to understand what seems to be a rule of the actor-audience relationship: 'the more I applauded, the better, it seemed to me, did Berma act'.[8] But all the applause cannot dispel his sense of disappointment:

Nevertheless, when the curtain had fallen for the last time, I was disappointed that the pleasure for which I had so longed had not been greater, but at the same time I felt the need to prolong it, not to relinquish for ever, by leaving the auditorium, this strange life of the theatre which for a few hours had been mine, and from which I would have torn myself away as though I were being dragged into exile by going straight home, had I not hoped there to learn a great deal more about Berma from her admirer M. de Norpois, to whom I was indebted already for having been permitted to go to *Phèdre*.[9]

The experience of this theatre-goer, then, is one in which anticipation gives way to disappointment, in which pleasure is bound up with anxiety and even perhaps pain and illness, in which acting is confused with a vulgar interruption, in which the transcendent possibilities of the world's greatest dramatic poetry appear to pass by almost unnoticed in a 'deliberate monotone', and success appears as dependent upon the audience as it is upon the artistic capability of the actor. Yet for all this, for all the confusion, anxiety and disappointment, it is an experience which he cannot bear to bring to an end, and to which he will repeatedly seek to return.

It is this confusion – of attraction and repulsion, compulsion and disappointment – experienced in the modern theatre, that is the principal subject of this book. I offer Marcel's experience of the modern theatre as emblematic of a more general and familiar experience of theatre in modernity. By modernity here I am referring to the phase in our history inaugurated by the industrial revolution in Europe, characterised by technological progress at the service of capitalist growth, in which the city is the centre of economic and political power. It is a modernity in which the theatre is shaped by new patterns of economic production, and, in particular, by the organised and pervasive division between work and leisure. As a place where work and leisure meet – in the forms of the actor and the audience – the theatre is perhaps inevitably going to be a place where there is a little doubt as to what is supposed to happen when producers and consumers come face to face.

Marcel's experience of this encounter is one of pleasure attended by pain, of uncertain satisfactions and contradictory impulses: an experience, in short, of what Jonas Barish calls – in a book dedicated to the theory and practice of theatre-hating – an 'ontological queasiness'[10] associated with the theatre. In the modern theatre, as exemplified by Marcel's experience, this 'ontological queasiness' seems to be at the heart of the matter: he doesn't know whether he wants to 'be' there or not, and he is not sure who anyone else is 'being' there. Of course, as Barish frequently shows, much 'theatre-hating' turns out to be a conflicted kind of love.

This ambivalence certainly characterises my own relationship with the theatre. Theatre, being queasy, makes me queasy. That such queasiness is widespread, that we find theatre uncomfortable, compromised, boring, conventional, bourgeois, overpriced and unsatisfactory most of the time, is I think not only generally accepted as true, but also generally accepted as part and parcel of the whole business. Theatre's failure, when theatre fails, is not anomalous, but somehow, perhaps constitutive. What

I want to argue here is that it is precisely in theatre's failure, our discomfort with it, its embeddedness in capitalist leisure, its status as a bourgeois pastime that its political value is to be found.

Theatre is a privileged place for the actual experience of a failure to evade or transcend capital. A performance of Racine's *Phèdre*, for example, fails to transport the spectator from the reality of his modern life, because it is, of course, part of modern life, part of capital. It is for this reason, above all, that the theoretical and artistic practices that have developed in a critical relationship to the theatre, often linked to the profession of performance, while of enormous value to an artistic and critical thinking that seeks to oppose or resist capital, neither can nor should leave behind altogether the practice and the institutions of theatre. If the promise of performance is to have redemptive force in this context, it has it only in so far as it remains in dialectical tension with the theatre that it constantly seeks to transcend. If performance and performance studies are committed – to varying degrees – to acts of ideological critique within capitalism, their claim as regards theatre is largely that they are more effective, that the challenge they offer to prevailing codes, values and oppressions is fiercer, more immediate and ultimately, more of a challenge.

What theatre perhaps does, within the formulation I am sketching out here, is to hide and to reveal both the oppressions and the challenges. It is in the imperfections (several of which are the key topics of this study) of its miming of the ideological structures of a given social organisation that theatre, perhaps, almost inadvertently, or with a coy slyness, discloses the weaknesses and blind spots in its own structures. Theatre is guilty, and knows it, while performance still makes some claim to innocence. In the decrepit, marginal, artificial and commodified institution that is the modern theatre you perhaps have to look much harder and with greater ingenuity for your resistance or your challenge, than you do in the more explicitly oppositional, self-consciously antibourgeois terrain of performance. Part of the thesis of this book is that such hard looking and ingenuity may be rewarding, and that the disclosure of guilty secrets in the theatre is an important complement to the invention of new public truths in performance. I therefore hope to show, in the section that follows, how a theoretical approach to theatre might be reconstituted from the heart of a discourse – the discourse of performance – that appears to promise that it might be possible to move beyond it.

From the promise of performance to the return of theatre

This promise of performance appears to have had three almost simultaneous foundational moments. If performance has developed its own historiography it almost certainly rests upon the theoretical assumption that these three moments may be understood as part of the same project. The first moment might be broadly defined as the emergence of theatrical or other practices that explicitly reject, oppose, expose or move beyond the framework of theatre – the term 'performance art' is often used to name these practices. The second would then be the moment at which these and other practices (from snake rituals to park ranger presentations, via the Brooklyn Academy of Music) start to be addressed from the interdisciplinary perspectives of performance studies, and no longer from within categories developed for appreciation of autonomous aesthetic production such as painting or drama. The term 'performance studies' is often used to describe these critical approaches. A third moment may be located in the emergence of 'theatricality' as a key (and negative) term in the understanding of certain post-modern art practices.

If this third moment has become inextricably (and perhaps accidentally) linked to the name Michael Fried,[11] the second is equally, if not more strongly bound, to the name Richard Schechner.[12] For the 'Fried' moment, theatre is not art enough, while for the 'Schechner' moment, art itself is not enough.[13] The relationship of many of the makers of 'performance art' to the idea of theatre might be summarised as, 'I can't name my practice, but I know it is not theatre', an expression of the fear that they can not be untheatrical enough (a sort of flipside of the 'Fried' moment). In fact, the antitheatricality of much performance art, with its conventional insistence on the presentation of 'realness' rather than the representation of the real (or anything else),[14] finds a strong and contemporaneous echo in the seemingly antitheatrical theatre practices of Peter Handke, Richard

Foreman or even the later work of Samuel Beckett. The fact that all three of these antitheatrical practices are so unavoidably theatrical in their engagement with the question of theatre may suggest that the strongest inflections of the antitheatrical prejudice are to be found within theatre itself.

If we are seeking to explain what is wrong with theatre, some avenues offer more fruitful exploration than others, and the focus of the present study reflects this. As I have suggested above, the disciplinary formation of performance studies, the 'Schechner' moment, makes no claim to address this problem at all directly, mainly because in its inclusion of theatre within the (arguably) broader category of performance, it seeks to address, in its own disciplinary interests, those things which link the various practices and institutions that constitute its field. Any investigation that looked too closely at what might be specific to theatre itself would risk undermining the viability of the field's self-definition, which depends upon knowing what theatre is like rather than what it might be in itself, in what its 'ontological queasiness' might consist. That is not to say that the consideration of theatre as such in the anthropological terms proposed by performance studies, especially in its inaugural 'Schechner' moment, does not yield considerable understanding. However, in seeking to establish what is wrong with theatre, a more historically and culturally specific approach is required, one which speaks of theatre at a particular moment and as a cultural institution in a particular historical and geographical location.

The present study concerns itself primarily with what we routinely understand theatre to be, in Western industrial or post-industrial modernity: a modernity in which Proust's Paris, 'the capital of the nineteenth century',[15] figures as the first great location. It is a theatre in which one group of people spend leisure time sitting in the dark to watch others spend their working time under lights pretending to be other people. It is a theatre that knows its own history, claims its place in the discourses of the arts, while acknowledging, with more or less good grace, its position in the economies of capitalist leisure.

Part of the argument advanced here is to suggest that what is wrong with theatre is most intensely and obviously wrong with *this* theatre and its sense of its own history; that aspects of theatre that have enjoyed, at least in their historiography, continued service from Athens in the fifth century B.C. to the present day, may have always been wrong, but certainly appear more wrong now. Indeed, this suggestion is in effect the condition of the present work's possibility, in that the wrongness of theatre is currently taking shape in a form that can be understood in terms of a specific relationship with the present historical moment. While it is hard to determine, for example, whatever one's suspicions, whether the meta-theatricality of Shakespeare, Corneille or Calderon might be a symptom of this wrongness or, rather, a signal that the theatre is (becoming) aware of something wrong with itself, it is possible to argue with some credibility that modern work articulating anxiety about its own form as its central subject matter (from Handke's *Offending the Audience* to Forced Entertainment's *First Night*) puts the question of theatrical undoing squarely on the table. Martin Puchner has done enormously valuable work on the aesthetic history of this tendency within modern theatre, showing convincingly that modernist theatre (from Wagner, through Joyce, Yeats and Stein, to Brecht and Beckett) offers a sustained 'resistance' to theatre and to theatricality as a value, and that in doing so, it performs acts of reform and rehabilitation in which theatre's 'wrongness' becomes the motive for experimental theatrical production.[16]

It is therefore to two significant texts that both make use of the term 'theatricality', but which are frequently used in support of the discourse of performance, that I now turn. Firstly, there are aspects of Michael Fried's arguments over literalist art that require elaboration. A second line of argument, Josette Féral's, more clearly associated with the emergence of performance as such, will complement and enlarge upon the opening made by Fried. What I am seeking to do in relation to both Fried's text and my subsequent discussion of Féral's essay, is to locate, somewhat against the apparent grain of these texts, an identification of theatre with a certain kind of unease, and, in that unease, a possible 'ontology' of theatre that might permit its reinstatement as a fruitful area of theoretical and political inquiry in spite of, if not because of, the cases made against it or the alternatives to it offered by the discourses of performance.

As generally understood, Fried's concerns over the work of artists such as Donald Judd and Robert Morris centre upon the fact that the work in question is not self-sufficient. It does not, as Fried claims the modernist painting he espouses does, absorb the viewer, permit her a moment of self-transcendence in contemplation of the work. Instead it forces the spectator to acknowledge what Robert Morris calls 'the entire situation',[17] 'including, it seems', as Fried notes, 'the beholder's *body*'.[18] In Fried's characterisation, then, the modernist work that he champions offers the possibility of a spectator who is all consciousness, who has vanished, as it were, from the scene of her own spectatorship, receded into the complete darkness of a non-existent auditorium the better to contemplate the wholly unsituated picture that is suddenly almost both subject and object of this act of contemplation or absorption. The work of the literalists against whom his critique is levelled, by contrast, insists upon the facts of co-presence in the act of spectatorship, either refusing or unable to evade them. The nature of this co-presence is what leads Fried to describe the experience of literalist art as possessing 'a theatrical effect or quality – a kind of *stage* presence'.[19] It is not possible to identify Fried's use of italics for emphasis in this essay with any programmatic intention, although the predominant effect is to call to mind or simulate the effects of spoken emphasis, to impart a certain intensity to the articulation of certain terms. It is interesting, nonetheless to note the emphasis given to the words 'stage' and 'body' in the development of this argument, as though the body were the last thing we might expect to find engaged in the aesthetic encounter, and as though the stage were a degraded place where presence is standing in for something far more serious (in this case, literally, absence, of course). Fried's rhetorical strategies aside (persuasive though they are), it is the awareness of one's body as a presence in a situation that seems to constitute the condition of theatricality in this argument. Theatricality functions here as a disturbance, almost uncanny, of the proper relations of the spectator to the art. Fried suggests that the encounter with the literalist art object is like an encounter with another human being, and one that appears to be intensely theatrical in its circumstances:

In fact, being distanced by such objects is not, I suggest, entirely unlike being distanced, or crowded, by the silent presence of another person;

the experience of coming upon literalist objects unexpectedly – for example, in somewhat darkened rooms – can be strongly, if momentarily, disquieting in just this way.[20]

The proxemics are inducing discomfort. Someone is too close or too far away, in a 'darkened' space, too. Where first Fried suggests that it is the awareness of oneself, of one's own body or *body* as part of 'the entire situation' that disrupts one's encounter with the work, it is now hinted that it is the intimation of an encounter with a 'silent' other that is 'disquieting'. This seems, wonderfully, to go right to the heart of the theatrical setup, where, one is tempted now to suggest, the encounter with another person, in the dark, in the absence of communication, is also an encounter with the self, and thus the occasion for all sorts of anxieties, anxieties that one might begin to discuss under headings such as narcissism, embarrassment or shame (as Chapters One and Two will do). What Fried objects to in the objects of Judd and Morris seems to be the way in which they subjectivise the spectator, turn the spectator into an audience that thinks too much of itself, that exposes itself somehow to its own gaze, that puts itself, improperly, upon the stage, in place of the work that was supposed to have engineered the transcendence of such categories altogether. The objects turn themselves into you, and you into them, and instead of a plenitude in oneness experienced in the moment of absorption, comes a constant to and fro, an unbecoming becoming, in which the action takes place in a kind of in-between, neither onstage nor off, accompanied by the rattle and clatter of unseemly machinery in the wings. In modernist abstraction, there are, of course, no wings.

Although this account of theatricality might seem, at first sight, to be the very antithesis of the theatrical set-up, in which the distinction between onstage and offstage, the work and its audience is supposed to be clear cut, in reality, because the people who are co-present to each other in the theatrical set-up are always alive, this kind of interchange, however embarrassing, however much we seek to avoid it, is always already there, built into the structure of 'the entire situation'. In this sense, then, Fried offers an account of theatricality that stresses distantiation and interaction over illusion and absorption, suggesting, I think very helpfully (and in almost complete accordance with the thinking of Bertolt Brecht), that the prevalent notion that theatricality can subsist under conditions of illusionism is an historical misunderstanding of the form. One implication of Fried's account of theatricality that does not seem to have been followed through in this context is the possibility that the absorption he sees in modernist painting is the partner (rather than some kind of paradigmatic replacement) of theatrical realism. By this account, both modernist projects (realism and American abstract painting) seek to eliminate the spectator from the set-up, to hide the full extent of 'the entire situation', in both the phenomenological sense intended by Fried and a further political sense (that economic and other power relations in the relationship between artist and audience are hidden by both realism and abstraction). It is in the tension between the pictorial values of illusionism (sustained by conditions of spectatorship in which the darkened auditorium becomes the norm) and the co-presence that had previously underpinned theatricality, that many of the present day symptoms of theatre's 'wrongness' manifest themselves. This is especially true in the case of stage fright, a modern phenomenon that will be examined in detail in Chapter One, but also has significant implications for the consideration of embarrassment and shame in Chapter Two. In seeking to avoid 'stage presence' Fried is sparing himself the fear and blushing that it invariably brings with it. At the same time he starts to offer a model of theatricality that begins to sound like plausible grounds for 'ontological queasiness'.

In apparently seeking to suggest some justification for Fried's position, Josette Féral offers what has become an influential description of performance as a practice that rejects its dependence upon the theatre. Féral's essay, 'Performance and Theatricality: The Subject Demystified'[21] is not only an early statement of what Jon McKenzie describes as the second phase of performance studies (after the so-called 'theory explosion'),[22] it is also the point at which European discourses around theatricality (especially those of late twentieth century French philosophy) intersect with the discourses of performance. It is in Féral's theorisation that performance is generally thought to emerge most suggestively as a redemption, or at least an escape from the fallen and degraded condition of theatre's theatricality. Féral proceeds from Fried's notorious claim that '[a]rt degenerates as it approaches the condition of theatre,' to suggest that performance achieves what Derrida maintains theatre cannot, namely, an 'escape from representation'.[23] Claiming that theatre cannot escape either representation or narrativity (the latter on the basis that 'all the current theatre experiences prove as much, except perhaps for those of Wilson and Foreman, which already belong to performance'[24]), Féral appears to accede to Fried's fierce exclusions.

However, in this accession there lurks a little doubt: not only are we working on the basis of a double conditionality – we must accept Derrida's account of theatre's inevitable entanglement with representation and also the empirical claim that all theatre is implicated in narrativity – we are also invited to ignore or exclude from theoretical consideration precisely that work which is perhaps most exemplary of the theatre of that moment: the theatre of Richard Foreman and Robert Wilson, on the odd grounds that it has already become part of performance. Féral's uncertainty, throughout her essay, over whether Foreman and Wilson are making theatre or performance already helpfully suggests that whatever clarity her justification of Fried may bring, it will be a clarity constructed, for the purposes of argument, rather than presented as definitive. While Féral is sometimes read as distinguishing performance (good and new) from theatre (old and bad), she is actually engaged in a much more subtle interplay between the two terms.[25] The redemptive promise of performance may be on offer, but it is by no means a certain bet.

To begin with, Féral's account of the relations between theatre and performance suggests something much more problematic and dialectical than the promise of redemption. Performance is simply not going to achieve, in the name of (modernist) art, the leap free from the degradation of theatre. Any such leap will carry with it something of the theatre, probably something more substantial than just the trace of sand on a long-jumper's shoes. Féral's suggestion of a practice that doth protest too much its own independence from theatre invites the question of whether performance's rejection of form and fixity in favour of 'discontinuity and slippage'[26] is in fact any different from Artaud's call for a theatre beyond representation. Already, performance seems to stand subject to the same critique of its self-proclaimed foundations as is developed by Derrida in relation to Artaud's theatre:

> That performance should reject its dependence on theater is certainly a sign that it is not only possible, but without a doubt also legitimate, to compare theater and performance, since no one ever insists upon his distance from something unless he is afraid of resembling it.[27]

The fact that performance is here characterised as being afraid of 'resembling' theatre suggests that the anxiety over mimesis (a possible philosophical root of the antitheatrical prejudice) is still very much in play in this relationship. As Féral suggests, there is most unlikely to be an anxiety over mimesis unless some kind of mimesis is at work. Instead of offering a theatre-performance relationship in which performance redeems theatre from its entanglement in mimesis, Féral presents performance as occupying a mimetic relation to theatre (even if that mimetic relationship may be one characterised by rivalry and a desire to kill). She then offers a sequence of (mainly) spatial metaphors in which the relation might be understood. In all of these metaphors what is striking, and enormously useful for the present study, is the way in which they emphasise the continuing operation of the apparatus of the theatre, its enduring appearance as a stage on which things, including things with faces, appear or come to light.

> Performance explores the underside of that [today's] theatre, giving the audience a glimpse of its inside, its reverse side, its hidden face.[28]

In particular, what this turning upside down, inside out or around achieves is a revelation of how the processes of representation work to produce subjects on stage, or rather, in this revelation that goes beyond the subjects that theatre would have appear, '[s]ubjects in process'. In Féral's experience, which one might suppose to be strongly shaped by responses to the work of Robert Wilson, it is a kind of slow motion theatricality that allows this revelation, and with it this turning and inverting of the space of the stage. The idea that theatre experiences a kind of inside-outing, which performance permits us to identify as such, will be an important strand throughout this work. The connection between subjectivity as process and this inside-outing is particularly important, and seems to be something that

theatre does, rather than performance. It is not that performance turns theatre inside out but that performance has allowed
us to notice that turning when we see it. Performance, then, is
neither theatre's redemption, nor its undoing. Theatre does its
own undoing.

That this is the implication of Féral's essay becomes clearer
still in her next spatial metaphor, in which she claims, in terms
that are specifically Derridean, that 'performance indicates
theatre's *margin*'.[29] As Féral explains, far from being something
excluded or other, the margin is that which in fact constitutes
'what is in the subject most important, most hidden, most
repressed, yet most active as well'.[30] Not only, then, is performance that which allows us to see theatre as itself, by showing it
turning itself inside out and revealing its operational guts, it is
also that which frames it up. It is both gut and skin, the core of
the business as well as its shop window. The margin, Féral
suggests, 'refers to' all those things in theatre that seem not to
be part of its theatricality, by which she means here, it seems, its
representation and its narrativity. In becoming aware of this
framing up we are invited to see what lies not outside the frame,
but beneath or within it, that which the frame is hiding. Again
performance, by being a margin, acts as an agent of revelation. If
it is operating redemptively here, it is a fierce and unforgiving
redemption in which theatre is compelled to face up to something deep within itself, and redeem itself in an act of self-
recognition rather than on the free ride of self-transcendence.
This redemption is no gift, more a straight talking-to.

Féral's final metaphor suggests that by means of this reference, this pointing to all those things that theatre would rather
not own up to, performance has opened up some kind of backstage space in which theatre can keep these things of darkness,
and feed off them:

Performance can be seen, therefore, as a storehouse for the accessories
of the symbolic, a depository of signifiers which are outside of established discourse and behind the scenes of theatricality. The theater
cannot call upon them as such, but, by implication, it is upon these
accessories that theater is built.[31]

Here we realise, I think, that performance was here all along,
and has not just arrived like a deus ex machina either to save

theatre's day or to put a stop to the whole sorry affair. It is only in our reluctance to face up to these things, to theatre's construction upon a set of unassimilable accessories, that has given performance's intervention upon the scene the quality of revelation. The search for what these vital accessories might be is one way in which this project could be described. I want to use as my first clue in this search the possibility that these 'accessories' lurking backstage (which turns out to be onstage if we perform the inside-outing Féral describes) may have something to do with the 'disquieting' nature of the (perhaps) human presence Fried finds in literalist art, as well as Barish's 'ontological queasiness'. The 'accessories', for the purposes of this book, are the apparently marginal or unwanted events of the theatrical encounter, that will turn out, of course, to be somehow vital to it: stage fright; embarrassment; animals; the giggles; failure in general.

In acknowledging the influence of Féral's work on the orientation of this project it is also worth noting a reverse proposition offered by Elin Diamond, who suggests that instead of performance appearing as theatre's repressed, it is the theatre that we might today understand as the repressed of performance.[32] Diamond's formulation is clearly a seductive one for the present project, in that it suggests the possibility of an analytical operation in which theatre can be returned. However, there is something about theatre, at least as it is conceived here, that resists the topography of depth implied by psychoanalysis. It would be tempting to follow Fredric Jameson and suggest that the aim of this project might be to bring to light the 'political unconscious' of performance and to name it theatre. But there is no unconscious in the theatre, at least from this vantage point. Everything is there, out in the open. The production is taking place here and now, and not in some incessantly revised and self-revising past. The backstage is part of the 'entire situation'. The events, encounters and phenomena that this study addresses are not hidden or hiding. On the contrary, they are 'in your face'. The accessories are in plain view. That they have largely been ignored until now is not, I think, symptomatic of any repression. These phenomena are perhaps so unavoidable, so intrinsic to the occasions and institutions of theatre that to talk about them at all would be to risk being thought stupid, banal, literal-minded, or worse: unprofessional. The experiences of being scared, embarrassed or overcome with giggles – along with other peculiar and significant affective states encountered in the theatre – have so far fallen outside the scope of theatre studies perhaps because they are thought of as the kind of things that the non-professional theatre-goer might take an interest in. In establishing itself as a discipline, in relation to any of its parents or elder siblings, such as rhetoric or literature or even history, the study of theatre has tended to emulate the operations of the older disciplines, looking for those aspects of the theatre that most readily make themselves available for the kind of critical and theoretical attention considered viable in the other disciplines. More recently, at least in Britain, the disciplinary anxiety has tended to arise most acutely over the supposedly vexed relations between theory and practice. Both the present valorisation of practice and the earlier anxiety about relations with the 'parent' discipline of English literature require the exclusion from professional study of those things that mere theatre-goers might find intriguing about their experience of the theatre. What seems to be at work here is an antitheatrical prejudice within the discipline of theatre studies itself, which seeks to distance itself from the (supposedly) naïve greasepaint fantasies of the amateur in order to legitimise itself as a bona fide discourse on aesthetics or history.

Kleist's *Über das Marionettentheater*

The theatre involves a face-to-face encounter. I have started to suggest already in this introductory chapter, what might be at stake in such an encounter, whether the stakes be social and political (relations between producers and consumers) or psychological and aesthetic (being made aware of oneself when trying to forget oneself). I have also started to show that such an encounter will always be compromised by its circumstances: there is no unmediated relation to be found in the theatre. This theory of the modern theatre as a constellation of bungled, missed or difficult encounters is not completely new. It is in fact inspired by an early nineteenth century text which I will explore in some detail in the pages that follow, as a way of explaining my choice of topics for the chapters that form the remainder of the book.

I want to try to construct a framework for the chapters that follow out of the materials of Heinrich von Kleist's *Über das Marionettentheater*, a short narrative in dialogue, written in 1810, a year before the author killed himself.[33] It is a dialogue in which a stage performer appears to argue for his own removal from the scene. Although Kleist's text is often taken to be promoting the perfection in grace that is only achieved by the puppet or the god, it may also be read as a subtle repudiation of such ambition, in favour of a theatrical practice that knows its own limits, sensing its own wrongness in the face-to-face encounters between any who fall between these two poles, for whom grace can only ever be an aspiration.

In the most famous passage of Kleist's essay (which is often the only one to be discussed, at least in relation to the practice of theatre) Herr C., a dancer at the opera, gleefully explains to his interlocutor (the unnamed narrator of Kleist's story) that simple puppets are capable of more refined and graceful movement than even the most highly trained virtuoso human performer. The advantage claimed for the puppet over the human is 'my dear fellow, a negative one, namely this: that it would be incapable of affectation'.[34] The absence of self-consciousness is the precondition of grace:

when consciousness has, as we might say, passed through an infinity, grace will return; so that grace will be most purely present in the human frame that either has no consciousness or an infinite amount of it, which is to say either in a marionette or in a god.[35]

That is to say, the human frame attains this state of aesthetic grace only by being inhuman. There's nothing wrong with theatre as such, it's just the people in it I can't stand.

In his account of Kleist's essay, Paul de Man notes that this

idea of innocence recovered at the far side and by way of experience, of paradise consciously regained after the fall into consciousness, the idea, in other words, of a teleological and apocalyptic history of consciousness is, of course, one of the most seductive, powerful and deluded topoi of the idealist and romantic period.[36]

One might extend this critique into a suggestion that the structure of this delusion also informs the antitheatrical positions adopted by both Michael Fried and the advocates of performance art's 'real'. The self-consciousness that follows 'the fall' involves, of course, representation. Things are no longer purely present to us in an unmediated stream of knowing, but appear as shadows and degraded simulacra. This post-lapsarian succession of stand-ins is a theatrical state of affairs. In seeking to move beyond or evade representation, then, performance artists like Marina Abramovic,[37] in their insistence on the 'real' are trying to achieve what Jean-François Lyotard calls, in an essay inspired, it seems, by Kleist's, 'pure, punctual presence',[38] a condition of oneness and absolute singularity, that might be compared to Fried's account of the experience of the viewer of modernist painting. In neither case is there anything but the thing present; there is not even the 'minimal temporal hold' of synthesis,[39] in which the apprehension by the self of the thing can register, and with it the apprehension of the self by the self. Lyotard himself recognises that the idea of this kind of unrepresented presence is 'problematic',[40] but wants to hold onto its possibility, even if it 'cannot be conceived, or experienced, or felt'.[41]

The logic of Lyotard's account of Kleist is that only in the complete absence of consciousness, and, with it, the capacity for the temporal synthesis that registers repetition, could this 'pure act' be experienced.[42] Kleist, therefore, in his presentation of this aspiration to grace, which Lyotard characterises as the aspiration 'to exemption from syntheses, forms, becomings, intentions and retentions, from repetition, in a word . . . to that unique pinch or that 'pinch' of the unique',[43] dramatises the impossibility of its realisation, the continual agony of being caught within this 'deluded topo[s]',[44] the experience of '[t]he impotence of holding to a material instant, the pain of an impossible sainthood'.[45] For artists like Abramovic, however explicit they may be about the impulse to move beyond the merely theatrical in search of a 'pinch' of the real, the reality of their work is closer to 'the pain of an impossible sainthood' than it is to the achievement of this inhuman grace.[46] The experience of pain and impotence (or at the very least an endless nagging frustration) involved in the attempt to move beyond representation will be a subtext in much of what follows, in this chapter and beyond, and will be resumed again in relation to what one might tentatively call Lyotard's theatrical aesthetics in Chapter

Four. For now, what matters is Lyotard's recognition that it is the exposure of the impossibility of realising the aspirations to inhuman grace that animates Kleist's text, rather than the rehearsal of the aspiration itself. As I shall argue below, it is the continued presence of the human on the scene of Kleist's stories that ensures that this is the case.

De Man, then, in arguing persuasively that Kleist's purpose is larger than the restatement of this familiar topos of the aesthetic ideology, observes that the essay 'is not composed as an argument but as a succession of three separate narratives encased in the dialogical frame of a staged scene'.[47] It is in the staging, and its rhetorics, that the apparent restatement of this topos is seen to undo itself. For de Man, Kleist's is one of a series of key texts in which the category of the aesthetic is shown, in the historical moment of its articulation, to be unstable, disarticulated. Like Kant's 'Third Critique'[48] and Hegel's 'Lectures on Aesthetics',[49] Kleist's essay 'is not an uncritical acceptance or use of the aesthetic for pedagogical or ideological purposes but rather a critique of the aesthetic as a philosophical category'.[50] Kant and Hegel famously require 'an adequate aesthetics' in order to ground their respective philosophical systems,[51] but in seeking to develop such an aesthetics, they, like Kleist, find themselves actually engaged in 'the undoing of the aesthetic as a valid category'.[52] De Man explicitly contrasts in his essay Kleist's vision with Schiller's famous instrumentalisation of Kant, in which he imagines the 'aesthetic state' in terms of a room of dancers engaged in patterned, systematic and harmonious action. For de Man, Kleist's troubled sequence of dialogic encounters vividly exposes the totalising violence of Schiller's vision. My own reading of Kleist shares with de Man this resistance to the aesthetic ideology, and a conviction that Kleist's text performs such resistance with considerable dexterity and grace. It also seeks to identify in the Kleist text not only those aspects of the text – especially those which I take to be most pertinent to a discussion of theatre – that seem to reveal how theatre might contribute to an 'undoing' of 'the aesthetic', as does de Man, but also the ways in which these moments might also point towards my own concern with the undoing of theatre.

The famous story of the puppets is followed by the narrator's own account of how a young man of my acquaintance had . . . by a chance remark lost his innocence before my very eyes and had afterwards, despite making every conceivable effort, never regained that paradise.[53]

Herr C. responds to this narrative with his story of the bear infallibly capable of distinguishing real fencing thrusts from feints. Both these narratives demand close reading, and in particular the kind of close reading that must be applied to staged scenes, in which attention has to be paid to figures who are visible but who do not speak. Far from simply reinforcing the conclusions drawn from the example of the puppet theatre, and lending weight thereby to the pseudo-conclusion of the essay itself, these additional narratives or scenes attach a troubling set of additional meanings, which are, in turn, highly suggestive as to what sort of critique of the category of the aesthetic Kleist might be offering.

The young man loses his innocence because he sees, in his own reflection in the mirror while drying his foot after bathing with the narrator, a resemblance to a sculpture they had both recently seen in Paris. The young man comments on this, and when the narrator (either to test the young man's grace or to combat his vanity) suggests 'he must be seeing things',[54] attempts to repeat the gesture to prove it, and fails. Thereafter

all his charms deserted him. An invisible and incomprehensible power seemed to settle like an iron net over the free play of his manners and a year later there was not a trace left in him of those qualities that had in the past so delighted the eyes of people around him.[55]

This scene may be the narrator's attempt to support the ostensible theme of the dialogue (innocence lost through self-consciousness, the fall into the symbolic order), but in opening his mouth on this subject at this stage in the proceedings, he is also exposing the presence of a subtextual commentary on theatre itself. In the first place, it is not, apparently, the young man's consciousness of his resemblance to the aesthetic object, nor yet his staging of resemblance for an audience, so much as his *repetition* of that resemblance for an audience, that destroys his graceful innocence. It is not the knowledge that you are doing something, or even doing something for an audience, it is the knowledge that you are repeating something which is the problem with theatre. Not only is repetition a pressing problem of technique – the reconciliation of the necessity of repetition with the equally exacting necessity of apparent spontaneity is what drove the thinking of both Diderot and Stanislavski – but it also points to the disquieting possibility that the activities required of a theatrical performer are more like those of any other worker (the repetitive development of a skill and its daily exercise for wages), than they are like those of the new bourgeois idea of the artist, whose work is supposed to be spontaneous and free from the disciplines of wage labour.

The nature of this performer's relationship with his audience adds a further dimension to this exposure. It is not just that the repetition of the gesture might be construed in terms of work, it is that this work may bear a peculiar dimension of erotic exploitation. The young man appears to be naked (such is the usual state of the kind of statue he suddenly sees himself resembling, and of people drying themselves after bathing) in the eyes of an older man with whom he has been taking a dip. This is in a scene that has already been introduced to us as belonging to the 'loss of innocence' genre. The scene is therefore inescapably erotic, even suggesting perhaps that some sexual act has already robbed the youth of his 'innocence'. The narrator's account of the scene, in which the moral is to do with the deadly consequences of seeing yourself as an aesthetic object, emerges instead, perhaps, as a strong misreading of an encounter in which the problem is more to do with the recognition of oneself (and others) as sexual and theatrical objects (and one's reiterability in the mise en scène of both desire and theatre). The sense that something improper has been going on is somehow compounded by the knowledge that the two have recently been in Paris together (and we all know what sort of things go on there), and by the sense that the relationship between them is that of teacher and student. The scene is strangely imbued not just with work and sex, but with power and its possible abuse. Why, for example, does the narrator deliberately provoke the repetition that he seems to know will destroy the youth's innocence? It is as though the narrator/audience has used superior social or economic power to call up a performance that he knows will damage the performer. The audience-performer relationship here is one of erotic exploitation, in which a young man with perhaps precocious talents (for aesthetic appreciation and catching the gaze of women) is put too soon upon the stage of repetition.

Even stranger still is the narrator's final observation on this episode, in which he testifies to the presence of a witness who saw it all and will corroborate 'word for word' the truth of the story.[56] This witness appears late on the scene, revealing what we thought must have been an intimate and probably erotic bathing experience to have been performed for an audience. The promise that this audience can repeat the scene 'word for word' further suggests that the scene figures as a staging, since a repeat performance is apparently guaranteed. The narrator's introduction of this witness may perhaps be motivated by some anxiety about the narrative's credibility. Perhaps the narrator thinks that Herr C. will be drawing the same conclusions about the strong misreading of a sex scene that I have advanced above, and brings in his witness as if to reassure that nothing inappropriate could possibly have happened. In doing so, of course, the narrator simply compounds the perversity of the scene, by unwittingly turning the sex act he was trying not to reveal to Herr C. into a sex act performed for an audience – an audience who will repeat the act, 'word for word' if called upon to do so by Herr C. The narrator who figured first for us as an audience to a scene of innocence lost, is revealed as an actor in a scene of innocence taken. Might Kleist perhaps be suggesting that the theatre audience is just such an actor, and that erotic exploitation is an inevitable part of the theatrical experience? Of course if puppets replace humans on stage this troubling relationship is happily avoided. Attention is necessary, then, to the possibility that Kleist may be talking more directly about theatre than he appears to be. Perhaps the reluctance to face up to this in most of the more well-known commentaries on this text, including de Man's, is just one further example of the way the antitheatrical prejudice functions.

Herr C. responds to the narrator's revelations about the sexual mise en scène involving himself, the young man and the witness, with a third narrative, and rather puzzlingly claims the narrator 'will soon see its relevance here'.[57] What follows is the story of how Herr C. first humiliates the son of Herr von G., by outfencing him, and is then led by Herr von G. and his sons 'to the wood store',[58] where he is to meet his match. Watched, we presume, by the boys von G. and their father, Herr C. finds that the bear is able to parry his every thrust and to identify his every feint.

The relevance is by no means clear, and Herr C. makes no attempt whatsoever to explain what the meaning of his anecdote might be. Instead, he moves directly to draw his pseudo-conclusion, on which this last anecdote has no obvious bearing. The glaring absence of any relevance within the terms of the pseudo-conclusion suggests that the relevance Herr C. is so confident the narrator will see must be found in other terms altogether. How, then, might the figure of the bear be relevant to the consideration of theatre that Kleist is half-invisibly conducting?

The animal is not doing something a human could do, only better. This is not a reiteration of the idea that the unselfconscious can do things the self-conscious cannot. The animal is doing something that is simply not possible. The animal seems to possess a knowledge that cannot be explained. The animal is not using this knowledge to be a better fencer than any human; it wields no foil but simply parries with its paw, and it is, in any case, tied to a post. It is an act, surely, a performance laid on by the family von G. for their own amusement. The spectacle is an inversion of bear-baiting, in which the bear baits the fencer for the entertainment of onlookers. Bear-baiting stands of course adjacent to the theatre, or even interpenetrates it, sharing the theatre space with the plays of Shakespeare, for example. Kleist seems to be inverting theatre's neighbour to say something about theatre.

The uncanny here is that the bear appears to recognise the difference between a real action and a pretend one. The bear knows what animals are not supposed to know: the difference between acting and being. Not only is this a knowledge animals are not supposed to have, it is, at least in this example, a knowledge that no human can possess either. The lack of such knowledge beyond this particular example would involve a more general inability to distinguish between the real and the feigned. The temporary acquisition of such inability is the precondition of theatre because the willingness to take the feigned for the real is what allows theatre to entertain. A supernatural knowledge that precludes such a deliberate self-deception excludes the bear from the pleasures of the theatre.

Two further features of the scene are peculiar, and both are to do with the way the man looks at the bear and the bear looks back. First, the narrator comments that 'the bear's seriousness discomposed me',[59] and then the bear is described as 'looking me in the eye' when it ignores the narrator's feints.[60] The bear's seriousness discomposes because it insists that this is not play, at least not for the bear. Presumably it is similar to the moment in the fencing match when one player looks into his opponent's eyes and sees that he intends to kill him for real and not just tap the spot on his chest to score the point. A moment at the end of *Hamlet*, for example. It discomposes also because the seriousness of the bear's look betrays the bear's ignorance that it is being exploited for the purposes of entertainment. The bear that knows the difference between acting and being, and therefore cannot ever appreciate the theatre, is unaware that its own utterly earnest self-defence is being 'matrixed' as performance.[61] This could be rephrased to show that what the bear can't distinguish is acting from acting (in the sense that to act is to feign action and the word act therefore always means its opposite). What looked at first like an inversion of bear-baiting turns out to be bear-baiting raised to another level. The bear turns into a machine, and the willed action of the bear's fencing partner is just a matter of pulling levers and ringing Pavlovian bells.

But that is not quite how the power relations are configured in this particular account. Here we must also take note of the worrying fact that the bear looks Herr C. in the eye 'as though he could read my soul in it'.[62] Herr C. confronts the fear that he has become an actor, whose outward show communicates an inner state. In a face-to-face confrontation with a bear presented first as antagonist, and then as fellow actor in a comedy for the von Gs to enjoy, he suddenly sees the bear as audience and he doesn't like it.

Meanwhile back in the framing narrative, Herr C., the professional performer who hates to be looked at by bears and who would like to see humans replaced on stage by machines, suddenly seems to fear that his own performance as storyteller has been less than convincing:

"Do you believe this story?"
"Absolutely!" I cried, applauding him in delight, "I should believe it from any stranger, it is so very likely. How much more so from you!"[63]

Herr C.'s sense of himself as performer is over-emphatically confirmed by the outbreak of applause. Applauding someone you are talking to strikes a deliberate false note. 'Nice show!' you are saying. Irony reigns. You turn your interlocutor into an actor. If someone is trying to persuade you that something is true, and you applaud, you are admiring the performance of persuasion rather than conceding the truth of that of which you are being persuaded. The narrator's phrase 'it is so very likely' is a highly unconvincing attempt to sound convinced. The tone suggests, 'very convincing. Not!' And why is this story, that is so convincing that he'd believe it from a stranger, still more convincing coming as it does from his acquaintance? This statement might perhaps make sense if read in an inversion conditioned by the irony of the narrator's applause. I wouldn't believe it from a stranger and I believe it still less coming from you, you creature of the stage!

'You will soon see its relevance.' The story of the bear is relevant, not to the pseudo-conclusion, but to the underlying investigation of the conditions of theatrical performance conducted by Kleist. Its relevance will be seen in terms of the conditions of seeing that obtain in the theatre. Conditions of sexual and economic exploitation that make it hard to look the theatre in the face without blushing. For the bear is the only figure in the narrative who seems to possess the capacity to look you straight in the eye. Herr C. and the narrator find this particularly difficult.

In addition to the narratives, the dialogic frame of Kleist's text 'abounds in stage business'.[64] De Man reads this choreography of glances, nods and snuff as emphasising 'the self-consciousness of the representational mode';[65] a way of alerting the reader to the fact that scenes of persuasion are being staged, and that we should pay attention to the mechanics of persuasion rather than fall for the idealist delusion of which the interlocutors appear to be persuading one another. But they are also scenes of scenes, that speak of staging as well as persuasion. While de Man's insight is to slip backstage to look at how the mechanics of persuasion are operating, his blindness, artfully enough staged for us of course, is perhaps not to see the story of theatrical self-disgust at work on the stage itself. Where de Man's quarry is the materiality of language itself, in Kleist's text (as the fact that eventually undoes all ideology), mine, perhaps easier to track, is the possible materiality of theatre in the same text, and what undoings might be achieved by way of an attention to the materially theatrical. Helmut J. Schneider helpfully suggests the purposes of such a reading, when he notes how Kleist's articulation of the idealist discourse of grace is sharply anti-idealist in its force. Kleist's essay, he writes,

> turns the value hierarchy of the classical discourse [on grace] upside down, or, more exactly, inside out. It questions the priority of the interior over the exterior, the spiritual over the corporeal, the meaningful over the accidental, the metaphor over the literal, the signified over the signifier, the soul or mind over the body.[66]

To the body and exteriority might be added the theatre and its economy. Consider, for example, the staging of the discussion about mechanical legs manufactured in England to allow amputees to dance:

> "I wonder," he said, as I looked down at the ground and was silent, "whether you have heard of the mechanical limbs that craftsmen in England make for people who have lost their legs?"[67]

Why is the narrator unable to look Herr C. in the eye at this point? And why, as the conversation continues, does this apparent signal of embarrassment transfer across to Herr C. himself?

> I remarked, in jest, that there he had found the man he was looking for. For a craftsman capable of making such a remarkable leg would without doubt be able to construct him a whole marionette to his requirements.
> "And what," I asked, since he himself now, rather taken aback, was looking down at the ground, "what exactly would you require of the skills of such a person?"[68]

As the nub of the issue apparently under discussion comes into view, with the possibility that the craftsman who makes mechanical legs might be able to manufacture a marionette capable of surpassing human performance skills, both men appear to be looking at their feet. Is there something embarrassing about the idea of the machine replacing the human? Are our heroes ashamed of the fantasy they are sharing?

What they seem to be avoiding is precisely that which the triumph of the non-human performer would abolish, and which the bear uncannily simulates: that moment in the theatre when the performer and the audience make eye contact, the mutual recognition of two humans as present to one another. They look at their feet to avoid the gaze that would acknowledge that they are engaged in a theatrical encounter. Only the bear can look you right in the eye.

In not looking at one another they are also overlooking something that the entire pseudo-argument of grace obtained by way of unselfconsciousness rather too visibly, in Kleist's mise en scène, overlooks. The puppets only achieve their transcendence of human gracelessness by means of human labour. It is precisely this question of labour, in the form of the craftsmen who make mechanical legs, that is coming into view at this point. The shared fantasy which occasions the embarrassment of the downcast gazes is the fantasy that a realm of human experience might be possible that does not depend upon human labour. The embarrassment is not at the content of the fantasy itself – the replacement of humans by machines – but at the sheer scale of self-delusion that the realisation of such a fantasy would entail. The abolition of labour.

Two abolitions in one, then: labour and eye contact. Might one suppose that the discomfort that occasions the downcast eyes of embarrassment is a discomfort that knows the relation between these two? That in the act of mutual recognition, two humans present to one another might also recognise the fact of labour as an unavoidable part of the human condition, even, or perhaps especially, in the moment at which their aesthetic fantasy would seem to depend upon the failure to recognise this material fact? It is certainly the case that once the issue of labour is raised in relation to Kleist's text, the relations between the humans and others within it take on a new aspect. For a start we find ourselves witnessing a dialogue between an amateur and a professional, in which the professional reveals professional secrets, but shrinks from addressing fully the extent of the human labour that might be involved in the perfection of his profession. Next the amateur (the narrator) figures himself as a professional, as the teacher of the young man. Finally Herr C. presents himself as the expert fencer who easily outperforms the young von G., but who meets his match at a site of labour: the wood store.

His match, though not human, seems to be tied, literally and metaphorically, to a role within human entertainment. One of the conventional distinctions that might be made between the entertainments of the circus and the bear-baiting pit on the one hand, and the bourgeois theatre on the other, is that the obvious commercialism of the former is precisely what the latter is seeking to escape in its embrace of the aesthetic as the terms upon which its place in society is to be properly understood. This attitude to the relations between the theatre of art and the merely commercial is exemplified in the narrator's surprise at having found the supposed artist, Herr C., apparently wasting his time on the vulgar form of the puppet-theatre, which is to be found, of course, in the marketplace, rather than within the presumably neoclassical space of the opera house. The fantasy of the aesthetic here is one in which the artist is presumed to be engaged in autonomous and unalienated exercise of his or her faculties, rather than working for wages in the entertainment industry.

One can easily indulge in the fantasy that the poet, the painter, or the composer, whose work is accomplished in your absence, might simply create art for its own sake. It is much harder to keep this delusion intact in the presence of workers who are doing their work in your presence. The prostitute who is both seller and commodity is emblematic of modern capitalism for Benjamin, because she makes visible the nature of the underlying economy. The moment you recognise the actor in similar terms, a certain awkwardness or embarrassment comes into the relationship. Of course, such embarrassment only really surfaces at moments of crisis, at which the reality of the economic relation is somehow precipitated into view. While some of an audience's unease when asked, say, by Annie Sprinkle, to inspect her cervix during a performance, is clearly related to the sexual politics of this particular encounter, the issue of Sprinkle's professionalism (as a former sex worker and in her present role as performance artist) is also clearly at stake here. Sprinkle is inviting her audience to realise and thus defamiliarise through their participation in this inspection, the underlying economic relationship of prostitute-client/performer-audience, and to see them in the same light, as relations conducted within the sphere of capitalist leisure industries.[69]

The unease of face-to-face encounters between producers and consumers, between professionals and amateurs, might then be one of the many highly symptomatic side effects of Kleist's critique of the aesthetic ideology, and a further indication of why the theatre might figure as an object of scorn or suspicion for those for whom the aesthetic remains a viable category. Perhaps the professional theatre's deep distaste for 'amateur dramatics' may be partially accounted for in terms of this unease: what is lacking in the performances of the 'amateurs' is precisely that which the professional would routinely seek to deny, namely 'professionalism'. That is to say, the only difference between amateurs and professionals is work. If amateurs were paid to do it they would have done enough of it to do it better, or rather, to do it professionally. The actor is not the spontaneous creative genius of the autonomous aesthetic realm, but a labourer in the same economy as everyone else.

In a text whose ostensible concern is the demonstration that the aesthetic can only be obtained through the transcendence of technique, the argument is made dependent on a theatrical mise en scène that undoes itself by systematically revealing that there is something improper and shameful in the theatrical apparatus, and that this impropriety and shame is somehow linked to labour. The aesthetic ideology is exposed as depending for its construction on a theatrical foundation, and upon human labour. In undoing itself, the mise en scène that is Kleist's argument undoes the aesthetic, by hinting, darkly, that similar structures might operate more widely than we would like to believe. The persistence of theatre is due, perhaps, to the peculiar pleasures that are taken when these undoings reveal themselves.

These pleasures are the subjects of the chapters that follow. The choice of these subjects, and the experiences that animate them, has been guided both by my own sense, in the theatre, that these are the distinctively theatrical experiences, and by the hints, derived from Kleist, that theatre is all about face-to-face encounters, that animals (and children) belong on the stage in ways that make strange our sense that it is an adult human business, that sexual and economic exploitation are always on the scene, and that, above all, it is when it goes wrong, falls short of grace, that theatre is most itself.

From an ethics of performance to an affective politics of theatre

So, to pick up the clues of queasiness and disquiet, I shall say again: there is something wrong with theatre. You watch it happening. You are there, and its 'hidden face' is in your face. You are one of the 'accessories'. The theatre is structured upon the face-to-face encounter, and it is around the ethical, aesthetic and political problems of such encounters that the wrongness of theatre appears and organises itself. The theatre does its work while you watch. In the theatre you always know you are there, at the scene of the action, at the site of production. Seeing yourself there, and others there, and facing up to the nature of your relationships with these others, is what disquiets the mind and degrades the art. Each of the core chapters of this study therefore examines a different instance of the face-to-face encounter.

In Chapter One, stage fright will be approached theoretically as a product of the highly compromised face-to-face encounters that take shape in European urban modernity, in which it is perhaps the absence of reciprocity in the encounter between professional and consumer that produces the pathology. Chapter Two considers the shame and embarrassment attendant upon expectations of reciprocity generated by the experience of direct address and face-to-face contact between actor and audience in the theatre. Chapter Three places the animal on stage, with the initial hope of moving towards a theatre in which these human face-to-face encounters can be eliminated by the extreme 'otherness' of the animal, but admits eventually that the animal on stage forces a politicisation of the face-to-face encounter in the recognition of the histories and politics of labour and its exploitation upon which the theatre operates. Chapter Four finds in the mutual collapse of helpless laughter shared between performer and audience, not an unproblematic community of mirthful faces, but a stupefying encounter with the other and with the self, that threatens the breakdown or collapse of the theatrical system. In each case, there is something going wrong between the faces.

All this talk of faces will bring to many lips the name of Emmanuel Levinas.[70] It is clear that Levinas's ethical philosophy has come to play a significant role in recent thought about the ethics of performance, and while I am generally sympathetic to this ethical turn in recent work on performance and theatre, the present work seeks to offer an account of the face-to-face encounter that is rather more compromised, by history, economics, and, above all, politics, than the purity of an ethics that is grounded in a recognition of the singularity of the other would appear to generate. For Levinas, it seems, the face is not actually any face in particular, but rather the figure of the pre-ontological possibility of an encounter between subjects. Face-to-face encounters in the theatre may carry something of the frisson of such an absolute alterity, but Levinas himself would surely be among the first to caution against the over-literal transfer of his own idea of the ethical face-off into the concrete particularities of a theatrical encounter. Not only are Levinas's faces abstracted from any historical or even onto-logical contingency, the ethics that he would derive from the face to face is an ethics that would refrain from authorising any specific moral or political programme. While there is certainly no intention here to authorise any specific political programme, I do want to resist an ethics without content. Not only are the faces I discuss actual or potentially real faces, worn by historical actors, with genders, class positions and so forth, but my own ethical positions (whether Levinas likes it or not) are shaped historically by my own gender, class position and so forth, as well as by affiliations and commitments to specific others to which and to whom I wish to remain faithful. The problem with Levinas, for one thus encumbered with pro-gramme, is that without some grounding in the concrete, his ethics would seem either to forbid anything (on the basis that any action relative to any potential other might be a violation of the relation of alterity), or to permit everything (on the basis that a rejection of any discursive act on the part of an other would be a violation of the relation of alterity). An ethics that does not permit the theatre-maker or spectator to make mean-ingful distinctions between, say, a performance by Guillermo

Gómez-Peña and a piece of racist propaganda would seem not
to be an ethics at all. Or to offer a less clear-cut example, an
ethics that does not allow me to experience intense physical and
political discomfort in the predicaments generated for audiences
by the work of Societas Raffaello Sanzio is an ethics that is too
far removed from concrete actualities to be of much daily use.
The theatre I am interested in most is a theatre that invites us
perversely to enjoy our ethical discomfort and to think politically
about the sources of such enjoyment. To some extent, the
implications of Levinas's thought, particularly in its phenomenological aspects, might permit precisely such an enjoyment.
As Simon Critchley suggests, the sensuous enjoyment and love
of life is the basis of subjectivity for Levinas:

Levinas's work offers a material phenomenology of subjective life,
where the conscious I of representation is reduced to the sentient I of
enjoyment. The self-conscious, autonomous subject of intentionality is
reduced to a living subject that is subject to the conditions of its existence. Now, for Levinas, it is precisely this I of enjoyment that is capable
of being claimed or called into question ethically by the other person.[71]

I would suggest, though, that it might only be in the self-conscious
and the intentional enjoyment of one's enjoyment (including
the enjoyment of discomfort) that a politics of the theatrical
face to face might be elaborated, and that even in this more
down-to-earth formulation, Levinas offers a thinking that is
too far removed from the contingencies encountered by actual
subjects with intentions to properly account for the experience
of theatrical affect (which, needless to say, was never one of
his intentions). The problem with the ethical turn in the study
of theatre and performance perhaps lies not so much with
Levinas's thought, but with the idea that anything substantial
by way of guidelines for the conscious encouragement of the
good life could be derived from it, or that it has anything to
say about the specific problems of theatre. Similarly, a 'material phenomenology', to use Critchley's term, might be the
basis for a fruitful examination of the ethics and politics of
performance, and, of course, theatre, but only so long as it is
a phenomenology that refuses the idealist 'bracketing out' of
the contingent.[72]
    What I then propose, through the examination of these differ-
ent instances of the face to face, is that a certain failure of

relation in this encounter lies at the heart of the theatrical experience. That is to say that when the promise of a direct face-to-face encounter between two human beings is made within the theatrical set-up, either the act of delivery or the act of collection is always compromised. While we look for something to take place in our presence, and thus to facilitate some kind of meaningful communication, we actually find that the circumstances – the material conditions, if you like – in which this encounter takes place compromise the moment and inhibits the communication. Something fails to take place amid what does take place. Across the footlights a human encounter produces stage fright, embarrassment, unseemly laughter or the absolute collapse of the communicating medium. There is an ineptitude or clumsiness in the relationship, a miscommunication or a dropped connection. Alan Read, in a book which takes the ethics of theatre's face-to-face encounter as one of its organising principles, notes of what he calls a 'lay theatre', a theatre, that is, that falls outside the conventional economies of theatrical production, that

it is not inept, but neither can it deny the reality that stares all theatre in the face. That when something goes wrong in the theatrical fiction, a corpse here, a collapse there, it rarely forces cancellation but an increased level of attention and participation from the audience. This curious anomaly is no justification for the inept, but it hints at the misplaced ineptitude that so much theatre represents.[73]

Read is proposing, I think, that in a theatre that is less heavily insured against the risks of going wrong than most professional ventures, one that does not rely for its perpetuation upon routinely going right, we might glimpse something of theatre's 'margin' or 'inside'; an anomaly that points unerringly to something wrong with the theatre that wants so desperately not to go wrong. That we might look for the 'corpses' and the 'collapses', and value these 'anomalies' in spite of the fact that they appear to offer meagre returns for the rational investor. Theatre's 'misplaced ineptitude' may lie in its over-investment in that which it 'represents', while its properly placed ineptitude, its wrongplaced rightplacedness, might lie in an under-investment in mastery, technique, and perfection and a counter-investment in some kind of failure to master the techniques of perfect representation.

It may have something to do, then, with the space between representation and its failure.

Because Read makes the face-to-face encounter – the fact of co-presence – fundamental to his notion of theatre, he starts to argue for an ethics (in a progressive theatre) that most theatre might actually, in practice, choke at or stumble over. For what emerges, in the compromising of the face-to-face communication by failures properly to represent, is a kind of discomfort, a sense of not knowing quite where to put oneself when things go wrong, when ineptitude strikes. It is as though theatre depended for its life upon the success of that person up there in the light convincing you down there in the dark that they are someone else, and that something politically and socially important rests upon the success of this persuasion, while at the same time the very same process could only survive by acknowledging the fatal opposite of that success, the fact that the person up there is in not in fact someone else at all. You are both here, there's no transport out for either of you. The face to face is both offered, then, and withheld, made available and turned down, an opportunity and a threat. What is painful in theatre's attempt at the face-to-face encounter, its movement towards the ethical encounter, is the way that it is either already trammelled in repetition or completely exceeds the theatrical frame that would allow it to signify. What this study looks at, therefore, are moments, apparently anomalous, to pick up Read's terminology, and apparently (only apparently) meaningless, which seem both to underpin and undermine the functioning of theatre as a mode of ethical or political communication. What this bafflement returns is a different kind of politics, a politics rooted in shame rather than mutuality, a politics that moves beyond the kind of ethics that seeks to ground itself in appropriate management of the face to face. A bafflement that suggests that all forms of theatrical management are inept.

Failure, then, is constitutive. That there is something wrong with theatre is the sign that it is theatre. Because this failure rears up in all those moments when the intensity of human interaction is simultaneously offered and withheld, this failure is experienced, not simply as the outcome of discursive operations and the intellectual recognition of, say, the closure of representation, but as affect. For each instance of the face-to-face encounter gone wrong, I argue that there is a particular feeling and that each feeling has meaning. What we experience as affect in these moments of undoing is an apprehension of our own position in relation to the economic and political conditions of our theatre-going. In the crudest terms, I hope to show that in the modern theatre, something of our relationship to labour and to leisure is felt every time the theatre undoes itself around the encounter between worker and consumer. When we experience something of theatre's 'ontological queasiness', pry too deep into the backstage darkness, or witness the whole apparatus turning itself inside out, we are experiencing something of this political relationship. While it may always have been thus, it is experienced all the more intensely now, under conditions of capitalist modernity.

There is something very literal-minded about this project. I tend to assume that when someone writes the word theatre, they mean theatre. My use of philosophical or theoretical texts therefore has a certain vulgarity. Féral's essay is reprinted in a collection devoted to the explication of the concept of 'theatricality' as a central trope of contemporary French thought. While this project draws sustenance on occasion from such thought, in particular the work of Kristeva, Derrida, Deleuze and Lyotard, it does so not simply in the belief that this philosophy that concerns itself with theatricality has something to offer to the study of theatre, but also in the cheekily literal-minded expectation that an examination of what such thinking cares to call theatre might enjoy some 'blow-back'; that in reading the theatricality of philosophy as an account of theatre, something of the operations of that philosophy might clarify.

1 Stage fright: the predicament of the actor

In an 'awful hole'

In *An Actor Prepares*, Stanislavski's young persona Kostya recalls some of his first experiences of stepping on to a stage. These experiences do not of course come direct. Stanislavski's text, like Kleist's *Über das Marionnettentheater* and Diderot's *Paradoxe sur le comédien*, is a loaded dialogue, in which the author's identity is parcelled out into two characters, one knowing and one naïve. The naïveté of the naïf is always a construct of the knowingness of his interlocutor. The forms of innocence and ignorance articulated by the naïf are defined by the knowledge of the knowing. This is especially clear in the Stanislavski text, in which Kostya appears as a young version of Stanislavski, studying under the expert guidance of the elder Stanislavski, figured in the text as the Director, Tortsov. Kostya's first experiences of setting foot on stage are therefore fictionalised in order to give the best possible logical starting point for the sentimental education Stanislavski himself intends to offer. Kostya's first steps must therefore introduce the most basic problems confronting the actor. They appear under the heading 'The First Test'. Kostya has arrived early and tries to prepare himself for the rehearsal ahead.

> I went out to the front of the stage and stared into the awful hole beyond the footlights, trying to become accustomed to it, and to free myself from its pull; but the more I tried not to notice the place the more I thought about it.[1]

The auditorium is in darkness. But the knowing Stanislavski knows what lies in the dark, even if Kostya cannot. However vivid Kostya's imagination he has no direct personal experience of what it is like for this 'awful hole' to contain other living human beings. But it is surely Stanislavski's own knowledge, his own personal experience of playing to a real audience that makes the hole 'awful' for Kostya. Indeed, as the text reveals a little later, it is not the darkness itself, but something else that confronts Kostya with an 'awful hole'. His attempt to get used to being on stage seems to consist in resisting its pull. He needs to free himself from some kind of compulsion. Is the hole sucking him in, tempting him to a plunge across the row of footlights and into . . . the pit? There is both attraction and repulsion in this encounter; push and 'pull'. His technique for resisting this compulsion is to try not to think about it, to put the 'awful hole' from his mind. This has the predictable effect of intensifying the whole ghastly experience.

He helps a workman pick up some nails and starts to experience 'the very pleasant sensation of being at home on the big stage'. But this comfort is short-lived, and soon he is in the auditorium, waiting for his turn to play his scene (from *Othello*) on the stage. Waiting drives him into a state in which he longs to get through the ordeal of acting on the stage. He is afraid of returning to the stage, but this fear has 'a good side' which is not fully explained here,[2] although the implication is clearly that it takes his mind off the particular details of what he is about to do. Again the mature Stanislavski's hindsight is at work here; Tortsov knows, which Kostya cannot, that a certain nervous tension and emptiness of mind can work in an actor's favour. The time has come for Kostya to play his scene. For a moment everything is fine, but then the curtain rises, revealing once again the 'awful hole'.

But the minute the curtain rose, and the auditorium appeared before me, I again felt myself possessed by its power. At the same time some new unexpected sensations surged inside me.[3]

Now the pull of the 'awful hole' is described as a 'power', and as something that has 'possessed' Kostya. Once again, he is not free, but compelled, by some occult force. This mysterious force appears to be inducing 'sensations' within him, sensations whose 'surg[ing]' suggests something somatic as much or as well as psychological. Indeed a little later, describing a moment of anxious expectation in the dressing-room, Kostya feels himself 'almost nauseated'. Stanislavski does not really specify what these 'sensations' might be, but points instead to their specific triggers, including a pleasant 'semi-isolation' in which the darkness above, behind and to either side of Kostya hems him in with some degree of comfort. At the same time these darknesses force him to attend to 'the public'. Again, it is not darkness as such that makes the 'hole' 'awful', since darkness is now all around and comforting. Some particular awfulness is associated with the presence of a 'public' in the 'hole', even though, at this moment, the public consists only of Tortsov and Kostya's fellow students. His 'fears' – presumably those conjured up by the 'power' and the 'pull' of the 'awful hole' – also impose upon him, he notes, 'an obligation to interest the audience'.[4] In his exposure the unseen eyes are making demands upon him, which he internalises as 'unexpected sensations', rising up in his body, and commanding him to act. The sense of being under an obligation throws him off course. As he progresses through the scene he is in extreme haste: 'My favourite places flashed by like telegraph poles seen from a train'.[5] The supreme modernist technological embodiment of speed rushes him past icons of technological communication rendering him incapable of communicating as he wishes. Technique appears to be working against itself. Again he appears to be acting in the grip of an irrational compulsion brought on by the encounter with the 'awful hole': 'The slightest hesitation and a catastrophe would have been inevitable'.[6] The text breaks off on this semi-ironic note of unknowing. A catastrophe of some kind has clearly occurred. Tortsov has seen the train-wreck, while Kostya congratulates himself on having outpaced the nameless danger.

Eventually the day of the exhibition performance dawns, and Kostya comes face to face with the full horror of being on stage. Stepping on stage he is at first blinded by the lights, which 'seemed to form a curtain of light between me and the auditorium. I felt protected from the public, and for a moment I breathed freely'.[7] Even this comfort speaks of a knowledge of the discomfort which is to come. Protection implies danger. It is only 'for a moment' that he can breathe freely. Only momentarily can he command the most basic unconscious action. The nameless force, the power, the pull, is here revealed, with its full somatic impact, as the public, a force that restricts his breathing, and after this moment of respite, it bears down upon Kostya, to hurl him into a catastrophe from which, paradoxically, he will salvage his first moment of real acting:

> but soon my eyes became accustomed to the light, I could see into the darkness, and the fear and attraction of the public seemed stronger than ever. I was ready to turn myself inside out, to give them everything I had; yet inside of me I had never felt so empty. The effort to squeeze out more emotion than I had, the powerlessness to do the impossible, filled me with a fear that turned my face and my hands to stone. All my forces were spent on unnatural and fruitless efforts. My throat became constricted, my sounds all seemed to go to a high note. My hands, feet, gestures and speech all became violent, I was ashamed of every word, of every gesture. I blushed, clenched my hands, and pressed myself against the back of the armchair.[8]

Once again the fatal combination of fear and attraction exerts an intensely physical force upon the neophyte actor. The 'awful hole' has revealed itself as more terrifying than mere darkness. The contents of the hole are what make it 'awful'. The introjection of the public binds Kostya to a terrible task. The obligation to entertain the interest of the public arouses the desire to rip out his guts for them, lay before them his innermost being, but at the precise moment of this compulsion comes the hideous recognition that there is nothing in there. He discovers a nothingness within himself that he has never before encountered. He confronts the impossible task of squeezing out more emotion than he has. He wants to express liquid from his body but has no power to do so. He is paralysed. His means of communication petrify, cease to become part of his flesh, as though the public were a Gorgon. He starts to lose command of his voice, which makes high pitched sounds. He is being robbed of his adulthood, forced into an immobile, helpless, squeaky state of being: a state of infancy. Everything he attempts brings him shame and he rages vainly against this obloquy, reddens and stiffens in the grip of his own incapacity.

But it is precisely in this moment of his most complete abjection that the seeds of his modest triumph lie. Torn from all those basic things in which he experiences himself as a sentient and conscious being – breath, speech, movement, face, hands – his helpless rage allows him to 'cut loose from everything about me'.[9] He is no longer himself, his subject-object relations shattered, he utters the 'famous line, "Blood, Iago, blood!"' and suddenly feels 'in these words all the injury to the soul of a trusting man'. His emotion roused by rage at his helpless infancy is transformed into the rage of Othello, and 'through the audience there ran a murmur',[10] that signalled for Kostya that he had momentarily achieved the goal of the actor.

What Stanislavski is suggesting here, in his narrative fiction of Kostya's first steps on the stage, and in the evocative language with which he colours the experience, is that there is some necessary connection between the 'awful hole' and the ability to act emotion with conviction. This is not simply to say that an awareness of the audience is vital to histrionic communication; in fact Stanislavski's training techniques tend to work in the opposite direction, encouraging a disregard for the presence of the audience. Rather, Stanislavski's parable of the birth of an actor suggests a sequence of vital but damaging encounters with the idea of an audience, in which catastrophe, paralysis and fear are both prerequisites and direct fuel for the truthful presentation of human emotion in the theatre. As Stanislavski works through the various stages in an actor's training, other sources are found to preserve, stimulate and access resources that will help the actor in his aim. These sources often depend for their efficacy upon techniques which exclude the audience from the actor's view, drawing the actor's attention in, into the self, the memory, and holding him or her within the various circles of attention from which the auditorium is ruthlessly excised, allowing the experience of 'Solitude in Public':

You are in public because we are all here. It is solitude because you are divided from us by a small circle of attention. During a performance, before an audience of thousands, you can always enclose yourself in this circle like a snail in its shell.[11]

But the initial moment, the founding crisis upon which the possibility of truthful acting seems to depend, is a bruising physical and psychological encounter with the audience that leads to the actor's complete failure and a collapse into the experience commonly known as 'stage fright'. The violent exposure of this experience is that of a snail ripped from the protection of its shell, or rather, the infinite vulnerability of the slug that has never even known the comforts of a shell.

This is what Tortsov knows and Kostya cannot. The ironic play between the young and the mature Stanislavski pivots on this (and the irony is weirdly doubled by the fact that Kostya is playing Othello in a scene with Iago, the worldly-wise man who plays on the emotions of others in order to engineer tragic catastrophe). The catastrophe that Kostya believes himself to have avoided in his rehearsal of the scene is witnessed by Tortsov in the knowledge that, unavoided – experienced in its full force – it is the first step on the path to truthful acting. At the very start of the elaboration of his famous system – still the most substantial and influential source for actor-training in the West – Stanislavski makes stage fright the precondition of theatrical success. He also does so in terms which are highly suggestive for an analysis of what this strange phenomenon might be.

A very 'modern' hole

The emphasis placed above upon the technologies of the railway and the telegraph may not have been misplaced, and Stanislavski's metaphors may prove to have been very precisely chosen. Stage fright is a phenomenon of modernity. The term first makes itself visible in Mark Twain's *Tom Sawyer* (1876), and stage fright itself is receiving public attention in print by 1891, when Adolph Kielblock published *The Stage Fright, or How to Face an Audience*.[12] Before turning to Kielblock's rather illuminating early observations on the subject of the face to face, the idea that stage fright is specifically modern needs some justification by means of a historical positioning. As suggested at the outset, in the choice of Proust's account of 'Berma's' performance of *Phèdre* in Paris, this is the historical positioning that defines the primary scope of this entire study: it deals with the theatre of modernity, the theatre of the darkened auditorium that knows its own history, reflects and theorises upon its own origins, while participating eagerly in the worlds of commerce, leisure and entertainment that define its social place within modern capitalism. Although aspects of this study will step back beyond the moment of modernity, this is the theatre that will function, as it does for most people in the West today, as normative.

In 'The Metropolis and Mental Life' Georg Simmel offers one of the most succinct accounts of the way in which human psychology at the end of the nineteenth and the beginning of the twentieth century is determined by the particular existential pressures of modern urban living.

Three aspects of this determination appear to bear directly upon questions relating to professional actors in general, and the threat of stage fright, in particular: professional specialisation, the 'calculative exactness of practical life' and the cultivation of the 'blasé attitude' as the basis for social interaction.

According to Simmel, then, the modern city intensifies the social division of labour:

the concentration of individuals and their struggle for customers compel the individual to specialize in a function from which he cannot be readily displaced by another . . . In order to find a source of income which is not yet exhausted, and to find a function which cannot readily be displaced, it is necessary to specialize in one's services. This process promotes differentiation, refinement, and the enrichment of the public's needs, which obviously must lead to growing personal differences within this public.[13]

The actor in the modern city is a professional specialist. The specialist can best secure his or her livelihood by the acquisition of specialist training, that sets the specialist apart from the non-specialist in a particular field. The actor is no exception to this. In the introduction to *Twentieth Century Actor Training*, Alison Hodge notes that,

It was not until the beginning of this century [she means the twentieth] that an explosion of interest in the power and potential of actor training took hold in the West.[14]

Although she does not name the experience of modernity as such, she refers to two aspects of modern life as catalysing this explosion:

partly through a growing awareness of the rigorous training in Eastern traditions but also through the widening influence at the turn of the century of objective scientific research.[15]

The encounter with Eastern traditions is clearly a function of imperialism – with perhaps the emblematic moment being Artaud's encounter with Balinese theatre at the Paris Colonial Exposition of 1921. No immediate connection with stage fright presents itself here (although it would be very instructive to find out to what extent the phenomenon is found outside Western modernity, were such an outside actually to exist). The impact of scientific research, which will also be felt in the development of psychoanalysis – an issue that will be addressed momentarily – is more immediately relevant here, in that scientific inquiry readily leads to the development of methods of enhancing professional efficiency. As Hodge notes, the studios, academies and laboratories set up 'throughout Europe and the United States' in the wake of this explosion of interest are not simply designed to investigate the nature of the acting process, they are 'ultimately' to 'prepare the actor for work'.[16] Scientific rationality and the urban marketplace determine the new social position and career trajectory of the professional actor.

Closely associated with scientific rationality is the spread throughout social relations of 'calculative exactness',[17] most evident in everyday life in the intensified regulation of personal time by the economy. As Simmel puts it:

The technique of metropolitan life is unimaginable without the most punctual integration of all activities and mutual relations into a stable and impersonal time schedule.[18]

It is interesting to see living in modernity described here in terms of technique, not least because it permits an immediate transposition into any specialism defined by technique (including, of course, acting) of the behaviours required for modern living. More important for now, however, is the issue of the timetable. As soon as public transport in the city runs to a timetable any fluidity in curtain-up or curtain-down times that might once have been permitted is now out of the question. As part and parcel of their specialisation, actors will be expected to submit themselves to the regulation of clocks and bells. Stated in its crudest form, the industrialisation of entertainment means that actors no longer stand in attendance upon the whim of a court or patron, but dance to the tunes of the working week and the last bus home. Beyond this immediate practical consideration – which is not negligible – there is a wider question of psychic impact. The punctuality necessary to urban living is just one element in a wider calculation. The professional specialist must calculate a career. The actor acquires an agent and becomes acutely conscious of day-to-day success or failure in the competitive employment market. The sense of a livelihood and thus a life at stake becomes part of the daily routine. Henry James's Gabriel Nash, in *The Tragic Muse* (originally published serially in the *Atlantic Monthly* in 1889) describes the way in which modern life makes a mockery of the theatre professional's aspirations to make a contribution of artistic value, as he explains why refined people despise the theatre:

It will be known better yet, won't it? when the essentially brutal nature of the modern audience is still more perceived, when it has been properly analysed: the omnium gatherum of the population of a big commercial city at the hour of the day when their taste is at its lowest, flocking out of hideous hotels and restaurants, gorged with food, stulti- fied with buying and selling and with all the other sordid preoccupa- tions of the age, squeezed together in a sweltering mass, disappointed in their seats, timing the author, wishing to get their money back on the spot – all before eleven o'clock! Fancy putting the exquisite before such a tribunal as that! There's not even a question of it. The dramatist wouldn't if he could, and in nine cases out of ten he couldn't if he would. He has to make the basest concessions. One of his principal canons is that he must enable his spectators to catch the suburban trains, which stop at 11.30.[19]

As part of the calculation required to survive in such conditions, the professional actor, like every modern urbanite, must adopt the 'blasé attitude'.[20] The 'blasé attitude' is a paradoxical psychic formation – a modern social variant on the proper detachment of Diderot's comédien – in that its apparent indifference marks a 'highly personal subjectivity'.[21] Each individual in the modern metropolis must, in order to sustain a sense of self against the seething mass of other individuals with whom fleeting contact is made, develop a pose of indifference, or even 'latent antipathy' to all the others.[22] This not a matter of social breakdown or failure, but on the contrary, it is essential to the conduct of social life in the modern city:

what appears in the metropolitan style of life directly as dissociation is in reality only one of its elemental forms of socialization.[23]

Of course, this individual sense of self may itself be sustained if not determined by the specialisation discussed above. The actor, for whom, as Stanislavski's training dictates, observation of and empathy with other people are key elements in preparation for a role, is nonetheless also compelled by the alienation inherent in modern living to establish and maintain the distance of the 'blasé attitude'. Despite, or rather, because of, the necessity to observe and empathise with others, the actor is in fact the most 'blasé' of all (apart, of course, from psychoanalysts). The actor must be professionally 'blasé', treating empathy and fellow-feeling as means to a professional end. So blasé in fact that he or she must be able to pretend not to be, and must at the very least simulate an interest in the lives and feelings of others. Whatever tension is involved in the maintenance of the 'blasé attitude' for most citizens of the modern metropolis, is liable to be heightened for the actor, because the relationship between feeling and calculation, or between inner disposition and external attitude, lies at the heart of his or her professional life.

Three further inventions of modernity should be added to those features delineated by Simmel, in order to focus more directly on the conditions of theatrical production: the unconscious, theatrical naturalism and electric light.

The growth of scientific interest in the mind, and, in particular, the development of new forms of depth psychology, including, of course, psychoanalysis, makes the actor, as much as anyone, aware of the human mind as an object of study. The concept of the unconscious, and, most importantly, the idea that it might be the source of all kinds of hitherto unexplained physical and mental conditions, is of particular importance. The possibility that psychoanalysis might be able to start explaining, or at the very least, naming such conditions, creates in itself a new situation for the actor. This is not simply to suggest that actors who become aware of psychoanalysis and the models of their mental processes that it offers inevitably start to exhibit the kind of symptoms that the new discipline is looking for, but rather that both modern acting and psychoanalysis share origins in a particular social and political situation. Indeed, Fredric Jameson suggests that it is precisely those aspects of modernity identified by Simmel that create the conditions in which psychoanalysis becomes possible:

The conditions of possibility of psychoanalysis become visible, one would imagine, only when you begin to appreciate the extent of psychic fragmentation since the beginnings of capitalism, with its systematic quantification and rationalization of experience, its instrumental reorganization of the subject just as much as of the outside world.[24]

For the actor, what may be important here is that in the modern experience of calculating a life there emerges a notion of the psyche whose proper place is the private space of the home, and which derives its structure from the essentially private relations developed and maintained within the family. The actor is required somehow to represent, through some mediation of her own life experience, aspects of this private psychic space in the rationalised public sphere of the bourgeois commercial theatre. She is therefore required professionally to embody what is experienced for most of her class as an intensifying split between the public realm and the autonomous psyche: to do in public what most people are increasingly learning to make private. If sexual attraction and family feelings are what come to define the new private psychic space of subject formation, it is precisely these key constituents of self that the actor is paid to reproduce in public. Both psychoanalysis and modern acting technique provide the actor with methods for conducting an investigation of the newly autonomous sphere of their feelings, and to do so for the benefit of a public. It is the conditions of modernity described by Simmel that permit the emergence of this new object of study (for the individual, for the actor, for the playwrights of bourgeois realism and their spectators). As Jameson argues:

with the coming of secular society and the desacralization of life paths and of the various rituals of traditional activity, with the new mobility of the market and the freedom of hesitation before a whole range of professions as well as the even more fundamental and increasingly universal commodification of labor power (on which the central discovery of the labor theory of value was itself dependent), it became possible for the first time to separate the unique quality and concrete content of a particular activity from its abstract organization or end, and to study the latter in isolation.[25]

In this case the new object of study might be described by the actor as 'my personal life', and it is in the fact that this supposedly new and separate experience must be deployed professionally and publicly by the actor that the possibility of a psycho-social crisis over the relations of inside and outside has its origins. While the separation of spheres that Jameson suggests presumably generates certain spaces of psychic comfort for most of the modern bourgeoisie (they can cry at home and act blasé on the street), the fact that the actor needs to be able to make use of the interior private experience for public purposes means that the fact of the separation of spheres is experienced over and over again as discomfort. The separation is never completed, forever repeated. This discomfort, which might issue in stage fright, might also be understood in terms of Richard Sennett's discussion of theatricality's 'special, hostile relation to intimacy'.[26]

Sennett suggests that the change in the relationship between public and private realms that occurs in the transition from ancien régime to European modernity creates four new phenomena for the modern self, each of which is highly suggestive for the present study. The first is intimacy in public: the development of social codes that require that public behaviour be governed by norms dictated by the standards of intimate relations. One might say, to put this very simply, that as the private sphere of family and sexuality is increasingly identified as the source for personal self-validation and authenticity, it becomes essential to convince others of one's integrity as a human self by displaying those qualities that make you a good, authentic person in that place that now matters most, that place where you come face to face with the truth of the other, in the intimate personal encounter or, in the revealingly awkward contemporary term, 'in' the 'relationship'. By the same token, the modern theatre demands that in order to win credibility from an audience attuned to such values, the actor must similarly display her integrity. The second echoes Simmel, as Sennett suggests that the modern city produces the experience of 'isolation in the midst of visibility to others',[27] a term that perhaps even consciously echoes Stanislavski's use of the term 'solitude in public'. The idea that you can be on your own in the city, carrying around with you in the public sphere the bubble of your private life seems to be an essential prerequisite for an acting technique that requires that you take your home to work. Sennett also suggests that the involuntary disclosure of emotion and the emergence of the performing artist as a public personality are major elements in the establishment of a distinctively modern public sphere. This combination has intensified enormously, of course, since Sennett first published these ideas, in the 1970s, with the cult of celebrity self-exposure becoming a dominant feature of the post-modern mediascape. Taken together, it is easy to see how these developments – largely understood here by Sennett as indicative of a theatricalisation of everyday life in modernity – will have had an enormous impact on the everyday life of the modern theatre. This narcissism of the recently elevated public personality, whose intimacies are public property, who is isolated in the visibility of the electric light, who simulates the involuntary disclosure of emotion through the reanimation of his own; these conditions lay the foundation for the eruption of the phenomenon of stage fright, particularly with the related emergence of new theatrical forms in which this very experience (of the self in modernity) also starts to become both the subject matter and the central form of dramatic expression.

The emergence of new theatrical forms, most particularly those of naturalism, requires from the actor an approach to character based on psychology, and, specifically, a psychology in which the impact of the outside on the inside is considered crucial, as it is for a naturalism that sees character as the product of environment. If theatre is to meet Zola's requirement (established in *Le naturalisme au théâtre*) that it emulate modern science and the realist novel and conduct a 'study of its characters' psychology and physiology',[28] the actor must pay attention to these new scientific discourses and work in accordance with insights they offer into contemporary reality, so that she or he can successfully simulate 'actual life on stage'.[29] Of course, never in the history of theatre has the social position of the actor been so similar to the social situation of the character: they are, at last, contemporaries, and more than that, members of the same social class. This means that the 'actual life' the actor is required to simulate is close enough to her own for her own life to become a private resource for public display. While Diderot feared that the actor's over-identification with the emotions of the character would be detrimental to theatrical representation because it would lead the actor to lose control of her technique, the new danger for the actor is that their new technique, along with the new forms and subject matter of bourgeois naturalist drama, might permit so intense an over-identification, that the actor might no longer be required to act at all, but instead just effectively to 'be' a version of herself. Theatrical naturalism and the training that develops to help sustain it become inextricably associated with the new psychological sciences, as the central subject of both resolves around the question of what it is to be a self in modernity. Stanislavski clearly owes much to Pavlov, Sechenev and Ribot,[30] while Freud offers massive retrospective credibility to the foundations of his 'system'.[31]

Colin Counsell also discusses stage fright in the context of Stanislavski's technique, oddly but interestingly suggesting that it might be described in terms of Shklovsky's concept of defamiliarisation. The connection between Shklovsky and Brecht's *Verfremdung* has been frequently discussed, and the possibility that both might be regarded as a kind of calculated stage fright, a stage frightening, is particularly fruitful. It suggests that by making certain of the distance between actor and character, fixing it as a distance, in advance, or keeping strange whatever the strange-familiar thing one might be presenting, the actor coolly evades all the sweaty and nausea-inducing anxieties associated with the uncertain transition between one and the other.

If psychoanalysis as a technology of self-production and naturalism are the first two inventions of modernity to contribute to stage fright as we know it, then electricity is the third. The introduction of electric light into the theatre followed swiftly after the invention of the incandescent carbon filament electric lamp in 1879. In 1881, for example, Richard D'Oyly Carte introduced electric lighting to the Savoy Theatre in London. Within seven or eight years most theatres in Europe had replaced gas with electricity. The significance of this development for the actual experience of the actor on stage is two-fold. On the one hand, it eventually allowed for stage lighting to be much brighter and more intense. Indeed, early objections to the introduction of electric light in the theatre often centred around the loss of the subtlety that had been achieved with gas lighting. Not only does the stage become brighter as a result of the introduction of electricity, the auditorium eventually gets darker. The contrast between the two is heightened. Electric light also allows for greater directionality: actors can be plucked from the surrounding gloom and thrust into its glare.

There is some confusion over the issue of the darkened auditorium. Some sources associate it quite directly with the new theatre of naturalism. Jean Chothia, for example, suggests that it was André Antoine's 1888 production of *La mort du Duc'd'Enghien* that introduced Paris to the darkened auditorium. She notes that:

The darkening of the house is a significant gesture in the creation of illusionist theatre, establishing once and for all the claims of the stage over the auditorium as the centre of attention. Whilst house lights in Paris had been dimmed they had not been completely extinguished before, even by Antoine.[32]

It seems reasonable to assume that Antoine is extinguishing electric light, since previous light sources did not permit a complete blackout. Although the objective of a darkened auditorium had clearly been conceived long before Antoine, even the relatively recent technology of gas lighting could only achieve a partial darkening. Donald C. Mullin cites visual evidence of much earlier attempts to achieve a dark auditorium in the case of the theatre of San Giovanni Crisostomo (1677) in Venice:

The most remarkable feature of the hall was the lighting provided for the auditorium: a chandelier was let down from a well above the ceiling when needed, and withdrawn when the play was in progress, leaving the audience in semi-darkness. Subsequently, this method of dimming the house was occasionally used elsewhere, but the majority of houses preferred to keep the audience chamber illuminated throughout the production.[33]

The aim of a darkened auditorium figures even earlier, in the theoretical work on theatre and stage design in the sixteenth century, advocated by Leone Di Somi and Angelo Ingegneri but, according to Wolfgang Schivelbusch, 'these theoretical proposals had no practical effect on the Renaissance and Baroque theatre, as the social role of the theatre demanded a brightly lit auditorium'.[34]

The social role of the theatre includes the display of wealth through clothing, the assertion of rank and class through position in the house, the deployment of the erotic gaze (flirting), as well as the conduct of other social and economic relations. All of these had to be done with the lights on. By the eighteenth century, however, the trend towards a darkened auditorium appears to have become firmly established through much of Europe. Schivelbusch suggests that the trend may have been more rapid in Germany than elsewhere. He hints that the theatre had perhaps obtained a higher aesthetic status in Germany than it enjoyed elsewhere, where its function as a social setting and an entertainment still predominated. Presumably this might be attributed to the Hellenism precipitated by Winckelmann and explored theoretically by Hölderlin and Hegel, as well as being evidenced in the work of Richard Wagner, whose

performances at Bayreuth took place before an almost totally darkened auditorium. This was a radical attempt to abolish the theatre as a social place and to transform it into a mystical one.[35]

Elsewhere in Europe 'the process of darkening the auditorium was slow; it proceeded by fits and starts'.[36] The advent of gas lighting in the early nineteenth century allowed far greater control over the level of light. Quite simply, it allowed all lights to be lowered or even extinguished at once without a whole army of candle-snuffers being employed. Gas lighting itself did not allow a complete blackout, since pilot lights remained on.[37] Electric light did permit this possibility, but as Schivelbusch notes, it seems that the strength of popular and professional notions of the theatre as a social space inhibited all but the most radical innovators such as Wagner and Antoine in their pursuit of darkness. Schivelbusch also notes, however, that the development of other forms of entertainment, including the magic lantern and the diorama, did depend upon the darkening of the auditorium even at a time when many theatres had not progressed very far along that path. The development of the cinema seems to have consolidated the tendency to darkened auditoriums more generally, setting a normative standard not intrinsic or even proper to theatre itself.[38] So, although the brightness of the stage and the darkness of the auditorium remain subject to some historical uncertainty, as well as considerable divergences in practice from one theatre to another and one country to another, a broad picture is discernible. At the time of the founding of the Moscow Art Theatre in 1897, the stage is almost certainly more brightly lit than ever before, and the auditorium darker. Indeed, the auditorium may even be darker than it should be. Such are the social and technological components of Kostya's 'awful hole'.

On this basis, then, one might offer an account of stage fright as an historically determined symptom, in which the circumstances of a particular social and economic situation combine with developments in theatrical form and technology, and impact in a very direct and specific manner upon the psychological condition of the actor. Urban life encourages latent antipathy between individuals as the basis for their social interaction. The habitual method for dealing with the latent antipathy of others is the development of a self-enclosing shell – the 'blasé attitude' – that might resemble the development of 'public solitude' as a device for managing relations between performer and audience. The public at large, perceived as harbouring latent antipathy for the performer, based purely at first on the fact that they are fellow inhabitants of the modern city, becomes, for the performer, an even greater threat, once they take the shape of a particular audience. The audience may now share an additional set of reasons for harbouring latent antipathy towards the performer. Each of them has paid money to see a performance at a specified time. The economic conditions of modernity mean that they are giving both time and money to the performance in question, which in the context of an increasing division of work and leisure, carries greater weight than ever before. Furthermore, the actor herself is acutely aware that her own specialised professional career depends, to a greater degree than in the past, on the approbation of the public. Trained to do nothing other than this, the actor is, at least theoretically, more vulnerable to the economic power of the audience than actors of an earlier period might have been. On the one hand, it is the economic power of the entertainment consumer in general that has strengthened in the modern city, and the audience as a body can therefore be more readily identified as the immediate source of employment, and on the other, increasing specialisation means that the economy offers fewer prospects for the out-of-work actor seeking alternative employment.

While working under these newly demanding social and economic conditions, the actor is simultaneously encouraged, if not actually obliged, to explore his or her own psyche. An actor's training based on Stanislavski requires a degree of introspection as the basis for successful simulation of emotion. The constant stimulation of 'emotion memory' means that the actor is asked to merge private and public life in such a way as to make his or her most intimate experiences and recollections the basis for professional success. It is not just the actor's professional credibility or employment prospects that are at stake when he or she steps on stage, it is his or her self: a negative response from an audience is no longer just a comment on professional accomplishment, it has become a judgement upon the inner self. This judgement is exercised in darkness. The actor under scrutiny is initially blinded by the light, and even when this effect fades as the eyes adjust, the auditorium presents an undifferentiated darkness.

This is the full reality of the 'awful hole' into which Kostya is plunged when he steps on stage. As a professional actor in the modern world, he finds himself standing in bright electric light under the scrutiny of people he can't see in an 'awful' dark 'hole'. He has grown up in a world where he has learned to treat all strangers with hostility and to assume that they harbour a latent antipathy towards him. He is earning a precarious living which is substantially dependent upon whether the hostile people in the darkness like him. This is the only thing he knows how to do. He has spent a great deal of time looking into the depths of his soul. He has been through specialist training that taught him never to look at the audience because that might turn him into stone. No wonder he feels horrible. Fortunately, a new theoretical discipline has found a name for that horrible feeling. It's stage fright, and it's fearfully modern. But there's no cure. So we end up with something that has a name, that has a history, but what is it?

Into the hole and out: diagnosis and cure

Most writing on the subject of stage fright is in search of either cause or cure, or both. The title of Kato Havas's book is typical: *Stage Fright: its causes and cures, with special reference to violin playing*.[39] Studies of stage fright from a musical perspective are numerous. Theatrical literature tends to avoid the subject. Glen Gabbard notes the existence of 'an unspoken conspiracy of silence . . . among performers'.[40]

Havas suggests why this might be the case:

In most cases stage fright is considered shameful, a kind of degrading disease, something akin to leprosy, which is best kept a dark secret.[41]

The musician's stage fright can be addressed more readily than the actor's. For a musician, stage fright interferes so directly and devastatingly with the technical apparatus of the performer that it makes performance more or less impossible. Shaking and sweating hands impede the delicate communication between player and instrument. The threat is readily understood as a physical one, a challenge to technique. In the case of the actor, public perception of technique is somewhat different. Although shaking hands and sweaty palms, breathlessness, temporary paralysis, dizziness, faintness or the inability even to think, and any of the other physical manifestations of stage fright are clearly debilitating for an actor, the public perception of what an actor is trying to do – pretend to be someone else – means that technique is thought of as internal and mental rather than external and physical. Stage fright for an actor is therefore regarded as some kind of mental malfunction. Clearly the mystificatory language in which much theatrical technique is discussed (and taught) helps shape public perception in this regard. While a physical disease may be scandalous enough for its sufferer to seek to hide it, mental illness still carries a far greater stigma.

Even in texts which discuss stage fright in general terms, and which do not address themselves as directly as Havas does to a particular musical context, references to musical performance or other public appearances (such as sermons, lectures, public speaking) tend to outnumber references to theatre. Non-theatrical examples are more readily understood, and remedies appear to be easier to propose, mainly because they can be offered in physiological terms. Although W. Ritchie was clearly an energetic charlatan (other titles in his copious series, available from the publisher's residence in Liscard, Cheshire, include *Perpetual Youth and Beauty*, *French in a Week*, *Personal Magnetism*, *Corpulency and its Cure* and *Hints to Ladies: or how to obtain a husband*), the prescription he offers in his 1915 pamphlet *Nervousness and Stage Fright: A Never-failing Remedy* is hardly out on a limb in stating that:

as all students of physiology know, there is at the base of the stomach a certain nerve centre which controls the involuntary actions, which is occasionally subject to derangement, and which can be restored to its natural state by a particular action of the lungs.[42]

The cause of stage fright is some kind of physical disruption and action to restore equilibrium can be readily taken. This is straightforward, scientific and requires no recourse to magic or mumbo-jumbo. Unfortunately the theatrical phenomenon, in opening up the possibility of mental illness, demands something more than a physiological fix, and almost immediately signals the intervention of magic and mumbo-jumbo. Adolph Kielblock, although unable himself to offer psychological expertise to assist his readers, at least acknowledges the need for such expertise:

it looks as though the psychologist, the alienist, – in brief the men who have made the exploration of the inmost recesses of the human mind a specialty, – might lead us out of the labyrinth; but they do not seem to have ever paid much attention to this branch of the science.[43]

While waiting for the alienists, then, Kielblock directs our attention to the mysteriousness of the phenomenon, in terms which are typical of the evasions deployed where superstition and stigma are at stake:

Some of the oldest and most popular actors, singers, musicians, lecturers, confess that they are still haunted by "the spell" every time they have to ascend the stage or pulpit, in spite of the most determined efforts to keep off the incubus.[44]

Stage fright appears here as a ghost which 'haunt[s]' the performer, as a '"spell"' placed upon the performer by some malign supernatural force, or even – and this is perhaps the most suggestive in relation to the discussion that follows – something that takes over and possesses the performer, stealing away all will and control. Clearly the word 'fright' is inadequate to express the phenomenon, as Kielblock himself notes, citing an unnamed reporter in an unspecified 'Western newspaper' who asks:

But what is stage fright? No one who has ever felt it can explain it to his own satisfaction. In most cases there is no fright at all, there is not the slightest sense of fear. It is the result of some magnetic or other influence which goes out from a crowd to an individual.[45]

In *Nerve Control: The cure of nervousness and stage-fright*, H. Ernest Hunt seems to sense the presence of similar forces: part magical, part scientific, when he notes that,

Thoughts and emotions are vibratory in essence, just as sound, light and heat . . . we are all aware of the contagion of fear, the infection of laughter . . . illustrations of the working of this law of sympathy.[46]

The magical faith in the power of science and technology expresses itself as a scientific certainty about the operations of apparently magical powers. This combination of speculative certainty and credulousness seems to be very common: the same tone is readily recognisable in Stanislavski's account of the interaction of mind and body. Far from being a naïve or primitive view, it almost certainly reflects general lay awareness of scientific and philosophical work that has been gradually breaking down the Cartesian dualism that had held until, say, the mid-nineteenth century. The work of Lewes, Ribot, Darwin, Sechenov and Pavlov all have major importance for a modern understanding of mind–body functioning and the processes of acting. Even Kielblock, for example, who is far from rigorous in his attributions and speculations, refers directly to Darwin in his account of emotional functions as they impact on the performer. Of course one of the most systematic and far-reaching scientific projects to have renegotiated the discursive relations between mind and body is psychoanalysis, and its founding notion that physical symptoms might have psychological causes is clearly of immediate relevance to the question of stage fright. So, in order to understand the mystery of the 'spell', the nature of the 'incubus' and to make sense of what the 'vibrations' might be doing, it is to psychoanalysts' accounts of stage fright that I now turn.

In making this psychoanalytic turn at this point, a note of methodological caution is required. While cause and cure remain the objectives of the psychoanalytically oriented writers, a consideration of whose work follows, those are not my objectives. A phenomenology will suffice in this instance; interpretation will be avoided. This is for two reasons. First, it is the fact that stage fright happens, and the way in which it is experienced, discussed and dealt with within theatre practice and its discourses, that is of interest here. The object of study is the theatrical, and inasmuch as stage fright appears as a central element in the experience of the theatrical, it falls within the scope of this work. Where stage fright stands as an index of a particular person's or group's psychological experience and development outside the specific context of its theatrical manifestation, it is none of my business. Second, there are problems of obviousness and deniability that arise when the 'psychoanalytic mise en scène' is mapped too closely onto the theatrical experience. As Joe Kelleher notes of his own almost unwitting psychoanalytic reading of a performance of Caryl Churchill's *Blue Heart*, at first there is a comforting sense of 'fit' between what is articulated on stage and what a psychoanalysis might articulate.

> The situation was unsettling, however. That is to say, the more obvious (in the sense of being irrefutably evident) my reading appeared to me to be, the more obvious in that *other* sense (the sense of a naivety that misses the mark of a greater critical interest) it also appeared.[47]

Since I have no duty of care arising from a desire to cure, the tool of cure, interpretation, is not for my hands. I shall therefore use psychoanalytic accounts as further descriptions of the phenomenon, and try not to draw any obvious conclusions.

Kielblock and his unnamed reporter are already suggesting in 1891 that stage fright is not in fact a form of fear, but might be better understood in other terms, perhaps as the surfacing of some kind of revulsion or phobia (that is to say that it is a feeling that is unhealthily disproportionate to the magnitude of its ostensible cause). This is certainly the general view of most psychoanalytic writers on the subject, who note that for stage fright to qualify as fear, actors experiencing it must have some demonstrably proportionate object to fear, must be in some genuine danger. Kielblock himself observes that in the case of stage fright 'the feeling of a risk is simply the result of a morbid state of the imagination'. Glen O. Gabbard suggests that, according to Freud's distinctions (in *Beyond the Pleasure Principle*) between 'fear', 'fright' and 'anxiety', stage fright is 'a misnomer', and 'stage anxiety might be a more accurate term to describe the phenomenon, as it meets the criteria of being both expected and prepared for'.[48]

According to Stephen Aaron, who has written the only book-length study of the phenomenon, and who has done so from a broadly psychoanalytic perspective, Gabbard's work reaches similar conclusions to both his own, and the other significant contributions to the field, those of Donald Kaplan in the late 1960s.[49] All are broadly in agreement that

Stage fright is a severe anxiety attack, a form of panic anxiety; it is sometimes called traumatic, disintegration or primal anxiety. For reasons that will become apparent later on, Kaplan (1969) is correct when he calls it "morbid."[50]

Aaron's list of the symptoms of such an attack correspond to those observed by Gabbard and Kaplan. I will enumerate them here, as listed by Aaron, without comment at this stage, but will return to consider them in detail as a group of symptoms later:

They can include dizziness, sweating, trembling, palpitations, nausea, dryness of the mouth, diarrhea, frequent urination, muscular tension, and, of course, respiratory difficulty.[51]

They concur that it is something that does not simply happen to people otherwise predisposed to neurotic symptoms, and that it has many causes, many or all of which may be present in any given appearance of the phenomenon.

Stage fright is an overdetermined symptom of all persons who must perform before an audience.[52]

They are also confident that, however disabling it may appear, stage fright is part of the creative process of the actor. For Gabbard, it 'adds a unique dimension to the vitality of live performance', because it places the performer in a relationship of 'interactional tension' and 'ambivalent empathy' with the audience.[53] For Aaron, whose book's title indicates the positive value placed on the phenomenon by assigning it a 'role in acting', it functions as a prophylactic and serves as an artistic problem to be solved and overcome. For Kaplan, stage fright has aesthetic value because it can be banished through the establishment of reciprocal relations between performer and audience. This reciprocity, he suggests, is an important element in the quality of the theatrical experience. Kaplan's position is possibly aberrant here, for an interesting reason. While Gabbard writes in the *International Journal of Psychoanalysis* and claims no particular theatre expertise, Aaron writes as a teacher and director of theatre, as well as being a clinical psychologist. Aaron's theatrical background places him firmly within the post-Stanislavskian tradition of American theatre production, and Gabbard, as a layman, seems to adopt assumptions about what happens in theatre that would be shared by those working in that tradition. Kaplan, although a psychologist, rather than a theatre practitioner, wrote both his pieces for *The Drama Review* (*TDR*), the publication most closely associated with the repudiation of that tradition in the 1960s. The value he places on reciprocity would seem to demonstrate an affinity with the participatory, non-representational theatre developed by, among others, the founding editor of *TDR*, Richard Schechner. In spite of this possible discrepancy in their views of what might be interesting or possible in terms of theatrical production, I shall, in what follows, treat Aaron, Gabbard and Kaplan together, and seek to identify a set of common themes, without always identifying their appearance in each of the texts, while taking examples of analysis from whichever text offers the clearest articulation.

The first key theme is loss of control. In stage fright the actor loses control of bodily functions, including the key functions of movement and speech which are his métier. Kostya, for example, in *An Actor Prepares*, finds himself constricted in breath, speechless, robbed of his capacity for gesture. Worse still, and highly suggestive for our psychoanalysts, this loss of control extends to other functions too: the performer stands in dread of pissing or shitting himself in some ghastly regression to a state of infant incapacity. The reactivation of experiences of phases of childhood development is, perhaps inevitably, the common feature of all the possible determinants for stage fright proposed in the psychoanalytic literature. What is not precisely specified by any of the three writers is the extent to which this loss of control might be understood as a failure properly to manage relations between inside and outside. The actor gets too hot or too cold: the membrane that is the skin is functioning poorly and failing to regulate flows between the outside world and the inside body. Sweating and clamminess seem to be trying to deal with heat inside by making the outside wet. Excessive urination, diarrhoea and nausea all involve a failure to keep in those things that one would normally push out, but only in the right place, and this, the stage, is not it. Respiratory difficulties involve a double failure: a failure to take in air for the extraction of oxygen, and a failure to breathe out in order to expel carbon dioxide. Clearly difficulties over inside and outside are highly suggestive in the context of a psychologically based technique for acting such as Stanislavski's, but at this point, a certain obviousness demands a termination of analysis, at least for the time being.

The second theme involves recognition of a sequence from 'blocking' to 'depersonalisation'. Blocking is described by Kaplan as

the momentary experience of complete loss of perception and rehearsed function.[54]

It is in this phase, of course, that control is lost, as the experience

erases all sense of control and aims at a total extinction of impulse by disconnecting the self from all avenues of functioning, including speech.[55]

This means that not only does the performer risk the bodily regression to infancy discussed above, but higher functions, including recently acquired memories of words and actions to be repeated on stage, are imperilled. Performers who have suffered stage fright speak of the way in which their minds go blank, and how for what seems like an unbearable duration they are unable to remember what they are supposed to be doing. For Kaplan the sequence appears to be truly chronological, with depersonalisation succeeding blocking the moment the performer is on stage:

Once on stage, blocking gives way to depersonalisation. This reaction is most often experienced as a split between a functioning and an observing self, with pronounced spatial disorientation.[56]

In fact the sequence may only be logical. It is quite conceivable, and in keeping with many accounts of the experience of stage fright, that the performer stands by as a helpless witness to his or her own malfunctioning. They watch themselves block, and it seems to last for ever. This depersonalisation, whether simultaneous with blocking or not, might also be read, from a theatrical perspective, as the basis for an acting technique based on *Verfremdung*, in that it seemingly allows a separation between what the audience sees – the functioning self – and what the performer is seeing and doing. This further suggests that what could be happening, theatrically rather than psychologically, in this moment of the most advanced stage fright, is a failure on the part of the actor completely to inhabit the role. The act of actorly transformation is unaccomplished, hangs in the balance. A collapse into the functioning self would presumably involve a resolution into role, as rehearsed functions return and control is resumed. A relapse into the observing self would halt the action, break any remaining illusion and suspend the play, with no character being produced to function in the framework of the production. This phase of depersonalisation, then, might be understood as a traumatic and prolonged act of *mimesis-as-poesis*, in which there is a moment of intense wavering between the presenting self and the self to be presented, the maker and what she makes. What the actor may experience as a long drawn out anguish, the audience may read as a momentary flicker, a suspension like that of a diver at the end of the springboard, not quite plunging into the text of the scene, held for a fraction of a second at a point where refusal remains an option. Such moments are occasions of what I have called elsewhere a 'semiotic shudder' where the audience has no way of knowing whether they are seeing an actor making themselves into a sign or an actor failing to do so.[57] They are about somebody being not quite where they ought to be, and flickering there. Again, it might be said, this time in relation to both role and text, that the performer is oscillating between inside and outside. If, as suggested above, *Verfremdung* might be seen as a kind of calculated and deliberate stage-frightening, it achieves its objective by arresting in advance any possibility of this thrilling but painful oscillation, simulating the divided state of stage fright but without any of the physical symptoms, as a kind of prophylactic or antidote.

Gabbard associates this depersonalisation with defence mechanisms designed to ward off separation anxiety and achieve separation-individuation.[58] Separation is the third common theme among our psychoanalysts, and it is at this point that some degree of interpretation or analysis (not, I promise, my own) must be presented, simply for the sake of clarity. Separation anxiety occurs in the young child when it learns to walk on its own. At first the child is 'enthralled with himself and his faculties', but thereafter develops an 'all-consuming, almost constant concern about the location of his mother'.[59] This 'poignant experience of sensing one's own helplessness and need' is 'reactivated' in the moment the performer steps on stage and experiences the momentary sensation that he is a child again, a child who is only pretending to be independent and autonomous and who, inwardly, is crying for the omnipotent symbiotic mother to rescue him from the plight in which he has discovered himself through his own self-assertion.[60]

Two aspects of this phase and how it is described need comment here. First is the supposed desire for a return to a 'symbiotic mother'. This implies a longing for a return to an earlier state in which the infant does not quite perceive itself as separate from the mother at all, but as part of the same organism or machine, connected either by the umbilical cord or by the mouth's attachment to the breast. The moment of stage fright is thus supposedly characterised by an ambivalent relationship to fluid physical aspects of the mother, and psychoanalytic accounts of the phenomenon would seem to make connections between this ambivalence and the specific physical symptoms. Whether or not we buy the notion that the actor who vomits from stage fright is expressing a ambivalent feeling about his mother's body and its various non-solid products, the operation of this metaphorical link in all the psychoanalytical accounts may be significant. The second is that the moment of self-enthralment described by Gabbard is the moment at which narcissism reaches its peak. This is the secondary narcissism associated with Lacan's mirror-phase, rather than the primary narcissism that the later Freud insisted preceded any ego development. Sandor Ferenczi connects this narcissism to stage fight in terms which are highly suggestive, in relation to the depersonalisation/ *Verfremdung* phenomenon, to the loss of basic physical control and also, lest we forget him, to the blushing young man-statue of Kleist's *Über das Marionnettentheater*.

Among persons who are embarrassed by "stage fright" when speaking in public or in musical or dramatic productions one finds that at such moments they have frequently fallen into a state of self-observation: they hear their own voices, note every movement of their limbs, etc., and this division of attention between the objective interest in the thing produced and the subjective in their own behaviour disturbs the normal, automatic, motor, phonetic or oratorical performance. It is a mistake to believe that such people become awkward as a result of their excessive modesty, on the contrary, their narcissism asks too much of their own performance. In addition to the negative-critical (anxious) observation of their own performance, there is also a positive-naïve, in which the actors are intoxicated by their own voices or other doings, and forget to bring about an accomplishment with these. The 'doubling of the personality' is often a symptom of inner doubt about the sincerity of what is said.[61]

Ferenczi's observation does not seek to account for those symptoms of stage fright typified by nausea, vomiting, and dizziness. These might be regarded, then, as a kind of excess in the phenomenon, something that does not appear to be necessary to the functioning of the malfunction and which therefore evades, to some degree, explanatory frameworks other than those offered by the child-mother dyad. To press this latter forward further at this point would be too obvious. Terminate.

Abject hole: first 'blow-back'

In the reading of Stanislavski above particular attention was paid to metaphor: not simply to the 'awful hole' itself, but also to the image of infant helplessness and the feeling of having been turned to stone. We might add to that, especially in the light of the consistent theme of confusion between inside and outside identified in the psychoanalytical accounts of stage fright, Kostya's feeling that he 'was ready to turn [him]self inside out'.[62] In the survey of the psychoanalytic accounts of stage fright a certain reticence has been observed, so as to avoid something that may be staring us, or Kostya, in the face. Let us not then fall prey to the temptation that insists on returning, and make too rapid an identification between the 'awful hole' and the vagina. It would be wrong to suggest that every, or indeed, any actor experiencing stage fright is reliving some infant anxiety about origins, membranes and fluids. The impact of modernity in both its general socio-economic form and its particular theatrical manifestation in psychological realism have been introduced into the discussion partly in order to forestall such a reductive acquiescence in the obvious. The obviousness begins to take on the character of a myth, once it can be seen as a function of a particular historical situation. (Psychoanalytic) myth as depoliticised speech, seeking to present as natural and enduring that which is in fact a changeable human product, offers a universal explanation of stage fright that ignores the possibility of its own role in the production of the phenomenon.

What if psychoanalysis has not discovered the (multiple) causes of stage fright, but reverse-engineered them? Stage fright may not be explained by psychoanalysis; it may have been an early invention of the discourse, so vividly does it seem to illustrate the otherwise inaccessible phases of infant development. So instead of gleefully pointing at the symptomatic use of metaphoric language by Stanislavski as evidence of his only half-knowing confession of neurosis, we might seek to view the psychoanalytic discourse itself as a metaphorical one, observing the same structures as the theatrical, while both in fact refer back to some as yet unnamed or even unnameable reality. A reality that is some kind of absence, a 'hole' itself around which the metaphorical discourses circle, unable to symbolise or otherwise make meaning of it. A meaninglessness at the centre of the discourses, created by the discourses themselves in order to ground their own functioning. The question of whether we believe a (psychoanalytic) word of it need not arise. The words suffice as testimony to the meaninglessness.

In order to retain a sense of this meaninglessness, or at the very least an uncertainty about meaning, I do not propose to use the work of Julia Kristeva on abjection as an explanatory device, but rather to examine it as a metaphorical system subject to a reverse symptomatic reading. In addition to reading Stanislavski to discover the Freud within, I hope to offer a reading of Kristeva that uncovers a certain, only feelingly acknowledged, theatricality. Peeling each back towards the other, I hope to suggest that both psychoanalysis and theatre may organise themselves around a central something, a something that they both need, as foundational moment, but can not, ever, discuss and must therefore always occlude or expel. The purpose of the reading of Kristeva, then, is not to complete the obvious connection by linking her state of vomit, fainting and membranes associated with the pre-symbolic mother-child relation to the actor who vomits, faints and can't tell his insides from his outsides. It is not to complete this interpretation, but to show how any such interpretation might always rest on metaphor. In forcing a metaphorical reading of Kristeva as a theorist not merely of stage fright but of theatre itself, I seek to avoid the trap of collapsing the theatrical and the psychoanalytic together into a mise en scène of universal consciousness (or unconsciousness), while insisting that they do share a common problem associated with representation, and which their recourse to similar metaphorical strategies underlines. In keeping with the resistance to interpretation that I wish to maintain, I shall focus exclusively on what Kristeva herself calls her 'preliminary survey of abjection, phenomenological on the whole'.[63] The curtain rises, and

> There looms, within abjection, one of those violent, dark revolts of being, directed against a threat that seems to emanate from an exorbitant outside or inside, ejected beyond the scope of the possible, the tolerable, the thinkable. It lies there, quite close, but it cannot be assimilated.[64]

Where are we? Inside a state of some kind, where something is looming. Looming over what? There already seems to be an above and below in this within. To be loomed over is to become aware of one's shrinking from, a curling down and inward, away from the looming which is felt as outside. So above and below is also outside and inside, and we are still within. There is an outside outside, too, but it may also be another inside, but it exceeds us, exacts too high a price upon our understanding. At least that is the way it seems. We do not seem to know what is going on here. That which looms, within or without this inside, is a revolt against this thing we cannot think, tolerate or even conceive as being. Whatever this thing is it is close by but we cannot make it part of ourselves and nor can we dissolve ourselves within it. We are radically separate from it without being able to know what it is, but we know its interests are inimical to ours. This may be why we do not yet know who we are, let alone where. Might we be looking into the darkness from the panicking solitude of a stage? Trembling in a space that can be both inside or outside: with the curtain down, just a drawing room, but with the (safety) curtain raised, a dangerous and exposing exterior. Or is it that we are trying to inhabit someone we are not, get inside someone's skin, seeking to hide ourself in here so that out there, somewhere, in the dark, quite close but separate, someone, something will take us for another, and facing up to the threat that in its 'thoughtless hunger' the 'awful hole' might not reciprocate and ground our self-transformation with its approval?

a vortex of summons and repulsion places the one haunted by it literally beside himself.[65]

Once again the haunting, the possession, and with it the push and the pull experienced by Kostya. His 'hole' appears here as Kristeva's 'vortex' from which a power goes out towards him, emanating exorbitantly, placing him under an obligation, possessing him with a compulsion. And where is he now? The 'spatial disorientation' is at its most intense: he is 'beside himself'. Where else, indeed, might he expect himself to be, here, inside this inside/outside place, the stage, but there, beside himself, his observing self looking at his functioning self, *verfremdet*?

A massive and sudden emergence of uncanniness, which, familiar as it might have been in an opaque and forgotten life, now harries me as radically separate, loathsome. Not me. Not that. But not nothing, either. A "something" that I do not recognise as a thing. A weight of meaninglessness, about which there is nothing insignificant, and which crushes me. On the edge of non-existence and hallucination, of a reality that, if I acknowledge it, annihilates me.[66]

In the hole there are real people, and in a real 'opaque and forgotten life' they will reappear as such. Right now, they are strangers, a thousand strangers, full of 'latent antipathy' but retaining that sense of the familiar in their strangeness that makes them uncanny. They are people but not the kind of people I recognise right now. It is that they are people that makes the fact that they are alien so frightening. The body-snatchers have invaded the auditorium. I can't make them out in the light that blinds me and plunges them in obscurity. Only if I were to hold my hand to my face, like Scully and Mulder and so many who came and went before them, shading my eyes at the dazzling approach of the alien craft (the one we made ourselves, of course), could I hope to drag them back into the real world, recognise Mum and Dad and all the others. But what good would that do me, since that is not the place where I am? I am in no position to drag anyone into the real world. Here, in this place, I cannot raise my hand to my face, because the stage directions determine otherwise. A new reality is coming into being, shaping itself around the presence of this 'separate, loathsome . . . "something" that I do not recognise as a thing'. A reality that is a hallucination into which I am being invited or compelled to step, at the risk of losing my self. In the hole the thing that is not a thing, that once was my fellow citizens, here, in the city, is pulling me over the edge and towards annihilation: it wants me to stop being myself, to become someone else, and in this moment, I waver, tremble, perform the semiotic shudder for them, before I go. The audience precipitates me out of here, and 'during that course in which "I" become, I give birth to myself amid the violence of sobs of vomit'.[67]

That elsewhere that I imagine beyond the present, or that I hallucinate so that I might, in a present time, speak to you, conceive of you – it is now here, jetted, abjected, into "my" world. Deprived of world, therefore, *I fall in a faint.*[68]

We could be going back the other way now, perhaps. It's hard to tell, what with all the spatial disorientation. I don't know whether I am coming or going, inside or outside. I'm sucked into this present, this here and now of my role, the here and now in which I can not raise my hand to the light (because you, you out there are not even supposed to be reminded that the light is out there with you), the present tense of the drama in which I am condemned to my routine of decanters and pistols, hats and furniture, and from in here I'd have to hallucinate my way back to where I imagine, fondly, you once to have been. And the moment I let that new hallucination take hold, remember that you are out there, really out there, in an out there I could just step off the stage into, annihilating my own here and now and pulling the whole house down about my ears, something of the harshness of you is felt in me as something and I fall out of myself. The scenery becomes scenery, the props props, I am me and it is so unbearable that consciousness cannot maintain itself. *Swoons.*

   It is a problem with mimesis. On stage you can't copy. You have to be there. As. Concretely as. And that is the way with mimesis: not just a copy but a new thing. A thing like the other thing. Whatever you do on stage you are making something. Even if you fail, you make a failure, you make a flop: you make a show of yourself. And it is in the confusion of this making, in the movement from one self to another, that all the trouble bubbles up:

Obviously, *I am* only like somebody else: mimetic logic of the advent of the ego, objects and signs. But when I *seek* (myself), *lose* (myself), or experience *jouissance* – then "I" is *heterogeneous*. Discomfort, unease, dizziness stemming from an ambiguity that, through the violence of a revolt *against*, demarcates a space out of which signs and objects arise.[69]

In order to inhabit the space of signs and objects as a sign myself, mimesis takes me through this moment of ambiguity. I shouldn't really experience it, perhaps; it may only be an old philosophical idea, but it seems to bring on this most awful sickness in me. Turning yourself into someone else can make you ill. We all know that: it's part of the mythology of the theatre. It's a Panic thing, so no wonder its scares the shit out of you. There's no need actually to believe that anyone turns into anyone else in order to believe in the existence of the symptoms and the reality of the underlying neurosis. It is not for nothing that theatrical types are routinely regarded as hysterics. And it's not just the people – the shape-shifters, the sophists and the rhetors, the haunted and possessed, the mountebanks, whores and paid entertainers – who experience this abjection in relation to their profession, their art that is not quite an art. There's something about 'the Business' that like 'the Family' arouses a certain more general social revulsion. If we accept that the antitheatrical prejudice is, at least in part, a revival or endless rehearsal of Plato's problem with mimesis, then we recognise that this neither artful nor artless commerce, this frivolous-serious play-work is caught up in all kinds of discomforting confusions, bound to rouse the ire of the authorities in disproportion to its real subversive potential:

It is thus not lack of cleanliness or health that causes abjection but what disturbs identity, system, order. What does not respect borders, positions, rules. The in-between, the ambiguous, the composite. The traitor, the liar, the criminal with a good conscience, the shameless rapist, the killer who claims he is a savior.[70]

Who are these people? They sound remarkably like stock types, rather than people Kristeva met on a day-to-day basis. They are theatrical types, and the theatrical is the borderline composite that makes us sick. And who, but the actors – the disgusting mimes themselves – could this be:

immoral, scheming, and shady: a terror that dissembles, a hatred that smiles, a passion that uses the body for barter instead of inflaming it, a debtor who sells you up, a friend who stabs you in the back.[71]

But, as if to confirm the fact that the metaphorical is working consistently across the theatrical and the psychoanalytic order, Kristeva (literally) characterises the abject, as

a cynic (and a psychoanalyst); it establishes narcissistic power while pretending to reveal the abyss – an artist who practices his art as a "business." Corruption is its most common, most obvious appearance. That is the socialized appearance of the abject.[72]

Where it first seemed that stage fright was the experience of abjection in the theatre, we now find that it is the experience of the abjection of the theatre: the meaningless ground without which it could not signify, but which it must expel, time after time, every time its fearful but corrupt practitioners resume their dreadful trade.

Face your fear

Donald Kaplan is not alone in prescribing reciprocity for an attack of stage fright, although I have suggested above that his ideas in this regard are not widely shared by those psychological writers who think of theatre in only the most schematic way. The idea that facing up to the presence of others in the theatrical encounter is the best way to quell the nausea is shared by Stephen Aaron, who maintains that even a negative response from the audience is reciprocity enough: the attack of fright is reversed, he says, due to 'the audience's acknowledgment, in whatever form it takes, of the presence of the actor'.[73] To test further the thesis that theatre's undoing occurs around the fulcrum of the face-to-face encounter, I would like to pursue this question of reciprocity a little further. Where acting techniques derived from Stanislavski – the fourth wall, public solitude, the circles of attention – seem to depend upon preventing reciprocity, even while they create the sickness that needs it, it might be supposed, especially in the light of the few hints dropped above regarding Brecht's *Verfremdung*, that other techniques might activate a reciprocity that would answer that sickly need.

An alternative technique, then, might offer the hope that, if an actual human gaze can somehow be plucked from the 'awful hole' and its owner thereby engaged in an act of communication, the sickness will pass. But, unfortunately, not only do the conventional relations between actor and spectator in the modern theatre make this eye contact (let alone anything more substantial by way of reciprocation) difficult to achieve, even in those circumstances where it can take place, it may exact from the spectator a price commensurate with the actor's gain. That price – paid in shame and embarrassment – is the subject of the next chapter. One sickness will be exchanged for another. Stage fright is the predicament of the actor in modernity. Its cure will be the predicament of the spectator – the embarrassment attendant upon the uncalled-for face-to-face encounter. While this chapter has examined the constitutive failure of theatre, around the actor's trouble with facing up to unknown others, the chapter that follows will explore a further dimension of the same problem: the other half of the double bind, in which the cure simply transfers the malaise to the other. The sick actor is replaced by the blushing spectator. From the actor 'embarrassed by stage fright', as Ferenczi has it, we will turn to the spectator, embarrassed at being called up as its supposed cure. The audience will fail to deliver.

2 Embarrassment: the predicament of the audience

Please don't look at me

In the Royal Shakespeare Company's 2000 production of *Richard II*[1] Samuel West, who played Richard, addressed some of his lines directly to the audience. I know this because it happened to me. I cannot remember the line in question, nor the moment in the play when it happened, but I distinctly recall that it happened, and that I found it embarrassing. I know I shouldn't have done. When I was young and Brechtian I was all for eye contact. I wanted the theatrical encounter to be acknowledged. I wanted to do it with the lights on. I thought it would be more truthful that way. It made sense, it was rational, direct, and blindingly obvious. In the RSC production of *Richard II*, the lights are on and the actors talk to the audience.

As Bridget Escolme has argued in a recent book, this production ran against the grain of current mainstream practice in Shakespeare production in its use of direct address. Her work on direct address in Shakespeare and on this production in particular is enormously useful for the way in which it both accounts for and subjects to critique current production practice in this regard.[2]

Direct address, at least in the modern theatre, in which the conventions of illusionism are firmly established, tends to signal some disjuncture between actor and role. At its simplest, it is the ironic aside in which the acknowledgement of the presence of the audience by the performer functions as a way of allowing a character to claim complicity with the audience, on the basis of superior shared knowledge of the reality of the fictional situation. In most accounts of acting technique it is therefore suggested that direct address tends to point up to an audience the fact of co-presence and emphasises thereby the presence and the agency of the performer, disrupting any illusion that what we are seeing is simply the 'character' in the fictional world of the drama being played. Much theatre history, including much influential work on Shakespeare's theatre, views naturalism as the telos of modernising developments in the Elizabethan and Jacobean theatre, and thus views direct address as one of a set of rhetorical conventions that a modernising theatre seeks to eradicate.

Escolme's analysis of recent productions of Shakespeare offers a vivid demonstration of the ways in which contemporary theatrical conventions, derived from late-nineteenth and early-twentieth century naturalism and realism, and governed by this teleological framework, work strongly against the performative potential of the plays themselves. In particular, she argues that it is in dialogic and sometimes reciprocal acts involving actors and spectators that theatrical figures construct the selves that compel attention and give pleasure. This is a persuasive line of argument, especially as it accounts for the success of performances such as Anthony Sher's, as Macbeth for the RSC, and Mark Rylance's, as Hamlet at Shakespeare's Globe. It works even more comprehensively to account for the complex performative action of the RSC production of *Richard II*. Where Escolme, quite properly, argues for approaches to the production of such plays that free themselves from the modern naturalist/realist legacy (including actor training in the Stanislavskian tradition), my own focus in this chapter is on the ways in which the continual compromise with this legacy produces affects and predicaments for the audience which are interesting in their own right. It is when direct address arises as a disruption to dominant conditions of spectatorship that it produces the kinds of discomfort and embarrassments that will be dealt with here. I should add that these embarrassments are themselves a kind of pleasure.

Perhaps because it is viewed as a technique on the wane, the mark of attachment to old traditions and resistance to the modernising of technique in the interests of an evolving 'naturalism', direct address is not much discussed in critical and theoretical studies of Shakespeare and his contemporaries. With the exception of Escolme's *Talking to the Audience*, it merits only occasional asides in the critical literature. One rather unusual exception to this is an extended and highly speculative soliloquy or 'thought experiment' conducted by Harry Berger, in a study of *Richard II*.[3]

Berger's work offers itself as a corrective to the stage-centred criticism that he sees beginning to exercise a baleful hegemony in the field of Shakespeare studies. He claims that the reading of an 'armchair' critic can offer insights into the nature of performance that performance criticism itself cannot. This claim is not without some merit, although its demerits will be more evident in the discussion that follows. In particular, he proposes a practice he calls 'decelerated reading . . . [in which] slowness derives in part from the complex and multidirectional acts of attention that characterise what I have been calling imaginary audition'.[4] In the decelerated reading of imaginary audition, attention is paid not simply to who speaks, but to who responds, who is silent, where they are implied to be. It is a close reading attentive to the possibilities of staging, that seems to claim to be able to produce a richer elucidation of theatrical meaning than an account of an actual performance could achieve, confined as it is to the registration, in real time, of disappearing moments. In fact, there seems no reason why actual audition should not provide the material for just the same kind of decelerated reading. Indeed, decelerated reading may be precisely what Stanton B. Garner is calling for when he suggests that accounts of performance might usefully respond to Clifford Geertz's advocacy of 'thick description' to ethnographers.[5] It may indeed be the case that the process of memorial reconstruction through the act of writing that is every performance critic's burden is a fertile site for the reading Garner, Berger and Geertz are all looking for. This entire discussion of direct address is itself an attempt to place in the thickest possible set of ideological and historical frames, a single moment in a single performance, the moment at which Sam West, playing the part of Richard II, looked me in the eyes. You don't get much thicker than that.

Berger's 'thought experiment' is worth citing at length.

I imagine that as I am watching a play, at a certain moment an actor/character looks directly at me. How shall I respond? Several options are open, and the choice among them will be conditioned partly by the metatheatrical signs the play as a whole emits. If I suppose it is the actor who looks at me, I can either ignore his look or else assume he is picking me out as a momentary target in the audience; I might feel called upon to return the favor by acting alert, responsive, displeased or bored, and in doing this I am free to choose a simulation that matches my actual feeling or one that hides it. Whatever I decide to do, I am playing the theatrical role of a spectator who perceives himself to be present to the actor in the physical space of the theatre that we share and fill. But the situation changes if I imagine that it is the character rather than the actor who looks directly at me . . . Then . . . I cast myself as a fictional character . . . or I imagine myself absent.[6]

Several issues deserve attention here. First of all, it is not entirely clear why, other than because of Berger's commitment to the privileged critical vantage point of the armchair, this incident has to be imaginary. As W.B. Worthen points out, the act of imagination appears incomplete:

> Berger's sense of the "structure and conditions of theater" tends to assume the conditions of modern theatre as normative: silent audience, darkened auditorium, clear boundaries between stage and audience, acting and behaviour, onstage and offstage.[7]

Because he does not imagine himself in a specific theatre, in a specific time and place, watching a specific performance of a specific play, Berger's experiment depends on some very thin description. It is not just that it brackets out, in a phenomenological sense, all kinds of material that would not be regarded as immediately given to his imagining consciousness, but that would be exerting an influence of some kind on any particular real play-goer, it falsifies the situation by its apparent dependence on certain default normative conditions. One theatre Berger clearly is not imagining himself to be sharing and filling with the actor/character, for example, is The Globe, where the play to which he is soon to devote such critical attention received its first performances, in daylight. Another is The Pit, the theatre in which Samuel West looked at me, in a white box space where the audience and the actors were evenly lit. In fact the absence of any specific conditions of social, economic or cultural production might invalidate the 'thought experiment' altogether in the eyes of some critics of a materialist tendency.

Be that as it may, even with all this put in brackets, Berger's thought experiment raises some unexpected and useful questions that bear directly upon the question under consideration – embarrassment. He identifies two main ways in which he might choose to respond to the gaze he confronts; one based on the supposition that it is the gaze of the character, the other based on the perhaps more realistic supposition that it is the actor's. Once again the imaginary nature of the confrontation allows a degree of laxity in relation to theoretical possibilities that simply do not hold up in practice. Even if we allow for the existence of such a person as 'the character', a suspect permission in itself, the experience of being looked at by someone in a public place tends, as Stanton B. Garner observes, in his critique of Berger's position, to make us more acutely conscious than usual of the real flesh-and-blood actor behind whom the represented character presumably stands:

> But if this analysis (what Berger calls the "textualisation of the audience") has the virtue of implicating the audience in the perceptual duality that characterizes performance as a whole (like the actor, I become other than myself, to the point of rendering myself the absent or fictional correlative of the actor's performance), it does so at the expense of the actuality that constitutes the ground and the other side of theatrical fictionality. If this actuality can only fully manifest itself at the cost of the illusion it sustains, the real proximity of performer to spectator nonetheless makes itself felt throughout the actor's performance and the audience's response.[8]

In responding to the imagined gaze of the character, Berger's imaginary decision to 'cast' himself as an attendant lord is understandable enough. The RSC production of *Richard II* depended for some of its performative efficacy on just such a process: David Troughton as Bolingbroke, for example, enjoined us all to stand to register our attendance and complicity in the deposition he was setting in motion. But it is not only the actor who remains hidden in such a transaction as Berger's 'casting'. The actuality of the actor, as Garner points out, is related to the actuality of the auditor. Imaginary audition clearly cannot encompass this relation, which only becomes fully apparent in the actual experience (but might perhaps at least be acknowledged by a 'thought experiment' described more thickly). The decision to cast oneself as an 'attendant lord' is in many respects very similar to Berger's alternative response, to 'imagine myself absent'. In both cases Berger is removing himself from the scene. He avoids the gaze, not by refusing it or averting his eyes, but by refusing to acknowledge his own presence, averting himself, as it were, making himself somehow invisible. Easy enough to do in the imagination, and possible, perhaps (although I doubt it) in a darkened auditorium, but by no means the most obvious or straightforward response.

When the scenario based on Berger's other supposition about the identity of the imaginary person looking at him is examined the situation emerges as *identical* but even more *odd*. Supposing that it is the actor, Berger makes the peculiar choice of *pretending* to be a member of the audience. He imagines himself 'act[ing] . . . responsive'. This is of course wholly unnecessary, since he is already just such a person, and he is responding, or imagines himself to be, for the purpose of this experiment. Yet, he cannot conceive of a response to the gaze of the actor other than in terms of simulation: 'Whatever I decide to do, I am playing the theatrical role of the spectator who perceives himself to be present to the actor in the physical space of the theatre.' This takes some explaining. Berger may be forgetting that this could happen in an actual theatre and that he could respond in actuality, and that he does not have to cast himself in an imaginary theatre every time he thinks of himself. Alternatively, it may be the case that there is something about the encounter Berger imagines that he actually wishes to avoid. As I have suggested, this scenario is not only more peculiar than the first, but, in effect, identical. Every possible response imagined by Berger to the experience of meeting the gaze of an actor/character in the theatre involves the complete annihilation of his self. The actor looks and Berger fervently imagines the ground opening up. Any response other than the unfeigned return of the gaze, as himself, may be countenanced. He can't face the face to face, even in the theatre of his own imagination. At the heart of Berger's imaginary audition lies an embarrassment about the condition of theatre. Imaginary audition itself begins to look like a machine designed to simulate the theatre, but to do so without the theatre's inconvenient tendency to break down or sediment difficulty around the actual co-presence of actor and audience.

Garner, for whom the embodied phenomenology of Merleau-Ponty provides a framework for an understanding of the materiality of actual bodies in actual situations, identifies the key signifier of this reluctance to face up to things:

The reverse gaze catches me in the act of looking, challenging . . . the *ecstasis* by which I 'surpass' my corporeal boundaries through the outer-directedness of vision . . . In so doing, the reverse-gaze returns me to myself, forcing a corporeal self-consciousness that registers itself in a physical discomfort and in the tingling of embarrassment on my face.[9]

The 'tingling of embarrassment' is the flesh-and-blood sign of the difficulty of the encounter Berger must keep out of his mind even in the act of imagining it into being. The difficulty, as the more theoretical considerations that follow will suggest, is to do with the awareness of one's self as flesh and blood, being as body, the predicament of being physically here and now in a historical sense: social, exposed, subjected, disciplined, split.

The historical nature of this self-awareness needs clarification. In Berger's 'thought experiment' there is, as I have already indicated, an assumption of a particular normative condition of theatrical spectatorship, one, in fact, that is essentially the same as that assumed by the historical and institutional place of theatre that I have established as the ground for the present study. That is the theatre of modernity, with its brightly lit stage and darkened auditorium. I have suggested that Berger's argument is compromised by its unacknowledged attachment to this form of theatre. In acknowledging the historical specificity of the form of theatre assumed in Berger's 'thought experiment' there opens up a new dimension to the general argument over the embarrassment of the face-to-face encounter, in this particular theatre. In the case of *Richard II*, a play composed in relation to one kind of theatre is played in another. The modes of actor-audience address presupposed in the composition of a sixteenth-century play differ greatly, as the discussion above has already shown, from those that pertain in the theatre of modernity both Berger and I are taking as our own base assumption. The embarrassing thing about eye contact in the 2000 production of *Richard II*, then, may be that it is in the wrong place and the wrong time. Since the sixteenth century models of theatrical spectatorship have developed, in a reciprocal relationship with the development of new theatre architectures and theatrical forms. Modern theatrical spectatorship is a relationship set up to generate a particular set of pleasures, and it is in the confusion generated by action that departs from those that sustain this relationship, that the embarrassment occurs. We are in the wrong place at the wrong time, which is always embarrassing.

The emergence, in the theatre of the 1960s, of new modes of direct engagement between performers and audience generated considerable confusion and embarrassment for those spectators who retained an investment in the pleasures of the more conventional modern theatre. Helene Keyssar, writing in 1977, for example, distinguishes the audience participation tactics of this new theatre (she appears to have such groups as The Living Theatre and The Performance Group in mind), from earlier self-reflexive strategies like the aside or even Brecht's *Verfremdung*. On direct contact itself, she evokes a familiar experience:

> most of us will remember either remaining in our seats with relief that we were not the ones approached, or if 'contacted' by an actor, responding in whatever manner was least embarrassing.[10]

The original element of Keyssar's argument is that these moments of contact or participation are in fact distortions of recognition scenes in tragedy. In discussing the experience of pity and terror in the witnessing of such scenes as Oedipus' discovery of who he really is, and Lear and Gloucester recognising one another on Dover Beach, she argues that it is in such scenes

> that we discover one of the particular pleasures that theater can offer to an audience. In theater, because the audience is not in the world of the play, we can recognize each other and recognize something of ourselves without showing ourselves to one another. In ordinary worlds, we cannot participate in public revelation without yielding our own privacy, because we are mutually in each other's presence. In the theater, as Stanley Cavell argues, "We are not in their presence," but "they are in our presence".[11]

The modern theatre to which Keyssar is accustomed offers her, as a spectator, precisely that with which it threatens the actor: the experience of 'intimacy in the midst of visibility' that I have suggested in Chapter One is one of the determining causes of stage fright.[12] The actor is always at risk of 'yielding . . . privacy', in the act of self-revelation that is psychological acting, while the spectator is permitted to enjoy the feeling of intimacy that comes from witnessing acts of self-revelation in others, without disclosing anything of herself, safe in the darkness of her seat.

For Keyssar, the seat in the dark is not simply a comfortable vantage point from which to observe untroubled the passage of passion upon the stage, but it is the only place from which certain 'particular pleasures' can be experienced. There is therefore a kind of incivility in the theatre that breaks into this space and turns the lights on, demanding that the spectator join the actor in a shared space.

Richard Sennett, in a recent discussion of the development of public spaces in democratic Athens, reflected upon the peculiar characteristics of the *stoa*, a covered space between the agora itself and the buildings that enclosed it.[13] Here, in the *stoa*, you were in public and not in public, at the same time. You could address yourself to those outside in the agora, but they could not respond to you. You had the power of public speech without its responsibilities or consequences. The modern theatre makes of the stage a kind of *stoa*, from which the actor may speak without fear of contradiction, while making also of the seat in the house a kind of reverse *stoa*, where you may enjoy the public speech of others with no obligation to respond. There is in this set-up a fragile negotiation between vulnerability and safety, intimacy and publicity, responsibility and freedom, and what Keyssar seems to regret in the audience participation tactics of the experimental theatre of her period is its subjugation of this fragile ecology to the largely political imperatives of what we might want to call 'real' dialogic communication, and the spatial configurations that come with it. When the lights come on, she finds herself, rather like Berger, 'wholly befuddled' as to who she is, or, worse, she feels that

To be so seduced or to yield to assault by actors in a theater is not to free oneself of hiddenness and isolation, but to violate and lose oneself entirely.[14]

I am not sure that one can so easily be lost 'entirely', and suspect that being 'befuddled', perhaps only momentarily, is more the order of the experience. Keyssar seems almost to be unconsciously repeating, in negative, as it were, the radical and communitarian claims that The Living Theatre and The Performance Group made about their work and its assault on bourgeois subjectivity. It's the befuddlement, rather than the self-annihilation, that seems interesting. Perhaps my own example from *Richard II*, which does not arise from any grand claims to political efficacy or self-transformation, offers a more modest, but more appropriate position from which to extrapolate a little from Keyssar's argument. It seems that it is when we find ourselves in a grey area, where the lights could, as it were, be either on or off, or both, that embarrassment (and befuddlement, to which I increasingly suspect it must be closely related) is most likely to arise out of face-to-face encounters of this kind. If it is not clear what the rules are – whether we are meant to be in the agora-like rough and tumble outdoors of The Globe (or its contemporary reproduction), or the *stoa*-like chamber of public intimacy that is the modern theatre – then we don't know what responses to engage when the encounter comes. Keyssar characterises her experience of face-to-face contact – of loss of self, violation, and abolition of particular pleasures – in largely negative terms. My own use of the term 'embarrassment' to describe my experience with Samuel West might suggest a similar position on my part, which is far from my intention. Instead, what I want to suggest here, is that the 'particular pleasures' that Keyssar finds in theatre actually include the pleasure of embarrassment. That is to say that the moment, or even, in fact, the possibility of the moment of embarrassing self-disclosure in the event of the theatrical face to face, is essential to the self-recognition that we enjoy. If self-recognition is the pleasure that we gain, then some degree of self-disclosure is the price to be paid for it, and there is a particular pleasure in that very expenditure. Without it, the self-recognition comes free, and yields, perhaps, a little less enjoyment.

In addressing separately in this and the previous chapter the predicaments of actor and audience, I am deliberately leaving until later (until Chapter Four, to be precise) questions of mutual predicaments. But it is at least worth noting here that while stage fright, on the one hand, or embarrassment, on the other, may be predicaments and pleasures that are characteristic of the slightly uncertain space of the modern theatre, there may be moments of mutual befuddlement, or even stupefaction, in face-to-face encounters, that are of equal significance. There is therefore perhaps a particular pleasure to be had from a compromised, fleeting, flesh-and-blood mutuality, even if we don't understand it as it happens. Is not the pleasure of the one-night stand always bought at the cost of a certain embarrassment?

It is precisely this flesh-and-blood presence to one another, either in life or on stage (to pretend for a moment that one of these does not sit within the other, and the other within the first), that seems to be causing all the trouble for Kleist's various double acts in *Über das Marionettentheater*. Herr C. would like to see flesh and blood removed from the stage altogether, because of its incurable self-consciousness. Neither the narrator nor Herr C. can look one another in the face as they discuss the possible mechanisation of humanity, and stare at their feet instead. The young man imitating the statue (giving flesh and blood to a graven image, imitating the imitation), can't tolerate the gaze that knows what he is doing, blushes, and is incapacitated by self-consciousness. Only the bear can look you in the eye, reading your soul with a gaze of utmost seriousness. Wherever Kleist's figures become conscious of some kind of split in the self, between acting and being, between ambition and capacity, between image (self-for-the-world) and self-presence, they seem to buckle, lose face, doubling up in paroxysms of embarrassment. To use Garner's phrase, these moments 'return[. . .] me to myself', making the difference between me and my self tangible. The blood that flushes in my face is the sign of myself returning to me and my awkward recognition of the need to make way for this troublesome guest.

Kleist's staging of this series of moments of self-conscious collapse within the frame of a conversation between an amateur and a professional (and with it a range of relations such as punter/player, patron/artist, as well as all the difference training makes, for actors, dancers, students and bears) offers a social context of economies, disciplines and power-relations that compels a consideration of embarrassment that allows all these materialities in. The brackets imposed by phenomenology and the distortions generated by an armchair viewpoint fall away, and Samuel West and I and me (and myself) are revealed again as people engaged in a specific kind of theatrical relation, in a particular institution which both produces and is produced by specific economic conditions. For in the theatre of capitalism, the reverse gaze must always acknowledge, however tacitly, an intimate economic relation: I paid to have this man look at me, and he is paid to look. Our intimacy is always already alienated. It is a difficult intimacy.

The nature of this 'difficulty' may become clearer if the meaning of embarrassment is established more securely before theoretical considerations are allowed their head.

What is embarrassment?

Embarrassment *as* difficulty is the first key. Sharing origins with the word embargo, an embarras is 'an obstacle', and 'embarrasser' is 'to block'.[15] Barely used in English now, the noun 'embarras' includes among its meanings a number of particular instances of blockage or obstruction, including, for example, '1867 SMYTH *Sailor's Work-book.*, *Embarras*, an American term for places where the navigation of rivers . . . is rendered difficult by the accumulation of driftwood.' As a verb, the first meaning offered for embarrass is:

1. *trans.* To encumber, hamper, impede (movements, actions, persons moving or acting).

Something that might easily happen to either an actor or to someone watching an actor, then, and also, and this is crucial:

b. *pass.* Of persons: To be 'in difficulties' from want of money; to be encumbered with debts.

The nature of the obstacle is found to be economic, but in this context the "difficulties" seem to have become 'difficulties'. The function of these inverted commas is not quite clear here (they seem to be an obstacle, themselves, of some kind, impeding or complicating access to the meaning behind the sign), although the recurrence of this stylistic choice, dealt with below, may clarify a little.

The second and third meanings are offered thus:

2. To perplex, throw into doubt or difficulty.
b. To make (a person) feel awkward or ashamed, esp. by one's speech or actions; to cause (someone) embarrassment.
3. To render difficult or intricate; to complicate (a question, etc.).

So to embarrass might be to do something to someone by speech or action, to act or speak in such a way as to introduce obstacles or complications. One might imagine, if one were given to imaginary theatres, that the kind of speech and action that goes on in a theatre might be especially liable to render such complications: the simple confusion (or perplexity, or doubt) so prevalent and perhaps even unavoidable in theatre criticism between what the actor is doing and saying and what the character is up to is a perpetual source of difficulty to some people.

'Embarrassed' carries four possible meanings:

1. Of a road, a channel, etc.: Made difficult by obstructions. Now only *fig.*
2. Of persons, their movements and actions: Hampered by difficulties, impeded.
b. Involved in money difficulties.
3. Perplexed (in thought).
b. Confused, constrained (in manner or behaviour).

The 'involved' narrative is embarrassed, as is the person 'involved' in money difficulties. Money difficulties is a strange phrase, redolent of a degree of constraint. Involution seems to be curling some embarrassment back upon itself, and doing so where money is concerned. These difficulties need to be pressed further. 'Embarrassment', the noun, has two main senses:

1. The process of embarrassing (*rare*); embarrassed state or condition.
b. Of (or with reference to) affairs, circumstances, etc., often in pecuniary sense.
c. Perplexity, sense of difficulty or hesitation with regard to judgement of action; constrained feeling or manner arising from bashfulness or timidity.
d. Confusion of thought or expression.
2. Something which embarrasses; an impediment, obstruction, encumbrance. In pl often = "pecuniary difficulties".

The inverted commas reappear, as promised, and with them more than a whiff of euphemism, as though those working on the definitions cannot quite bring themselves to face up to the fact that some people have no money, or less money than they would like to have, that there are some people for whom the lack of money acts as an obstacle to action. The term "pecuniary difficulties" used here and the term 'financial embarrassment' to which their definitions repeatedly point, both reek of this linguistic constraint. It is like the use of the term 'women's problems'. The terms 'affairs' and 'circumstances' seem to be skirting around the issue too, perhaps partly because a degree of imprecision is necessary to the writing of definitions that are going to be serviceable, but, in the context of the patent embarrassment about 'money difficulties' – that odd stilted, constrained phrase – 'affairs' and 'circumstances' seem to be hinting at situations of such dreadfulness that they are spoken of only in hushed tones for fear that they would bring great shame upon the household were they ever to be noised abroad. Perhaps 'pecuniary difficulties' will prevent the resolution of 'women's problems'. Euphemism, the linguistic device designed to avoid embarrassment, brings it immediately to light. The secret that the dictionaries know but cannot speak, and in their not speaking so vividly expose, is that embarrassment is an economic condition. The task of determining the meaning of embarrassment appears to be an embarrassment, for those who are hired to do it.

In addition to opening up the various possible meanings of embarrassment itself, some articulation of the relationship between embarrassment and shame is vital here, because the theoretical considerations promised a while back derive from accounts of shame by the American psychoanalyst Silvan Tomkins and the Italian philosopher Giorgio Agamben, neither of whom speak of either 'embarrassment' or 'imbarazzo'. So we need to be very clear. The *Oxford English Dictionary* defines shame thus:

The painful emotion arising from the consciousness of something dishonouring, ridiculous, or indecorous in one's own conduct or circumstances (or in those of others whose honour or disgrace one regards as one's own), or of being in a situation which offends one's sense of modesty or decency.
2. Fear of offence against propriety or decency, operating as a restraint on behaviour.

The way in which the *Oxford English Dictionary* deals with these two terms might lead one to several initial suppositions about what distinguishes shame from embarrassment. Christopher Ricks, for example, suggests that embarrassment is an English thing, a sort of shifty Protestant, wet climate pseudo-affect, a pasty substitute for the red-blooded continental, fleshy, silk-knickered sensation that is shame.[16] Something of the hierarchy implied by Ricks's self-lacerating Anglomania would seem to operate in pragmatic terms. There is a certain moral seriousness attached to shame. Shame feels like a real feeling, while embarrassment feels like it's not even a feeling at all. Shame can wear capital letters without embarrassment. It has perhaps a certain tendency to glory in itself, to wallow. Philosophers pay it due respect. Embarrassment knows its place. It is to be found in the anthropology of the postwar American workplace (Erving Goffman) and in modest but reputable psychiatric journal articles.[17] It does not make theoretical claims, but subsists in the empirical. Where shame can define a culture (Ruth Benedict) embarrassment wouldn't presume.[18] Embarrassment is ashamed of itself, while shame has no shame.

It should come, then, as no surprise, that embarrassment plays only a very minor role in the extensive literature on shame. Its minority is perhaps what is important here. Léon Wurmser, for instance, sees shame as an affect and embarrassment as one of 'its cognate feelings'.[19] It is, he suggests, 'a mild form of shame proper'.[20] In its mildness, its minority, lies its impropriety. It is improper shame, shame in the wrong place, shame that ought to be ashamed of itself for manifesting itself at all and laying impertinent claim to the name of shame. That is to say, perhaps, the shame that shouldn't be seen at all, which is to say, of course, that it is, precisely, the shame that *is* seen, and all the more shameful for that, since shame really shouldn't be seen at all. Helen Merrell Lynd is perhaps exemplary here, in that embarrassment appears only in a footnote in her book on shame, where she suggests that

[e]mbarrassment is often an initial feeling in shame before shame is either covered up or explored as a means of further understanding of oneself and of the situation that gave rise to it.[21]

This is helpful, too, since it suggests that embarrassment may be to do with that aspect of shame that might appear, its flaring in the face, rather than its searing of the soul. One might even say that embarrassment is superficial where shame is deep. There is an episode of the American sitcom *Friends* in which Phoebe seeks to reassure Ross that 'this embarrassment thing is all in your head'. Phoebe is wrong. Shame is in there, on the inside, in your head; embarrassment is out there, in or on your face. Because this is a theatrical project, concerned with what appears, and not, finally, with what is going on inside, it is on embarrassment and on shame in so far as it registers on the face, that I shall focus.

It is beginning to seem that embarrassment may be articulated with shame in a triadic way: wherein embarrassment introduces itself as 'obstacle' in the service of shame-as-modesty, in order to deal with the underlying affect that is shame. Is embarrassment the social management of shame while being at the same time its revelation, its coming to view? You can hide your shame, but not your embarrassment. Embarrassment would not be embarrassed if it were not seen. Embarrassment is the blockage in face-to-face communication between human beings, that appears on the face when shame is experienced. While you might be able to experience shame alone without embarrassment, you can't when you are face to face with someone. Embarrassment embarrasses shame, in the sense of blocking its appearing. Yet at the same time as blocking the appearance of shame, embarrassment itself appears as an appearance of shame. It may, then, be possible to think of the relationship between shame and embarrassment as a relationship between inside and outside, between affect and appearance, between *psyche* and *socius*, a relationship that may permit us, at least for the purposes of this study, to think also of embarrassment as a minor shame, an appearing of shame, and, therefore, of course, as *theatrical* shame. It was embarrassment on my face when Samuel West looked at me, even if it may have appeared to be shame, and it is only because I chose to describe the experience as one of embarrassment, rather than shame, that this task of semantic distinction ever arose. In what follows the term shame will be used, because that is the term used by both Tomkins and Agamben (in translation), even if the idea of embarrassment as shame's appearance might sometimes be more appropriate. These distinctions made, I turn to Tomkins, ever conscious of the lurking embarrassment of the economic, which within Tomkins's text might perhaps be signalled by the non-appearance of the word 'embarrassment' itself.

Towards a politics of shame

In *Affect, Imagery, Consciousness*, Silvan Tomkins devotes considerable attention to shame and to the 'shame response'. For the purposes of this discussion, and bearing in mind the articulation of shame and embarrassment developed above, Tomkin's 'shame response' seems to correspond to the physical manifestations of shame, to the embarrassment, or blocking, of shame, and thus, to its appearance. 'Shame-response' is perhaps a euphemism. For the purposes of thinking about theatre, the most important aspect of this action is the fact that '[t]he shame response is an act which reduces facial communication'.[22] It is also closely linked to the experience of pleasure, interest and enjoyment, and acts as a break – obstacle, constraint, encumbrance, embarras – on the further pursuit of pleasure, interest and enjoyment (or displeasure and perverse enjoyment) derived from face-to-face communication. The terms in which Tomkins articulates this are highly suggestive:

> any barrier to further exploration which partially reduces interest or the smile of enjoyment will activate the lowering of the head and eyes in shame and reduce further exploration or self-exposure powered by excitement or joy. Such a barrier might be because one is suddenly looked at by one who is strange, or because one wishes to look at or commune with another person but cannot because he is strange, or one expected him to be familiar but he suddenly appears unfamiliar, or one started to smile but found one was smiling at a stranger.[23]

This experience of an encounter with the familiar-strange not only arouses thoughts of Freud's 'unheimlich', but also maps uncannily onto the experience of my encounter with Samuel West/Richard II. For example, I find myself 'looked at by someone who is strange': Samuel West is strange although he has been in my line of vision for over an hour, and becomes stranger in the act of looking at me because, in returning his look I see him differently – I notice his face as his face, rather than as an element in the ensemble that is the figure he presents. Also I am being offered, it seems, the possibility of communication. The desire to communicate is provoked by the look, the look that perhaps inevitably provokes and invites, yet the rules of the engagement clearly do not allow such a response on my part. Any response I may have felt myself being about to offer – a 'smile' perhaps, even if only a warming of the spirit through the eyes – is immediately inhibited by the strangeness of my interoculator. The fact that I cannot determine whether this is Samuel West or Richard II – the problem Berger in his armchair also faces – intensifies this problem. This is a problem of representation, and also, in a certain sense, a problem of ethics.

Someone is making claims on me and it's not entirely clear who. On the one hand, I feel obliged as a responsible and professional theatre-goer to comply with the contract I am being offered. Look for look is the deal. To turn my eyes away from his would be rude, and what's more, a betrayal of my own principles (those Brechtian principles of my youth). I have to return the gaze and hold it for as long as is required. On the other hand I have a resentful feeling that this is not entirely fair. Samuel West will at some point choose to move away, direct his gaze elsewhere, with no sense of obligation to me. I can live with that and I can even award myself some small moral consolation from the fact that I was man enough to look him in the eye, when others have visibly shirked their responsibilities and flinched away. But who exactly is it making this claim on me? Is it Samuel West or is it Richard II? When the ethical claim of the face-to-face encounter is deployed in this way, I feel I am entitled to know. And I am embarrassed because at precisely this moment the utter foolishness of the theatrical contract I have been going along with overwhelms me. I feel myself to be a fool for entertaining the possibility that Richard II might be asking something of me, and also feel Samuel West to be a fool for appearing in public pretending to be a medieval English king. The whole edifice of theatrical representation collapses and it's my fault for setting it up in the first place, or at least for going along with the project. I feel conned and found out at one and the same time. Shame heaped upon shame. Yet the rules of the game prohibit the shame response. By sticking to the contract I have ruled out the downward look, I must face it out, this encounter, brazen and unblushing. I am forbidden the experience of my own embarrassment. But in facing it out, it comes out on my face. I blush, as always, in spite of myself. The particular fierceness of this experience is later hinted at by Tomkins, although not fully explored in the theatrical context, when he observes that,

It is quite possible for an individual to be lost in admiration and excitement about another person, but with a minimum of awareness of one's own face and one's own self. The feedback from the face and chest constitute the awareness of excitement but such excitement appears to envelop the object of excitement and not to be localised on one's own face. One has only to look at the faces of a theater or TV audience to see that excitement can lift the individual out of his seat, his skin and his face, and place him experientially in the midst of the world created by the artist.[24]

The rupture in the machine of illusion, created by the reverse gaze, or even, perhaps, by the unexpected possibility of increased visibility created by the house lights coming up, is especially violent, because, secure in the dark the unobserved spectator has allowed excitement to work on the body, and on the face. To find oneself suddenly communicating this excitement to another person, and, what's worse, to a stranger who is strangely familiar, is to have one's desire outed. The theatre invites and seduces this desire and then, in the reverse gaze which is perhaps the key signifier of its ontological distinction from film and television, betrays it, dumping you back where you are, in your seat, to nurse the shame of having your desire thus exposed. Dumped back in your seat, thrown back upon your self, for

shame is an experience of the self by the self. At that moment when the self feels ashamed, it is felt as a sickness within the self. Shame is the most reflexive of affects in that the phenomenological distinction between the subject and object of shame is lost. Why is shame so close to the experienced self? It is because the self lives in the face, and within the face the self burns brightest in the eyes. Shame turns the attention of the self and others away from other objects to this most visible residence of self, increases its visibility and thereby generates the torment of self-consciousness.[25]

I put myself out of myself, all bright-eyed, only to find myself suddenly hiding myself. But unable to do so, because the ground does not open up, and instead, blood rushes to the site of my self, marking me out as the one who has exposed himself. The paradox of the blush as shame-response is that in the moment of reducing one kind of facial communication – the mutual look – I produce another. A communication that confirms to whomever would look the shameful fact of my self-exposure – yes, that really was me you saw out there – 'The very act whose aim is to reduce facial communication is in some measure self-defeating'.[26] Not only is embarrassment itself the appearance of some kind of breakdown in the representative structure of the theatrical machine, it is itself a breakdown of its own mechanism; a compound failure. Theatre starts to look like a pleasure and enjoyment machine designed to break down around its customers' acknowledgement of their desire for pleasure and enjoyment.

Meanwhile Tomkins starts to sound like Levinas. If one were to run this by Levinas (which will be done, in due course), one might find that Tomkins's shame is produced by the awareness of a failure properly to acknowledge the priority of the ethical relation proposed by the face to face. This ethical glitch has the potential to create embarrassment for either its perpetrator or for its 'victim', because, as Goffman observes, embarrassment can be felt *for* as much as *by* the *faux-passeur*.[27]

It is not only a question of representation and a question of ethics, but a question of political economy (one of the points at which questions of ethics and representation tend to converge). For it *is* the customer, after all, who is exposed here. I have suggested earlier that the 'dialectical image' in which the commodity appears in theatre and performance has the embarrassing effect of revealing the nature of the economic transaction underlying the performance. I will suggest later (Chapter Three) that both the neurotic language in which theatrical labour is discussed, and the constant harping on exploitation in respect of the human and animal bodies in the work of Societas Raffaello Sanzio betray a desire to deny the nature of the economic relationships in and through which theatre produces itself. While the discourses around labour and exploitation to be examined in Chapter Three will tend to expose the producer as producer in the eye of the consumer (who usually prefers to look away), the phenomenon of embarrassment arising from eye contact seems to expose the consumer as consumer in her own mind's eye, whether she looks away or not. In moments such as the encounter with Samuel West as Richard II, at least part of the embarrassment may stem from a recognition that the intimacy into which I am being seduced has been paid for. The intimacy is alienated: the familiar-strange is the strange-familiar.

If the experience of embarrassment can be understood then, as a shame response occurring within contexts which include political and economic relations, the self-consciousness that it signals has to be consistently understood as an understanding of oneself as implicated in, if not even, perhaps, constituted by such relations. This may be particularly important if the double nature of the self thus exposed in embarrassment is to be properly accounted for, since this doubleness or split seems to arise directly, at least within the terms established by the examples being discussed, from a sense of alienation, a positional discomfort in which one feels obliged to be in two persons/places at once, occasioned by uncertainty over market relations. Tomkins's account of shame and the shame response is almost exclusively psychological, and while it repeatedly refers to social contexts for the phenomena it seeks to explain, does not see psychological selves as political or economic productions.

The identification of a Levinasian tone in Tomkins's writing does not immediately suggest a quick route into deeper considerations of the political. However, in *Remnants of Auschwitz*, it is a brief passage of Levinas that plays a crucial part in Giorgio Agamben's attempt to arrive at a definition of shame that seems central to his account of the contemporary political subject. To situate the appearance of Levinas in Agamben's text, Agamben's own movement, throughout the book, from camp-survivor testimonies to political philosophy, is shadowed here. Before the citation of Levinas on shame, Agamben cites a recollection from Robert Antelme in which a student from Bologna is singled out from a column of prisoners to be shot. What Antelme recalls is that 'his face . . . turned pink. I still have that pink before my eyes . . . He turned pink after the SS man said to him, "*Du komme hier!*"'.[28]

Agamben regards this flush as a sign of 'the most extreme intimacy', namely 'the intimacy that one experiences before one's own unknown murderer'. The stranger takes on a terrible familiarity. Agamben compares this moment to the moment at the end of Kafka's *The Trial*, when Joseph K meets his murderers, and it is tempting to run this comparison back further, through moments in heroic narratives where those about to die in battle at the hands of unknown opponents beg to be allowed to know the identity of their killer. The student, Agamben, suggests, is ashamed for 'having to die, for having been haphazardly chosen – he and no one else – to be killed'.[29] The haphazard selection consigns the student to a role as random and meaningless object-victim while at the same time being an act of accidental but appalling intimacy. The student as the man whose life, its history, dreams and passions, is about to be brought to an end, is also the non-man whose selection for death has nothing to with him, his history, dreams and passions.

Agamben moves from this flush to cite what he describes as an 'exemplary analysis of shame' in Levinas's 1935 text,[30] *De l'évasion*, in which Levinas argues that:

What appears in shame is precisely the fact of being chained to oneself, the radical impossibility of fleeing oneself to hide oneself from oneself, the intolerable presence of the self to itself . . . What is shameful is our intimacy, that is our presence to ourselves.[31]

In a deepening of Levinas's analysis, Agamben follows Levinas's rejection of the idea that shame is imposed upon us by external factors, for example a sense of lack in relation to expectations of us held by others, either intimate or mediated by social norms. What he produces from this is a way of folding the political and economic conditions of self-production and self-consciousness *into* the intimate experience of self by self, in a subject whose responses are as much bodily as psychological. He seems to be producing a political body of shame:

To be ashamed means to be consigned to something that cannot be assumed. But what cannot be assumed is not something external. Rather it originates in our own intimacy; it is what is most intimate in us (for example, our own physiological life). Here the 'I' is thus overcome by its own passivity, its ownmost sensitivity; yet this expropriation and desubjectification is also an extreme and irreducible presence of the 'I' to itself. It is as if consciousness collapsed and, seeking to flee in all directions, were simultaneously summoned by an irrefutable order to be present at its own defacement, at the expropriation of what is most its own. In shame, the subject thus has no other content than its own desubjectification; it becomes witness to its own disorder, its own oblivion as a subject. This double movement, which is both subjectification and desubjectification, is shame.[32]

Shame as a physiological event, a bodily intuition, or shall I say, appearance, of a political condition is what seems to be at stake here. The flush of the Bologna student, then, is the action of a body that knows itself to be both everything and nothing, subject in and to a political regime where the mere inhabiting or possession of one's body is to be disciplined (Foucault) or killed (in Agamben's theorisation of 'bare life' as the body of the subject of modern bio-politics who may be killed with impunity).[33] It is knowing oneself to be such a body, such a 'bare life', both sacred and to be killed with impunity, that seems to be what the flush acknowledges. It is the way in which you appear as such. It is also perhaps, although Agamben does not press this point, except in the sense that he names the flush as a witnessing, a body aware of itself as being in view, picked out as the object of special attention in front of and in place of others. It is this appearing of oneself as 'bare life' that knows that in this appearing will come its consignment to this category, and thus, to death. More important than this fact of appearing to others, for Agamben, at least here, it seems, is the intimacy with oneself that comes from being compelled to attend one's own death. The self-witnessing is the real trigger, as if one were dreaming of seeing oneself executed, appearing to oneself as condemned to death. This intimacy is of course a 'proximity' rather than an identity, since the experience of intimacy depends upon the recognition of a certain distance from oneself. The folding in of the political within this self-intimacy becomes more explicit as Agamben suggests that one might think of shame as

nothing less than the fundamental sentiment of being a subject, in the two apparently opposed senses of this phrase: to be subjected and to be sovereign. Shame is what is produced in the absolute concomitance of subjectification and desubjectification, self-loss and self-possession, servitude and sovereignty.[34]

Embarrassment might then be the appearance of such a desubjectified subject. Elsewhere, in a short essay entitled 'The Face', Agamben writes about this experience of double subjection in terms of appearance, in a way that suggests that it might be helpful, however problematic, to talk about the 'flush of pink' on the Bologna student's face, as embarrassment rather than shame. When I am summoned up, as it were, by the face-to-face encounter, I blush because I appear, and because I know that I am locked in a structure in which I can only be as I appear. I can be nothing other than my appearance. That this reality should be on my face is clear from what Agamben writes:

We may call tragicomedy of appearance the fact that the face uncovers only and precisely inasmuch as it hides, and hides to the extent to which it uncovers. In this way, the appearance that ought to have manifested human beings becomes for them instead a resemblance that betrays them and in which they can no longer recognize themselves. Precisely because the face is solely the location of truth, it is also and immediately the location of simulation and of an irreducible impropriety. This does not mean, however, that appearance dissimulates what it uncovers by making it look like what in reality it is not: rather, what human beings truly are is nothing other than this dissimulation and this disquietude within the appearance. Because human beings neither are nor have to be any essence, any nature, or any specific destiny, their condition is the most empty and the most insubstantial of all: it is the truth. What remains hidden from them is not something behind appearance, but rather appearing itself, that is, their being nothing other than a face.[35]

The theatre is all about this appearing. It is an appearing in the face. In moments of embarrassment (or stage fright) what is happening is that you are suddenly aware of being made to appear, of the fact that you have your being through your appearance. The discomfort, the embarrassment, is what comes with actually experiencing this as a reality rather than simply in theory, or, to put it another way, from the recognition that appearing is all you can do, that there is nothing else but appearing, here, that appearance is not just the flimsy opposite of reality. Theatre can maintain the illusion that it is only about appearance (in the flimsy sense), so long as it manages itself properly. The moment something of the inappropriate, or, to use Alan Read's term, the 'inept' intervenes, appearance emerges in its truth, as reality. A properly managed theatrical encounter will only allow us to see actors appear, which is untroubling, since we know that actors are all about appearing. The theatre that fails to manage itself properly, the theatre that falls into the wrong, or acknowledges its wrongness, succeeds in making people appear, on the stage and in the house, not as authentic unproblematic and unified subjects, but doubled, in an appearance that is both truth and simulation. The fond hope that there might be 'that within which passeth show' is dashed. This, surely, is what, finally, Harry Berger may be sensing when he imagines that in response to the gaze of the actor he might try 'acting alert, responsive, displeased or bored', and that in doing so he might find himself 'free to choose a simulation that matches my actual feeling or one that hides it'.[36] In being made to appear we strangely sense that all we can do is appear, and that to be recognised is thus to be betrayed.

This is not simply to rehash the rather meaningless notion that all human behaviour is performance, or even that 'all the world's a stage', but instead to suggest that there is something in the appearing that takes place in the theatre that seems capable of activating in an audience a feeling of our compromised, alienated participation in the political and economic relations that make us appear to be who we are. As the choice of a production by the Royal Shakespeare Company for the key instance of theatre to be discussed in this chapter might suggest, this feeling may only be possible, or may be experienced most intensely, within the compromised and alienating space of the bourgeois theatre. I do not wish to claim that embarrassment is the appearance of 'the radical' in theatre, simply that in considering this 'minor' affect, something of truth, and of what 'the radical' might desire could be uncovered.

If the central subject of the next chapter, which is the appearance of animals on stage, might seem to involve a surprising movement, I'd like to claim it, nonetheless, as a logical one, in that the appearance of animals on stage, allows, I hope to show, the appearance of humans in a specific historical, political and economic situation. At first sight, and especially with Kleist in mind, the replacement of humans on stage by animals might offer some kind of escape from all these embarrassing face-to-face encounters. According to Kleist's Herr C., the theatre would be better off without human performers. We would be spared the blushes and the vomiting, just so long as all the performers lacked self-consciousness. Such is the appeal of the puppet, clearly, and also, one might start to suspect, the appeal of the animal performer. After all, as Bert States observes, 'there is always the fact that it doesn't know it is in a play'.[37] This is a relief, since all the blushes and the vomiting arise from the consciousness of self that is intrinsic, it seems, to the acts of performance and spectatorship that being 'in a play' entail: since as Herbert Blau persuasively suggests, 'what is universal in performance is the consciousness of performance'.[38] If the animal doesn't know what it is doing, and means nothing by doing it, the only consciousnesses engaged in the act of performance are those of the spectators, who are thus free to indulge their meaning-making faculties without risking any embarrassing encounters. It is another kind of imaginary audition, where, because the performer's subjectivity is not at stake, the spectator's is not really engaged.

This state of affairs would be fine for Herr C., but as his own second story – in which an animal performer makes its enigmatic and frightening appearance – shows, at least one risk still remains. The animal performer might be a reader too, in which case the ghastly reciprocity of the theatrical encounter sets in all over again. With an added and deeply alarming twist. Only the bear can look you in the eye. While Kleist's humans seem to be trying to look anywhere but at each other, in embarrassments at their mutual self-disclosure, the bear, supposedly without a self to disclose, discomforts Herr C. intensely, by returning his gaze. The animal looks back. There is, of course, no escape.

3   The animal on stage

Mouse in the house

In the Winter of 2001, during a performance of Harold Pinter's *The Caretaker* at the Comedy Theatre in London,[1] towards the end of Douglas Hodge's long account (as Aston) of his forced incarceration in a mental hospital and his treatment with electroconvulsive therapy, I thought I saw a mouse make an entrance from downstage left, crossing in a shallow diagonal and disappearing underneath the bed on which Hodge was seated. Upstage of Hodge, and more or less dead centre, sat Michael Gambon (as Davies), on another bed. After a short while in which I had time to run through various possibilities in my mind as to the exact nature of the phenomenon I had witnessed, the mouse reappeared, crossing in a far steeper diagonal from under Hodge's bed towards Gambon, who slid his right foot to one side to allow it past, and to disappear again beneath this second bed.

Quite apart from the additional excitement generated by the double entrance-exit routine executed by this non-human performer, and the odd way in which its activity was matrixed both by the mythology of romantically decrepit West End playhouses and the fictional setting of Aston's dilapidated room, one striking consequence of the stage mouse was the kind of conversation which sprang up around its appearance. The most thoroughly mined line of speculation was not just anthropomorphic but also economic and professional. An actor I spoke to in the bar during the second interval claimed that he and the mouse were both represented by the same agent. News that 'it may be going to New York' led to inevitable deliberate misunderstandings in which the production was assumed to be going, the mouse with it, but Gambon not. The Equity status of the mouse was discussed. That the mouse could be simultaneously conceived as being represented, possessing an agent and a role in the economy of the theatre dependent upon these agencies of representation is not entirely whimsical or fortuitous.

We know who we expect to see on stage. We expect to see actors. This needs saying: we do not even expect to see human beings, in all their diversity, but, as their representatives, a kind of group apart, more beautiful perhaps, more agile, more powerful and subtle of voice. Creatures who have been chosen on the basis of some initially desirable attributes, which they have subsequently honed and refined by means of professional training. So when we get something else, it appears as an anomaly, and a worrying one at that. The worries tend to be about exploitation. In the specific case of animals, there is an uneasy sense that the animal on stage, unless very firmly tethered to a human being who looks like he or she owns it, is there against its will, or if not its will, at least its best interests. The dog safely accompanied by fictional owner (like Launce's Crab in Shakespeare's *Two Gentlemen of Verona*) is naturalised out of this exploitative scenario by its subsumption into the owner-pet dyad. Other animals, perhaps especially those that are not quite so close to the human hearth as the dog, or which have a history of participation in long-extirpated cruel and unusual entertainments (bear-baiting, cock-fighting) bring with them specific and uncomfortable associations. A particular version of this discomfort obtains in the circus, sometimes seen as an anachronistic survival from the bad old bear-baiting days, but objections to circus do not also involve the sense that the animals shouldn't be there. Or at least not in the double sense that operates in the theatre. In the circus the animals shouldn't be there simply because it's cruel to make them perform tricks for us, but also should be there in the sense that they always have been. They are, after all, circus animals, and many of them may even have been born in to it. In the theatre, by contrast, the animals are not part of the tradition, even if they may sometimes have performed nearby. There are no theatrical dynasties of animals. The theatre, as the preceding chapter has tended to suggest, is all about humans coming face to face with other humans and

either liking it or not liking it. The animal clearly has no place in such a communication. Thus when it does appear on stage, untethered from framings as a pet within the dramatic fiction, the animal seems doubly out of place. Not only shouldn't it be there, because it can't be in its own interests to be, but also it shouldn't be there because this particular kind of being there when it shouldn't is what we expect to find in the circus, whether we go there or not, and we certainly don't want the theatre contaminated by that kind of association. There is also a third sense in which it shouldn't be there, closely related to these two: it shouldn't be there because it doesn't know what to do there, is not capable of performing theatrically by engaging a human audience in experimental thinking about the conditions of their own humanity (assuming for the moment the animal in question is appearing in a relatively highbrow entertainment: the effect of an animal appearing in, say, the musical *Cats*, might be another matter). The impropriety of the animal on the theatre stage is experienced very precisely as a sense of the animal being in the wrong place. In the circus there are still a few tawdry reminders of nature. The space is wide and open. It is a tent with an opening to the sky. Beneath our feet is some temporary flooring that does little to hide the proximity of the actual ground, grass and earth. The circus moves on. The theatre, by contrast, rigorously excludes nature. It stays where it is, in the city. No natural light comes in. On stage, there is culture raised to the power of two, as temporary floors and walls simulate the rooms of our own homes and other built spaces. Don't lean against the wall or the cultural equation collapses. Bringing an animal in here is courting disaster. We'll have them in our homes, so long as they have been properly trained, but in the super-artifice of the theatre, we fear that even the best-trained creatures could run amok at any moment, and spoil everything, especially since we know, don't we, that they would really rather be anywhere but here.

This last issue (the issue of control) is presumably the source for the much-cited advice never to work with animals (or children), usually attributed to W.C. Fields. One suspects that a fair few children and animals may have shared amongst themselves the advice never to work with Mr Fields, but this cannot be confirmed. The question of children as theatrical performers is a topic in its own right, and awaits a full study. It therefore largely falls outside the scope of this chapter. To some extent, however, children and animals raise similar problems for the theatre-going audience, suggesting that their appearance together in Fields's advice is more than coincidence. There are instances where the nature of the dramatic fiction allows the child actor to be assimilated like the fictional pet into the world of the professional actor, but where this assimilation is incomplete (which is often the case), there are side effects that are difficult to contain. The child actor starts to appear as precocious. Some training for child actors seems to have the effect of accentuating this, with too-perfect diction and too-sweet smiles. The precocious child is uncanny and (on stage at least) unpleasant, because of its knowing, or not-knowing-enough imitation of the imitations of its adult colleagues. They tend to appear as mini-adults, and some of our unease at their appearance seems to arise out of a sense that they are learning, and displaying too much too young. In two entirely different registers, the issue of exploitation tends to arise. In the 1980s on British television there was a programme called *Mini-Pops*, in which young children, mostly girls, dressed like the female pop stars of the day and performed raunchy routines to well-known songs.[2] Their dress, their make up and the feeling that their engagement with their material involved a worryingly precocious sexuality led to considerable concern over the programme. At the far end of the entertainment spectrum, the appearance of six children in the Auschwitz section of Societas Raffaello Sanzio's *Genesi from the museum of sleep* led some members of the British audience to protest that the children were being exploited by their use in piece of theatre that addressed issues beyond their understanding.[3] Similar concerns over the exploitation of performers who were not readily identifiable as actors, in the shapes that audiences are used to seeing them in, were raised in relation to the same company's *Giulio Cesare*,[4] where performers with unconventional body shapes, including two anorexic women, played major roles. The performers were described by one critic as 'exhibits'[5] and the production was described by another as a 'freakshow'.[6] In general, with both animals and children, the concern over exploitation focuses on whether or not the animals and children know what they are doing, whether they are capable of giving properly informed consent to their own participation and whether their lives will be in any way damaged by their appearance on stage. No such concern is expressed over adult performers, except where sexual exploitation becomes a major issue, as, for instance, in controversies over lap-dancing clubs.

I have already started to suggest that this anxiety over the exploitation of animals (and children) is both on the mark and wide of the mark, uncannily full of insight to which it is clearly blind. Labour and its divisions are clearly at stake, but rather more seriously than the liberal accusations of exploitation would credit. What these concerns actually illuminate rather valuably is the reality of theatrical employment itself, irrespective of the status or ability of the employee, as involving a particular form of exploitation.

Signs of labour

Michael McKinnie has suggested that this predictable response to the apparent excess of exploitation in these scenarios might usefully alert us to the always hidden exploitation of mature, able-bodied human actors.[7] McKinnie points out that the theatre is an economic subsector in which work is clearly alienated. Picking up on this perception one notes how the employee's time is regulated with rigorous force by bells and curtains, how both the rehearsal process and the nightly routine of performances are dominated by repetitive activity, how wage levels are set in structures of extreme differentiation, how these are maintained by a huge pool of surplus labour which renders effective industrial organisation impossible, and how the core activity itself is both a metaphor of alienation and alienation itself: the actor is paid to appear in public speaking words written by someone else and executing physical movement which has at the very least usually been subjected to intense and critical scrutiny by a representative of the management who effectively enjoys the power of hiring and firing. The actor is both sign and referent of the wholly alienated wage slave.

Yet what these hirelings are paid to produce, in the perspective stage and through the tools of psychological illusionism, is usually the fully rounded autonomous character, rich with the complex subjectivity which is the birthright of the bourgeoisie.

And the technique by which they produce these figures of bourgeois subjective autonomy works with uncanny efficiency to
hide the means of production: we see plays, not work, and the
success of character-production is routinely attributed to the
entirely free and spontaneous creativity of the autonomous
(non-bourgeois, bohemian) artist, who, of course, either never
did a day's work in his bloody life or literally (sic) sweated blood
to lay her creation before the public. The neurotic way in which
theatrical labour is discussed is surely a symptom that points to
the existence of a genuine underlying state of affairs, but one
which rarely, if ever surfaces as a political grievance in any
meaningful way. What the children and the animals do, therefore, is point through this neurosis to the alienation of the actor
and to the economic conditions of her presence on the stage. So,
to return to *The Caretaker*, it is clear that in this accidental
performing mouse we enjoy a fleeting glimpse of the bourgeois
subject's construction by the capitalist mode of production, and
its continued reproduction in a space that modern capitalism
figures as the absolute other of labour: entertainment.

The mouse, of course, means nothing by what it does, and it
is this, suggests Michael Peterson,[8] that gives the presence of
animals a distinctive quality on stage.[9] What I would like to
attempt to argue, however, is that that which appears distinctive about the stage presence of an animal can be viewed otherwise and made to figure as a clue to the nature of human stage
presence, which it more closely shadows than has generally
been accepted in accounts of the animal on stage. Lest the
mouse itself, so small, so accidental, prove too fragile a frame
on which to build a theory of theatrical labour, other animals
on other stages will be brought in (not, unfortunately, two by
two) to allow this argument to develop.

By not meaning anything by its appearance the mouse
appears less than human. Peterson is quite right to affirm that
'the presence of live animals introduces a non or anti-intentional
force',[10] an observation related to animals who are supposed
(intended by others) to appear, but which must clearly also
apply to those whose appearance is uncalled-for. This 'force',
Peterson suggests, 'lends itself to the perception of difference
and to an encounter with the uncanny'.[11] The lack of intention
presumably highlights the intention applied in performance by

humans, and herein lies the accentuation of difference, while the uncanny presumably arises from the illusion of intention generated by animal activity matrixed in performance in such a way as to fabricate intention. Above all, the intention to make a show of itself. By stepping on stage, even the mouse in *The Caretaker* is matrixed in such a way as to have intention readily imputed to it. The stage alone appears to be matrix enough to generate this uncanny effect. If this is the case then no animal can ever take the stage without producing the illusion of intention. As Peterson seems to acknowledge, 'live animal performance can never fully de-humanize the non-human animal'.[12]

Its participation, whether willed or unwilled, intended by others or entirely accidental, in the human activity of making a show automatically puts it in the place where that which is shown is also theorised (that place called the theatre) and where even the mouse in the house cannot evade the labour of meaning-production. Therefore the difference Peterson alludes to is at least partially effaced: although still visible as less-than-human, by sharing the stage with us the non-human animal is co-opted into patterns of intention, and through deep-seated impulses of anthropomorphism, appears as less less-than-human than it would in the wild. The more uncanny the less different.

Still some remainder resists semiosis. Semiotics, argues Peterson 'cannot tame what is wild about the signifier'.[13] What is it that semiotics would tame? The wild remainder that evades semiotic recuperation appears to be a kind of disruptive presence. As Robert Bresson, as part of an argument designed decisively to separate his cinema from the theatre, points out: 'On stage a horse or a dog that is not plaster causes uneasiness. In the theatre, looking for truth in the real is fatal'.[14] What Peterson calls 'the disturbing presence of an animal' seems to assert an irreducible phenomenality, yet at the same time to allow of the possibility of semiotic labour.[15] For Peterson also, intriguingly, argues that this

disturbing presence . . . could be framed, repeated (although not too often), distanced, abstracted – ideally, silhouetted – until it became one sign among many. But of course *no theatre person in their right mind would do such a thing.* Reduced to a sign, an animal contributes nothing to performance but expense and inconvenience.[16] [my emphasis]

By looking further at animal bodies and animal signs in Romeo Castellucci's *Giulio Cesare*, I think it is possible to see how, whether or not he is in his right mind, Castellucci does in fact employ animals as signs, in spite, or perhaps even because of, the expense and inconvenience involved.

Of course in *Giulio Cesare* an early modern sensibility figures classical antiquity as a time and space in which animals most certainly are signs, whether they like it or not.

> Against the Capitol I met a lion,
> Who gazed upon me and went surly by
> Without annoying me . . .
>
> . . .
>
> And yesterday the bird of night did sit
> Even at noon-day upon the market-place
> Hooting and shrieking.[17]

It is the displacement that is uncanny and convinces Casca these are 'portentous things'.[18] The lion is rich with intention, checking out the unarmed Casca, acting surly – not a quality for which the lion is usually known and an attitude that suggests a recalcitrance entirely human – and deciding, clearly, not to annoy him, while the owl is performing 'owl' with great commitment but at a time when it ought to be asleep. These are animals that have shifted from their proper place in the 'natural' world, to appear as signs. They are animals that have come on stage. Although Cicero cautions the overeager semiotician that 'men may construe things, after their fashion, / clean from the purpose of the things themselves',[19] even he seems to accept that these things (lions, owls) have purposes, and events in any case will soon conspire to bear out the semiotic reading of animal as portent. That semiotics cannot tame the wild signifier is the mark of our modernity. This relationship between meaning, non-human animals and human modernity will be discussed more fully in relation to both Aby Warbug and Adorno and Horkheimer later in this chapter.

For now, let's have a look at the animals themselves. A horse stands at the back of the stage as the feeble, white, emaciated body of Caesar is washed and pinned to the floor. We know he is Caesar because his only utterance was the Caesar sign 'veni, vidi, vici'. During the action which signifies the assassination the downstage flank of the horse is painted in white with the words 'Mene Tekel Peres'. Later, the skeleton of a horse is wheeled in to occupy the same place on the stage as the real horse. The skeleton is here to mourn, Old Paint-style, the death of its master (Brutus). Its head is pulled back to the recorded sound of a mournful neigh. It silhouettes itself, becoming the horse in the credits of a sentimental western, seen against the setting sun. A seahorse, hanging from a string, does nothing, except perhaps frame, repeat, distance, abstract. It is not a horse, it is just called a horse (is this the case in Italian? Yes: *cavalluccio marino*) and so its status as a horse on this stage depends entirely on its being read as sign rather than sea-creature. This puts the signifier 'horse' into a circuit between three referents: the skeleton, the sea-creature and the 'real, live' horse. There is a fox, stuffed, and attached to a shallow plinth, which is dragged across stage by a cord of some kind, and whose tail falls off and is adopted by Cassius. And, of course, there is the ironic cat. The cat sits almost undetected downstage centre amid the rubble of the second half set (a bombed out auditorium, seemingly haunted by bits of taxidermy as well as the emaciated dying Cassius and Brutus), and at a moment of high emotion suddenly sets its head spinning with cartoon speed, stopping abruptly and precisely and then slowly rotating to fix the audience with a gaze that is both challenge and comment. Challenge: can you take it?/make anything of this? Comment: how foolish we are to read emotion into the movements of animals (for to hear sorrow in the neigh of a horse is surely as foolish as to find ironic comment in the gaze of an animated stuffed cat).

Only one of these animals is 'real, live'. The others perform a variety of functions whose cumulative effect is to erase difference, to undermine almost to collapse the certainty with which we humans are used to distinguishing sign from being. The relationship between these animals – the variously dead among them seeming to tug the living with them into the grave that is semiotics – and the living breathing humans performing alongside them seems to be one in which the uncanny disturbance of the animal is somehow displaced onto the human actors. The bodies of the humans on stage – not only the anorexic women of the second half, but also the fragile white-skinned old man,

the huge-torsoed seated Cicero (with duck mask), the laryn-
gectomised Anthony-actor, not to mention the vocal chords
displayed on the endoscope screen – are all much more insistent on their 'irreducible phenomenality' than these animals
are. Because the 'real, live' horse is dragged into the world of
signs by this network of relations between meaningful bodies, it
is, beyond question being used, in defiance of common sense,
as a sign.

'No theatre person in their right mind would do such a
thing'.[20] Peterson suggests that all such a use of a live animal
performer as sign can add to a performance is 'expense and
inconvenience'. What if expense and inconvenience are what
the theatre person actually wants to incur?

Animals have appeared frequently in Raffaello Sanzio's work,
and one, which has appeared in several productions, is the horse
which originally created the role of 'the horse who was a sign' in
Giulio Cesare. However, when the company appear outside Italy,
their own animals are unable to travel with them. I take it that
this is for a mixture of reasons, most, if not all of which,
I assume, are concerned to some degree with the regulation of
capitalist economies: quarantine restrictions that limit the freedom of travel of their dogs; legislation on the transport of
livestock. The horse therefore not only stands on stage at the
Queen Elizabeth Hall in London as a sign for itself and others,
but also as a stand-in or representative (local understudy) of the
production's original horse, and as a reference to the economies
of everyday and theatrical labour in which company members,
both human and non-human, take part.

In a production by Tehran's Theatre Bazi, called *The Mute
Who Was Dreamed*, there was a duck on stage throughout the
performance.[21] It was a white duck and it mostly stood on a
table either preening itself or gazing at or away from the audience. Occasionally it was incorporated into the human action of
the piece – embraced, moved. The problem, it emerged, is that
this was a stage duck. Like the stage child, something of a
confection. Attila Posselyani, director of the piece, asked to
comment on what a largely expatriate Iranian audience assumed
must be vast differences between what he is allowed to show on
stage in Iran and what he was allowed to show in this presentation at London's Riverside Studios, sidestepped the obvious

political land-mine – there were, after all, men from the Iranian Embassy with video cameras – and spoke instead about the problem of the duck. It is supposed to be a wild duck, and it is supposed to be male. This one was quite definitely tame, and according to Posselyani, female. One of my friends was absolutely convinced that it was 'acting'. The company had not been allowed to bring their own duck, and had been compelled to make do with an officially permitted duck. An application had been made to the Chief Government Veterinarian to obtain a license for the presentation of a duck on stage. The duck itself had been rented from a stage animals agency, and came with obligatory duck-wrangler, at a cost of over two-hundred pounds per night.[22] In 2004, Raffaello Sanzio had to rethink their planned London episode of *Tragedia Endogonidia* when it proved impossible to hire an elephant to appear on stage. In the episode finally presented in London seven or eight cats appeared, at a cost of 2400 euros.[23] Over four performances this worked out at around seventy-five euros per cat, per night. Some of the cats were only kittens.

The animals are therefore also signs of a certain amount of 'expense and inconvenience', and of labour in the context of managing a theatre company in a regulated European economy. Whether this background information is relevant to the spectator seems irrelevant to me. The expense has been incurred and the inconvenience suffered. The horse, for example, is clearly and visibly inconvenient (especially in the rather untheatrically tidy location of a modern concert hall) to all but the most superficial viewer, and it appears as excess (almost as conspicuous consumption) in the presence of so many 'plaster' animals who sign with just as much efficiency. In becoming an efficient sign with phenomenal 'noise' filtered out by the framing and repetition, the horse insists that this excess must have a purpose. The purpose is to point to the excess, expense and inconvenience. In a theatre production where the issues of exploitation repeatedly ask to be raised, it seems clear that the economic relations between animals and humans must be acknowledged as being in play.

The proposition that the animal on stage might work to highlight questions of labour, in ways that address directly the problems faced by Kleist's Herr C., is given highly suggestive support by the use of animals, both dead and alive, in Jan Fabre's production of *Swan Lake* for the Royal Ballet of Flanders.[24] To the conventional dramaturgy of the ballet developed around the music of Tchaikovsky and the choreography of Petipa and Ivanov, which itself concerns violent transformations of women into swans and vice versa as its central action, Fabre made a series of what might be termed tactical additions, all of which appear to have been designed to address the issue of labour at the level of form. While the conventional choreography handles the transformations of Odile and Odette into swans and back entirely within the vocabulary of classical ballet, Fabre introduced several elements in which classical technique was thrown aside. From time to time throughout the production one male member of the corps de ballet performed a floorbound dance of agonised metamorphosis, in which spasmodic contortions of his arms repeatedly failed to lift him into the air. His arms stubbornly refusing to become wings, his body crashed violently against the floor, again and again. A chorus of armoured knights performed a unison dance, in which the weight and constraints of their metal casings visibly and audibly prevented them from attaining the grace enjoyed by other choric groups (most particularly, of course, the swans themselves). During an earlier sequence of repetitive choric sequences involving four pairs of dancers, the skeletons of dead animals were 'flown' into the proscenium. The production as a whole was framed by the presence of an owl, seen first in a film sequence projected onto a front-cloth at the opening of the performance, and then again at each interlude, and subsequently, live on stage, tethered to the head of the dancer taking the role of Rothbart (the evil prince whose spell has imprisoned the Princess Odette in the body of a swan). Although the presence of the owl during a number of key scenes clearly worked in ways that stressed the owl's real material presence amid so much highly technical artifice (it squawked consistently against Tchaikovsky's score; another case of an owl performing 'owl' with great commitment), it also formed part of a network of signification in which the labour of ballet itself was made visible.

As I have suggested in the discussion of Kleist in the introduction, the grace to which human dancers aspire and to which only those without consciousness can attain is a grace to be achieved without visible labour. Instead of the human dancer visibly and audibly working against the limitations of physiology and the constraints of gravity, Kleist's marionettes seem to move, their feet barely scraping the ground, without putting in any effort at all. They don't even break a sweat. Of course behind them and all their kind lie other labourers (the puppeteers and the manufacturers), but the drive of an aesthetic based on the marionette is that all effort should be eradicated from the moment of performance, so that the audience experiences the work as spontaneous free play. We see plays, not work, again. Joseph Roach locates Kleist's essay at the start of a very particular Romantic approach to performance in which spontaneity and grace are achieved by means of technical virtuosity. In order to present the audience with the satisfying illusion of perhaps superhuman or even supernatural powers, long hours of repetitive and painful physical labour are required. Roach cites the virtuoso displays of Paganini in the concert hall and bel canto on the operatic stage, but reserves the paradigmatic place to the pointe technique of ballerina Marie Taglioni. Her apparently effortless transcendence of gravity was achieved at a price:

> The ballerina's body, like the singer's larynx of yesteryear, is tortured into shapes and launched into physical trajectories that are not in nature. In the absence of suitable automata or in spite of them, repetition of exercises must fix the positions and motions of the dance so indelibly on the artist's muscles that she becomes capable of transcending artistically extraneous impulses such as pain. The art of the dance is motion recollected in tranquillity.[25]

Or, work reproduced as play. In the case of Fabre's staging of *Swan Lake*, it is the animal skeletons that compel the audience to think about the bodies of the ballerinas. From the very start of the performance, the skeleton of a swan has been placed downstage left, in front of the proscenium. The skeletons (of horse, bear and other unidentified creatures) are lowered from the flies during sequences in which ballerinas are repeatedly and bluntly lifted and held, as if for display, by their male partners. The bodies of the ballerinas, displayed thus, as though in the museum from which the skeletons seem to descend, are there, in ballet terms, to make aesthetically gratifying shapes: to be geometry rather than biology. What the animal skeletons do is force the audience to consider the skeletons of the dancers too. Suddenly conscious of the fact of the skeleton, the effort of lifting, the tension of the poses, the audience becomes aware of the musculature at work in the fabrication of the spectacle. The struggles of the male dancer trying to fly and the chorus of armoured knights trying to dance both seem to allude to the same thematisation of work as an essential prerequisite of technique.

The appearance of the live owl, later in the piece, seems to work in relation to the human bodies and the animal skeletons rather as does the live horse in *Giulio Cesare* in relation to the various stuffed and skeletal animals with which it shares the stage. That is to say that a continuum of living and dead organisms, variously engaged in the making of meaning, and variously exploited, are put to work at the service of art or entertainment. Roach's observations on technical virtuosity and its physical cost might provide a fruitful reading of *Giulio Cesare*, in which the technical accomplishment of rhetoric is 'paid for' by the laryngectomy of the actor playing Mark Anthony, and in which the human labour of moving about the stage is mimicked or mocked by the automaton elements of the mise en scène (the cat, the horse skeleton, the chair that walks across the stage, the collar that vibrates around Brutus' throat to make his voice tremble). What seems to emerge forcefully from both productions is that the co-presence of animals (dead or alive), humans (alive) and machines (dead or alive or just uncanny) is what tends most readily to generate this revelation of labour in the act of play.

Of course this 'labour of reading' that produces a 'reading of labour' (both mine and Fabre's) is open to charges of anthropomorphism and violence, on the basis that it wrenches the animal from its animal-ness and places it within a world of human signification (indeed, it could be argued that just putting an animal on stage does this.) On the other hand, in Fabre's defence, if not in mine, one might say that this anthropomorphism and its attendant violence is precisely the thematic material with which *Swan Lake*, especially in Fabre's version, is grappling. The competing claims of non-violence (ethical) and the making of meaning (always potentially political) are at the heart of the argument that follows. The ethically motivated desire to resist making meaning out of animals on stage involves, I shall suggest, a suppression of affect and an evasion of political engagement based upon an ontological distinction between human and non-human animals that is not sustainable in practice.

This wholly understandable desire is clearly founded in an understanding of, and respect for, alterity of the kind that has characterised much recent ethical philosophy, including, of course, the work of Levinas, as well as other projects that take Heidegger as a starting point (either positively or negatively). Much recent writing on non-human animals, including the best recent work on animals in art and performance, displays an interest in alterity as part of a commitment to an ethical re-evaluation of relations between human and non-human animals. The work of Steve Baker, Alan Read and David Williams is perhaps exemplary in this regard.[26] Implicit in some of this work is the idea that we might let the animal be, in its alterity, and while this has clear and important ethical importance, it leaves certain valuable questions unasked. What if, for example, non-human animals are just like human performers – not, as some might suggest, because they are part of some deterministic bio-aesthetic web – but because they all work in a theatrical economy characterised by exploitation and the division of labour? The closing sequence of this chapter works under the shadow of this question, while ostensibly trying to offer the beginnings of an historical account of human-animal relations that might explain why it is that the exploitation of animal labour in the theatre retains its affect in ways that the exploitation of human labour in the same place does not.

Animal politics

Looking at animals in ways that 'let them be' 'as they are' occludes the historical. The tension between a properly historical account of animal-human relations and one that is merely ontological surfaces fascinatingly in the struggle to translate, adequately into English, Romeo Castellucci's explanation of what animals are doing in his theatre.

Il teatro contiene sempre, a mio avviso, un problema teologico. È stato così dall'inizio, fin dalla fondazione del teatro. Il teatro è attraversato da questo problema, dalla presenze di Dio, perchè il teatro nasce per noi occidentali quando Dio muore. È evidente che l'animale gioca un ruolo fondamentale in questo rapporto tra il teatro e la morte di Dio. Nel momento in cui l'animale sparisce dalla scena, nasce la tragedia. Il gesto polemico che facciamo rispetto alla tragedia attica e quello di riportare sulla scena l'animale facendo un passo all'indietro. Rivolgere l'aratro sui propri passi, vedere un animale sulla scena, significa andare verso la radice teologica e critica del teatro. Un teatro pretragico significa, innanzi tutto, infantile. Il teatro pretragico è, accelerando quest'immagine, l'infanzia. L'infanzia, intesa come "in-fanzia", cioè come la condizione di chi è fuori dal linguaggio. Quindi, se c'è una polemica nei confronti della tragedia è senz'altro legata al ruolo dell'autore, al moto della scrittura e quindi a questa incredibile pretesa di verticalità sessuata.[27]

This may be rendered in English as follows:

The theatre always contains, for me, a theological problem. This has been the case from the beginning, from the foundation of the theatre. The theatre is shot through with this problem, of the presence of God, because the theatre, for us Westerners, was born when God died. It is clear that the animal plays a fundamental role in this relationship between the theatre and the death of God. The moment the animal disappeared from the stage, tragedy was born. The polemical gesture we are making in respect of Attic tragedy is to take a step backwards by returning the animal to the stage. To turn the plough back on its own path, to see an animal on stage, means to go towards the theological and critical roots of the theatre. A pre-tragic theatre means, first of all, an infantile theatre. Pre-tragic theatre is, to extend the image, a theatre of infancy. Infancy understood as *in-fans*: the condition of those who are outside language. Therefore if there is a polemic regarding tragedy it is without doubt related to the role of the author, to the movement of writing and therefore to that incredible pretension of a verticality that is differentiated in terms of gender.[28]

In Romeo Castellucci's contribution to *Performance Research 5.2: On Animals*, however, entitled 'The Animal Being on Stage', the final sentence of this passage appears as follows:

Therefore, if such a polemic concerning tragedy exists, it is certainly related to the role of the author, to the domain of writing and its incredible pretence towards the author, whose body, as well as the animal's, mainly consists in a simple and, at the same time, radical reality: "being there."[29]

Clearly, Castellucci's published Italian text (much of which appears to be a more or less word for word transcription of an interview with Yan Ciret at l'Académie Experimentale des Théâtres de Paris), contains some difficulties at this point, which the English translators have sought to clarify (perhaps in collaboration with Castellucci) by rewriting.[30] The effect of the revision in translation is striking. Where Castellucci's Italian appears to refer to some kind of historical moment in the development of relations between animals and humans, the revision does not, offering instead something much more in keeping with a purely ontological account of their difference. A close analysis of the texts will open up the nature of this historical moment as well as the means by which it may be occluded.

The real problem in the text is the term 'verticalità sessuata'. Verticality, differentiated in terms of gender, is said to be an incredible pretension. What is it, and what is its relationship to writing and to the author? Along with language, verticality is one of a number of characteristics customarily understood to distinguish humans from non-human animals. In a sentence that follows immediately from a discussion of a prelinguistic state – "in-fanzia" – a reading that understands verticality in terms of a transition, either a child's transition from crawling to walking, or an historical transition from non-human to human animal seems legitimate. Castellucci may, then, be talking about the entry into language alongside the move from four legs to two, and with it, in a kind of bundling together of mythic origins, the assumption of authorship through the act of writing. Furthermore, the verticality that thus moves towards authorship must also be considered as differentiated by gender.

The acts of incredible pretension are therefore those in which the (male) human animal takes the historic step of distinguishing itself from other animals by standing up and giving them names; establishing dominion over them by means of dividing them one from another, in language. In the process he seeks – this, perhaps is the most incredible pretension – to mark that verticality as male, leaving the female behind. This is a triple differentiation: of human from animal, and of one animal from another, and of male from female human. This is because acts of authorship – including those of the tragic playwrights – are seen, at least in mythical thought, as part and parcel of a process of separation of the human from the animal, and also as an establishment of a male order (law and politics) in place of an order more strongly marked by female power. As Castellucci himself suggests, in a passage immediately following the passage cited, 'pre-tragic theatre . . . is linked instead to a presence or a power of a female type'.[31] This of course is the effect of the court of the Areopagus, at which the new law and order of the *polis* is affirmed over and above the (religious) claims of the Furies.[32] That the act of authorship on the part of the tragic playwrights seemed to involve the simultaneous expulsion of both gods and animals from the stage (which was, in its pre-tragic moment, outside language), would seem to underline this connection between writing and human (male) power. The assumption of authorship is then a pretension as regards the gods or God, as well as a division of labour between humans and animals, and among male and female humans. It is the invention of intellectual labour (writing, authorship) and thus, by definition, the simultaneous invention of manual labour. Intellectual labour, of course, will always and henceforth be adult human labour, while manual labour will always threaten to return its workers to infancy and animality. Historically it has been women rather than men who have more often run this risk of a relapse into states construed in terms of infancy and animality by means of exclusion from intellectual labour, and men who have sought to transcend such infancy and animality by dominion in the domain of authorship and its associated trades.[33]

The moment, then, seems almost too full of historical import. The polemical gesture made by Socìetas Raffaello Sanzio is to identify the disappearance of the animal from the stage with the inauguration of class and gender struggle through the division of labour. This moment figures, then, as the start of history itself. We are unquestionably in the presence of a myth of origins, in respect of which the restoration of the animal to the stage is a 'radical' act inasmuch as it gestures towards this cluster of origins. If the plough might be understood as an exemplary symbol of the labour that decisively moved the human animal above and beyond the other animals (along with its verticality and its writing), then Castellucci's image of the plough being taken back along its own furrow follows this very same trajectory – towards, of course, 'the theological and critical roots' of theatre. The radical act of bringing the animals back on stage consists in the way it brings this history back into view. Castellucci seems to be suggesting that the division of labour, the death of God, the establishment of human dominion over the animals and the birth of tragedy may all be seen as simultaneous, as moments of the same historical moment, and that the historical moment in question is, in effect, the moment at which history begins (made through labour and available through writing). Western theatre has kept the animal offstage in order to hide its origins in these moments of inaugural violence and the institution of divisions of labour.

The history that comes back into view once the animal is returned to the stage is a materialist history. It is, first of all, a history in which humans are to be distinguished from non-human animals not by some abstract schema or system of classification, but by an act of human will, as Marx and Engels suggest:

Men may be distinguished from animals by consciousness, by religion or anything else you like. They themselves begin to distinguish themselves from animals as soon as they begin to produce their means of subsistence, a step which is conditioned by their physical organisation. By producing their means of subsistence men are indirectly producing their actual material life.[34]

What Marx and Engels do not render explicit here, but which seems implicitly evident, is that this production of their own material life, by humans who thus distinguish themselves as humans, is achieved through the violent subjugation of non-human animals, either through hunting on the one hand, or domestication and sacrifice on the other. Humans come into being not simply by knowing themselves to be different, but by making themselves different, through the practical and material revision of their relations with other animals. The sense that human society came into being through a conscious action in relation to animals, of this kind, seems to have been strongly present in Greek thought too, where the Protagoras myth proposed an anthropology based on human success in an outright and violent conflict with other animals. The Protagoras myth tells how the Titan Epimetheus used up all his powers providing for the different animals and sorting out their mutual ecology, providing them with the interlocking set of capabilities and skills that would allow them to survive in the world, so that when faced finally with humans he had nothing left to give them, leaving them feeble, naked and unprovided for. Seeing them in this naked and feeble condition, his fellow Titan Prometheus took pity on the humans and was moved to steal from Hephaestus and Athena their technical skill along with the use of fire. With this gift came the establishment of human society as a defence of human capacities against the threat of the animals:

Since man thus shared in a divine gift, first of all through his kinship with the gods he was the only creature to worship them, and he began to erect altars and images of the gods. Then he soon developed the use of articulate speech and of words, and discovered how to make houses and clothes and shoes and bedding and how to till the soil. Thus equipped, men lived at the beginning in scattered units, and there were no cities; so they began to be destroyed by the wild beasts, since they were altogether weaker. Their practical art was sufficient to provide food, but insufficient for fighting against the beasts – for they did not yet possess the art of running a city, of which the art of warfare is part – and so they thought to come together and save themselves by founding cities.[35]

Thus the establishment of the *polis* and the art of politics itself originates in humans' need to defend themselves against the animals who are stronger than they are, in spite of human religion, speech, houses and agriculture. The development of a theatre designed as integral to the life of the *polis* – tragedy – is enabled then by the act that in establishing humans as distinct from other animals also establishes once and for all human physical superiority over them. The formation of human society, in the Protagoras myth, seems to be completed by this subjugation of the animals through the art of politics. Before humans developed the art of politics and began to live in cities rather than out in the open where they were vulnerable to the wild beasts, their real identity as human beings had not been established:

man's consciousness of the necessity of associating with the individuals around him is the beginning of the consciousness that he is living in society at all. This beginning is as animal as social life itself at this stage.[36]

Living in the open, the human, without politics, but merely social life, is not distinguishing him or herself from other animals yet:

It is mere herd-consciousness, and at this point man is only distinguished from sheep by the fact that with him consciousness takes the place of instinct or that his instinct is a conscious one.[37]

Marx and Engels appear uncertain quite how instinct has become conscious at this point, and indeed the distinction made here on the basis of the shift from instinct towards consciousness is a doubtful one, simply within the terms of Marx and Engels's own line of argument, according to which, the real distinction is the one that is actively made by humans in their production of their own means of subsistence. Unless they distinguish themselves in this way they may only be distinct 'in-themselves' rather than 'for-themselves' and the question as to for whom they might be distinct at this moment in their historical development is left hanging. The distinction on the basis of consciousness and instinct appears to operate only retrospectively, once there are philosophers capable of positing a historical moment in which such a distinction might have been in place, even if no one at the time had been conscious of it. More importantly, however,

This sheep-like or tribal-consciousness receives its further development and extension through increased productivity, the increase of needs, and, what is fundamental to these, the increase of population. With these there develops the division of labour, which was originally nothing but the division of labour in the sexual act, then that division of labour which develops spontaneously or "naturally" by virtue of natural predisposition (e.g. physical strength), needs, accidents, etc. etc. Division of labour only becomes truly such when a division of material and mental labour appears. (The first form of ideologists, *priests*, is concurrent.)[38]

In effect, the human distinguishes itself from the sheep once it starts to view the sheep as a potential instrument in the satisfaction of its own needs on a long-term, self-reproducing basis. Once the function of the sheep shifts from that of wild beast which may be killed and eaten, to beast that may be acquired and made to reproduce for the benefit of humans (milk, wool), the true distinction between humans and animals appears to fall into place. Crucially, then, the act in which the human decisively makes itself human, in producing the means of its own subsistence, appears to be the moment at which it has acquired the 'political' skills of animal husbandry.[39] A division of labour that began in the distinct roles of male and female human animals in the act of reproduction, is reinscribed at the level of production of the means of production (of which non-human animals are a key element) and again at the level of ideology, in which the origins of the power of the ideologists, who must include authors and tragedians as well as Marx and Engels's 'priests' are occluded. Once this division of labour, the first that is 'truly such', is in place, the idealist task of effacing the origins of priestly and authorial power can begin:

From this moment onwards consciousness can really flatter itself that it is something other than consciousness of existing practice, that it really represents something without representing something real; from now on consciousness is in a position to emancipate itself from the world.[40]

The pre-tragic theatre, material, feminine, infant and populated by the animal gives way to the tragic theatre that is ideal, male, political and only human. (Of course, it is only in the 'ideological' presentation of these differences that they solidify into such apparently 'self-evident' binary formations). The development of tragic theatre from its mythic origins in the pre-tragic theatre appears then as a potentially constitutive element in the establishment of a certain political order: that of the city and the class struggle, and simultaneously, of an ideological structure that, by appearing emancipated from material reality, is able to develop historical and mythical narratives of how that order came into being in terms that are far from material. Much of what is so compelling about Attic tragedy stems from the fact that this act of idealist mythologisation is incomplete, that the plays themselves are marked by the violence that they are seeking to overcome and obscure. It is in this sense that they most definitely are engaged in a 'debate with a past that is still alive'.[41] The coincidence between the historical narrative implied by Castellucci's highly compressed formulation and that offered by Marx and Engels in *The German Ideology* should not come as a surprise, nor should it, necessarily, be understood in such a way that the one narrative reinforces or lends credibility to the other. What this coincidence points to, rather, may be the degree to which Marx's historical thought was shaped by German Hellenism. As Jean-Pierre Vernant remarks:

For Marx, as for all educated individuals of his generation in Germany, Greece was the cradle of humanity. Marx was well aware that, outside Greece and even earlier than it, there had been other civilisations, other cradles. But as he saw it, none of these beginnings, none of these first steps so typically represented the infancy of humanity.[42]

Infant humanity takes its first steps (achieves verticality) in German Greece, and it is from German Greece that the grand historical narratives of the nineteenth century draw their mythic power.

The *Performance Research* text attempts something quite different, and in so doing replaces (mythic) history with timeless ontology, albeit not without some difficulty. Instead of functioning as a trace of an occluded history of violence, labour and domination, the animal, once returned to the stage as a polemical gesture, finds itself just 'being there'. It appears, it seems, as a raw chunk of the real, or even, perhaps as the originary 'real', if the strong sense of 'radical' is to be preserved. The issue is complicated, however, by the decision to insist that the body of the author shares this quality with the body of the animal. If this is to be taken seriously then the translated text is not in fact suggesting what at first it seemed to be, that the ontological distinction between human and non-human animals resides in the animal's capacity to stand outside representation. If it does stand there, as the text seems to suggest it does, then so does the author and the distinction collapses. Perhaps the solution lies in a reading which is attentive to the use of the word 'body'. The body of the author 'mainly consists' in 'being there', as a kind of material precondition of the non-bodily and highly representational activity of the author's writing. Of course, if this is the case then it implicitly leaves open the possibility that the animal's body, which also 'mainly consists' in this 'being there', could also become the basis for non-bodily activity or labour (involving will, self-consciousness and so forth). I am not at all certain that this is what Allsopp, Melis and Valentini intend. It seems more likely that they are trying to tease coherence out of a particularly compacted piece of text, and in doing so preserve some of its complexity while shifting it decisively (and to my mind, unhelpfully) towards meanings more congruent with the ontological view of human-animal relations than with the Marxist inflection I have started to articulate above. The ambiguity in

their text might best be regarded as the scar left in the Heideggerian flesh by the Marxist wound, the trace of a struggle between ontology and historicity, between idealist and materialist
accounts of the animal, the human and their respective places in
the tragic and pre-tragic theatre.

What was the animal doing on stage before the birth of
tragedy? What was the pre-tragic theatre? We simply do not
know.[43] The materialist history to which the return of the
animal to the stage appears to allude involves a prehistory of
which, as a function of our own ideological activity and as a
direct result of the division of mental from physical labour, we
no longer have any memory. Instead we have a set of relations
that would appear to presuppose, as their origins, a specific but
ultimately unspecifiable activity. One aspect of the work of
Societas Raffaello Sanzio since their first major engagement
with tragedy in the *Oresteia* of 1996 would seem to involve an
attempt imaginatively to reconstitute this activity through the
deliberate, even literal, reinstatement of those things we believe
we know tragedy to have expelled from the theatre, including, of
course, animals. Their decision to seek in the contemporary
world some means of making a vanished experience available
again (while acknowledging, of course, the fragility or even
futility of such research) echoes an earlier attempt, by the art
historian Aby Warburg, to find secrets of prehistory alive in the
present.

In 1923, while a patient of the psychologist Ludwig Binswanger, Warburg gave a lecture by which he hoped to demonstrate to
Binswanger the extent of his recovery and thereby secure Binswanger's consent to his departure from the nursing home.[44]
Warburg chose to speak about the survival into modernity of
the serpent ritual of the Hopi people of south-western USA,
and to explore the historical limits of technological rationality
through a reading of a performance with animal participants.[45]
German Hellenism had long since (from Winckelmann onwards)
seen parallels between Native American and ancient Greek
cultures, so for a scholar of classical culture like Warburg, the
attempt to use anthropological fieldwork as an alternative to
time-travel was a choice with substantial intellectual weight
behind it.[46] Warburg would demonstrate that he was in his right
mind by means of a rational performance about an irrational

performance, whose animal participants would somehow undermine the grounds, or at least the value of the rationality Warburg
was seeking to demonstrate in himself. In this respect Warburg's
text seems to prefigure the central thesis of Adorno and
Horkheimer's *The Dialectic of Enlightenment*, a text that has been
haunting the present discussion for some while, and which will be
addressed more directly below. Adorno and Horkheimer's discussion of the entanglement of enlightenment rationality with
myth, and the relationship between the domination of nature
and the division of labour are clearly of enormous relevance to
considerations of Attic tragedy and considerations of animal-
human relations. For the purposes of the present discussion,
however, the most immediately significant aspect of Warburg's
account is that the animals in the Hopi rituals undoubtedly
possess intention.

The Indian's inner attitude to the animal is entirely different from that
of the European. He regards it as a higher being, as the integrity of its
animal nature makes it a much more gifted creature than man, its
weaker counterpart.[47]

And in the specific case of the rattlesnakes collected in their
hundreds and held in the mouths of dancers during the serpent
ritual itself:

Here the dancers and the live animals form a magical unity, and the
surprising thing is that the Indians have found in these ceremonies a way
of handling the most dangerous of all animals, the rattlesnake, so that it
can be tamed without violence, so that the creature will participate
willingly – or at least without making use of its aggressive abilities, unless
provoked – in ceremonies lasting for days.[48]

For Warburg the meaning of this survival of the primitive amid
technological modernity is clear:

How does humanity free itself from this enforced bonding with a
poisonous reptile to which it attributes a power of agency [it makes
the rain come]? Our own technological age has no need of the serpent
in order to understand and control lightning . . . We know that the
serpent is an animal that must succumb, if humanity wills it to. The
replacement of mythological causation by the technological removes
the fears felt by primitive humanity. Whether this liberation from the
mythological world view is of genuine help in providing answers to the
enigmas of existence is another matter.[49]

When this experience of animals in performance is considered in relation to the use of animals in performance by Socìetas Raffaello Sanzio, the meaning of the animal is amplified. The animal on stage today is a phantom of an earlier animal presence which humanity had not yet violently compelled to succumb to its own rational purposes, nor stripped of its power to mediate. The animal became mute nature when humanity made it so. When the animal returns, although in part the (exploited) object of human economies, it brings with it as part of its phantom presence, the possibility of its will. Alongside Warburg's compromised advocacy for the modern is a thread of complicity with the old magic: 'the creature will participate willingly'. This observation is presented as reported fact, the record of a field trip. The effect in Warburg's text is uncanny; the rattlesnakes are effectively overheard saying, 'Shall we go along with this?', or 'I'm feeling matrixed but I don't mind'. Warburg himself seems to be saying, 'I've seen the snakes dance but, really, I'm alright'. What Castellucci's restoration of the animal to the stage therefore seeks to achieve is not to permeate his theatre with the muteness of animal matter, as some readings of his own texts might suggest, but rather to bring the possibility of animal will into a technological mise en scène.[50]

The moment Warburg witnesses is the moment of magic and mimesis. The dancers imitate the snakes and the snakes permit the magic to be performed. This is a moment that is soon to be succeeded by the practice of animal sacrifice, where, again, the question of consent is of vital importance. That there is some connection between animal sacrifice and theatre is fairly well accepted, even if the more contentious accounts of a direct transformation of the former into the latter – such as those of the Cambridge Ritualists, René Girard, and Walter Burkert – are now thought to be discredited, at least in their more ambitious 'grand theory of everything' claims.[51] Animal sacrifice was an essential element in all the public rituals of the city, including the festival of Dionysus at which tragedies were performed. Michael H. Jameson – in a collection of essays suggestively entitled *Performance Culture and Athenian Democracy* – argues that animal sacrifice (*thusia*) was the city's 'central and essential ritual' and therefore that '[o]ther performative actions such as procession and dance may be viewed as elaborations of aspects of *thusia*'.[52] As Pierre Vidal-Nacquet demonstrates in his analysis of sacrificial imagery in Aeschylus's *Oresteia*, animal sacrifice haunts a performance that deals directly and explicitly with the terms and conditions upon which human civil society is establishing itself.[53] More generally, as both Vernant and Vidal-Nacquet show, ritual patterns are taken up and used by tragic playwrights as a privileged way of exploring the place of the human in the order of nature: the proper or improper observation of ritual processes such as sacrifice appears in tragedy as a key to the validity of human political and social action. This is not simply a question of imagery; sacrifice is intrinsic to tragic form. In a 'performance culture' sacrifice appears to have at the very least provided the structures and contexts for the viewing of all other performance activity.

The consent of the animal – its willing participation in Athenian performance culture – is vital. In Vidal-Nacquet's reading of Aeschylus's *Oresteia*, in which the killings of Iphigenia, Agamemnon and then Clytemnestra are variously figured in terms of either hunting or sacrifice, the question of the legitimacy of the murders hangs on metaphorical parallels with the consent or otherwise of the animal in the conduct of *thusia*: 'domestic animals which are, in effect, the normal victims for sacrifice, must give some sign to signify their assent'.[54] If the animal does not give its consent, according to Marcel Detienne, the sacrifice is illegitimate: 'when some animals refuse to move toward the altar . . . the sacrificial ritual is perverted and corrupted by traits that carry it into the domain of hunting or warfare'.[55] The question of animal consent is clearly to be taken seriously: unless the animal lowers its head in a manner that can be interpreted as consent, the sacrifice cannot go ahead. It is not surprising then that those humans involved in the sacrifice should be deeply concerned to be sure that they are acting correctly. It is for this reason, supposedly, that '[a]s a general rule the sacrifice is carried out in an atmosphere of uneasy caution, as can be seen in words and gestures laden with ambiguity'.[56] The animal's consent itself is likely to be a gesture of some ambiguity, requiring interpretation, while at the same time the sacrificers seem to want to retain ambiguity for their own actions, lest they be too readily interpreted in an unfavourable light. The 'atmosphere of uneasy caution' is also a wonderfully apt description of the atmosphere in which horses appear on stage in the recent work of Socìetas Raffaello Sanzio – suggesting an affectual carry-over that testifies persuasively to some continuity between the unease of Greek sacrifice and our contemporary disquiet in the face of animals on stage.

The relationship between the animal's presence and the act of sacrifice is at its clearest in *Giulio Cesare*. The horse is led on stage and stands there throughout the scene in which the assassination of Caesar is played. The assassination itself is clearly played as a sacrifice, but one in which there is doubt and uncertainty. To the sound of buzzing flies, followed by farmyard animals, and finally human voices in song, Brutus first combs Caesar's hair and then bathes his feet, deliberately recalling the gesture of Mary Magdalene. Then Caesar, naked, is laid out on the floor, and a length of cord is used to tie him down, looped around nails in the floor. The figure of '. . .VSKIJ' has to intervene to compel a hesitating Brutus to act: 'Bruto! La linea dell'azione! . . . Si fa cosi!'[57] All the movement in this sequence is careful, deliberate, ponderously delicate and slow. Only at the point at which Caesar's death is signalled by his cry of 'Ah! Et tu, Brute, fili mihi?' does the man who has brought the horse on the stage now lead it off: 'Solo ora si capisce che non era quello animale da sacrificare': only now is it understood that it is not this animal that is to be sacrificed.

This 'uneasy caution' is contagious: the mise en scène, in terms of movement and sound, clearly designed to communicate and infect the audience with a sweaty apprehension. Something very similar happens when a horse is brought on stage in *Il Combattimento*.[58] In this case the *direct* connection with sacrifice is absent (although metaphorical connections might very easily be made), but the degree to which 'uneasy caution' attends the appearance of the animal on stage is if anything even more intense. The horse is led on, its body and head clothed and hooded in white. As with the entry of the horse in *Giulio Cesare*, the sound of the horse's hoofs on the stage floor suggest that something is out of place: this thing is too heavy and insufficiently cultured to step properly on this (pretend, temporary) floor. Unease and caution initially arise perhaps from the management of this disjunction. But it is ultimately the reason for the horse's appearance that really disturbs. In a chill, still, medical mise en scène, the horse is to have its sperm harvested. Veterinary vaginas are applied by men who look like operating theatre staff. The horse's penis is visibly manipulated. Once two collections of sperm have been collected the horse is led away. The technological modernity that made serpent rituals obsolete by developing power stations is here replacing one means of animal production (letting them copulate) with another (in vitro fertilisation). At least structurally speaking, this harvest of spermatozoa seems to stand in the same relation to the magic (of fertility rites) as sacrifice. There can barely be any doubt that the uneasy caution of this staging, communicated with undeniable affect to the audience, arises from felt anxiety over the propriety of what is taking place, its legitimacy both as spectacle (and remember that sacrifice is a performance for an audience) and as a human intervention in animal reproductive capabilities.

For Adorno and Horkheimer, sacrifice marks the moment where principles of exchange come in to play:

In magic there is specific representation. What happens to the enemy's spear, hair or name, also happens to the individual; the sacrificial animal is massacred instead of the god. Substitution in the course of sacrifice marks a step towards discursive logic. Even though the hind offered up for the daughter, and the lamb for the first-born, still had to have specific qualities, they already represented the species. They already exhibited the non-specificity of the example. But the holiness of the *hic et nunc*, the uniqueness of the chosen one into which the representative enters, radically marks it off, and makes it unfit for exchange.[59]

The economy set in place by sacrifice would therefore seem to stand in relation to its precedents in magic and mimesis, rather as does the labouring animal in the system of theatrical representation in relation to the radically 'other' thing-like material animal that Heideggerian thought might be seeking to recuperate through the fresh eyes of phenomenology. There is most certainly a hankering after the 'holiness of the *hic et nunc*' in some of the post-modern accounts of the non- or anti-meaning of the animal in contemporary art and performance practices, as well as in those practices themselves. That tension or interplay between these two orders – the order of sacrifice and semiotics on the one hand, and the order of magic and phenomenology on the other – persists in contemporary theatre is attested to by Bert

States's observation that theatre's relations with the 'real world' always involve a struggle within the image between sign and thing:

In the image, a defamiliarized and desymbolized object is "uplifted to the view" where we see it as being phenomenally heavy with itself. A transitional moment of shock signals the onset of the image: one feels the shudder of its refusal to settle into the illusion.[60]

What States registers here, most valuably, is that this tension, between sign and thing, between sacrifice and magic, as it were, is experienced in terms of affect: 'shock' and 'shudder'. The claim I am seeking to advance here is related precisely to this, a specifically theatrical possibility: that in the case of the animal on stage our economic and political entanglement with the animal is something that is not simply registered intellectually, but felt in the body. While it is often assumed that affects such as 'shock' or 'shudder' may be generated by the 'holiness of the *hic et nunc*', it actually seems to me, following States, that the intensity of the affect derives from the way in which the material body of the animal, for example, penetrates the membrane between its own 'realness' and its signification. What is released when this membrane is penetrated (during the shudder) is an as yet untheorised sense of what ties the two registers together: namely the labour of the animal at the service of a dominant humanity.

The economy inaugurated by sacrifice, in distinction to the economy of magic and mimesis, is an economy which seeks to hide its origins in domination. That is not to say that there is any ethical superiority in the earlier forms – they are as much a part of human domination as sacrifice itself. Nor, as Simon Jarvis warns in his lucid account of this issue in *The Dialectic of Enlightenment*, should we be tempted by the idea that the earlier forms are better because they are more honest in their frank and open acknowledgement of their violent dominion:

If 'sacrifice' is opposed to the still more archaic 'mimesis' and 'magic', however, perhaps these latter correspond to social transparency and to non-identificatory rationality? If we may not be nostalgic for sacrifice, perhaps we may be nostalgic for magic and mimesis? This would be a misconstruction. Magic and mimesis are themselves cognitive practices, rational attempts to control nature. As such they too exhibit not pure irrationality, but the incipient entanglement of rationality and domination. Adorno and Horkheimer do indeed argue that magic and mimesis do not yet conceal this domination by claiming to have themselves constituted, produced or legislated over those external powers which they seek to ward off or invoke. Nor do they yet treat what is spelled or imitated as a representative rather than an individual. Domination is thus not yet internalized and mystified. Magic and mimesis, that is, represent a stage before the unity of the subject, but not before rationality or before domination.[61]

If there were just magic and mimesis the shock we would experience in our encounter with the animal on stage would simply be the shock of recognising this domination. That is, if any shock would be felt at all. For there is no reason to be shocked, there is no scandal in magic. The scandal, if there is one, a scandal of origins of course, is to be found in sacrifice, where the cover-up begins, where enlightenment's entanglement with myth and its dependence upon domination starts to hide itself.

Sacrifice is not exactly where the killing begins, but it is where the killing starts getting turned into something else, where killing begins to make an effort not to feel guilty about itself. Warburg's snakes get out of the ritual alive; the domestic animals of the Greek *thusia* do not. There is also a crucial distinction to be made between animals in the wild and animals who are being raised by humans. What this reveals is that the animal raised by humans is dead already: bred to be killed and eaten. So we might add further terms to a growing list of binaries: holy, wild, live, phenomenal, magic – profane, domesticated, dead, semiotised, sacrifice. And it is precisely in the movement from one set of terms to the other that the animal on stage has its affect.

Tragedy seems to stand in a relation to sacrifice in which it simultaneously colludes in the cover-up and uncovers it to view; obscures and discloses some truth about the relations between humans and animals. The return of the animal to the stage threatens to push this scandalous revelation a step further. In Societas Raffaello Sanzio's *Oresteia*, the plough is indeed turned back along its own furrow towards tragedy's origins, when the carcass of a goat is hauled from a box on the stage floor (a box that represents the tomb of Agamemnon) and hung centre stage. Tubes attached to the opened-up chest of the goat allow

Orestes to manipulate them at a distance, controlling a flow of compressed air that makes the goat seem to breathe: 'il corpo stesso del tragos che ha ripreso, sia pur fittizamente, a respirare'.[62] Clytemnestra points at the reanimated body and 'esclama sotto voce: Re Agamennone e vivo'.[63] The killing of humans and the killing of animals starts to look and feel like one and the same thing, in a theatre where the exploitation of humans and the exploitation of animals seems to confirm both as equally subject to the division of labour, and the domination that comes entangled with enlightenment.

The animal, restored to the stage, does what anyone on stage always has the uncanny capacity to do: it looks back at those who look. Animals are only a safe (and exceptional) presence on the stage for as long as they are denied this capacity for looking back. The moment they do look back they disturb us by being just like us, or even, as in the particularly uncanny case of the fencing bear encountered by Kleist's Herr C., better than us in some impossible way. The strangeness of the animal on stage comes not from the fact that it ought not to be there, has no business being there, but rather in the fact that there is suddenly nothing strange about it being there, the fact that it has as much business being there, being exploited there, as any human performer. In the shudder, the unease, the disquiet and the caution with which we greet the appearance of the animal on the stage, we are responding to this looking back, and in that looking back the recognition of some kind of complicity in domination and submission. What we experience is a form of shame, I think, at being discovered in our own acts of domination, over animals and over ourselves. The truth of the division of labour makes itself felt, and what we are ashamed of is that we never saw it before, not until the animal returned to the stage and made us stare it in the face, smell it, sense it in our shuddering.

This may be the source of Derrida's discomfort when he finds himself naked in the presence of a cat:

> I often ask myself, just to see, *who I am* – and who I am (following) at the moment when, caught naked, in silence, by the gaze of an animal, for example the eyes of a cat. I have trouble, yes, a bad time overcoming my embarrassment.[64]

The shame or embarrassment he experiences is related to the fact that the animal itself cannot be naked and cannot experience shame at its nudity. It is a shame Derrida also traces to the fact that in his being he is following (this is the point of the punning use of 'je suis', which means both I am and I follow) the other animals. Arriving late, he, man, Derrida, is granted dominion over them, and names them. Late on the scene, one is tempted to say, breathlessly arriving centre stage from the wings, taking a cue from Derrida's own insistent theatricalisation of his thought:

I must once more return to the malaise of this scene. I ask for your forbearance. I will do all I can to prevent its being presented as a primal scene: this deranged theatrics of the *wholly other that they call animal, for example, a cat.*[65]

The malaise of this scene, the unease and caution with which the naked Derrida negotiates his sense of self with the cat, lies in the shameful and awkward recognition, in response to the returned look of the cat, that what is at stake here is yet another staging of the return of the animal, the animal that always belonged there, to the stage, and that with it come crashing in all those divisions, violences and sacrifices that went into establishing your human self in the first place. It's not a primal scene, because it's a scene that has been played out a million times before. The animal protagonist in this encounter is no alien. This cat is a familiar. The animals are always with us, there is nothing strange about them, except the strangeness we impose upon them in order not to see them looking back, in order not to experience, as affect, the shame of our violent shared history.

4   Mutual predicaments:
corpsing and fiasco

Laughter

Laughter may seem like a strange phenomenon to include among such anomalies and alien bodies as stage fright, embarrassment and animals. Is not the restorative power of communal laughter one of those things that most theatre at least sometimes seeks to produce or achieve? One might also complain that laughter itself has already been sufficiently recuperated, even elevated to a philosophical practice, by writers as distinct from one another and as influential as Mikhail Bakhtin[1] and Friedrich Nietzsche. In fact, such is the coercive power of canonical hilarity that the kind of writer who doesn't like eye contact in the theatre is more or less honour bound to sit silently, arms folded in his seat, as his companions split their sides at the mirth-inducing antics of the clowns and the comedians, warming his chilly soul with Howard Barker's grumpy observations that 'the carnival is not the revolution', and that 'the baying of an audience in pursuit of unity is a sound of despair'.[2]

But it is not an affirmative, joyous laughter, the laughter of subversion and unashamed delight in the pleasures of the grotesque that is at stake here. Instead, it is to minor forms of laughter, laughter that is not improper on the grand political scale, but improper in the more local sense of being unwanted, untimely and in the wrong place, that our attention now must turn. Carnival laughter not only takes place in the time and place in which it is proper for it to take place, whatever its particular impropriety, it is also, in the wake of Bakhtin's considerable theoretical influence, a laughter which is always in the right place at the right time in the eyes of the political left, because it is the laughter that opposes political power. Its wrongness is what is right about it, its transgressions acting in perfect harmony with the critiques of authority in whose service critical theory has deployed it. The laughter at issue here is by contrast amoral, apolitical, accidental. In place of the roar, the shriek, the howl and all the healthy, full-throated guffaws that signal the coming of community and the overthrow of grim-faced oppression come the snigger, the smirk, the giggle and the titter. These are laughters that swallow themselves, are choked and throttled, laughters that bring hands to mouths and force orifices closed against the threat of outburst. The register in which this bodily language speaks is not the rampant vernacular of pissing and shitting, the unimpeded flow of inside into outside celebrated in the carnivalesque, it is a register of clandestine secretion, of leakage, seepage, spluttering, in which lips press tight against one another to contain saliva and sound and buttocks clench together to hold back farts or worse. Instead of 'pissing myself laughing' I struggle not to wet myself. The 'I' and the 'myself' are both my body: my mind, in so far as it is engaged in this strangely mindless behaviour, is more witness to the struggle between powerful contending impulses than it is either referee or participant. In Bakhtinian terms, these laughters mark the site of the struggle between bourgeois decorum and riotous subversion. They are laughters that have a particular place in the experience of the theatre, for both performer and audience, few of whom will not, at one time or another, have experienced this particular and intensely physical struggle with themselves. For these minor laughters, the laughters of shame and embarrassment, the laughters that are always under conditions of suppression and containment, are also the laughters that spoil, mar or interrupt theatrical performance. That they should threaten the theatre from within, sneak onto the stage from the lips of performers, is the particular problem with which this journey into theatrical failure begins.

Corpsing

In Forced Entertainment's *Disco Relax* Cathy Naden appears as one of two women who seem to be survivors from a long and tawdry night of drinking.[3] Sitting behind a table loaded with bottles and cans, she cracks jokes, tests out the range of her obscenity and innuendo and engages an imagined courtroom with bravura rhetorical bathos. Much of what she does she finds hopelessly funny. At the moment when she laughs at her own foolish joke it is impossible to tell whether this is the appearance, the sign of laughter, or laughter itself. Are we witnessing the drunken woman laughing at how hopelessly funny she is being, or Cathy Naden herself, laughing at her own stupid performance as she negotiates her way through the score of a new piece which is only in its third or fourth public performance? Just behind her on the stage a mop-headed guitarist (is he playing that thing or pretending to play it?) looks on, a smile of amusement flickering onto his face as Cathy Naden laughs at herself. This seems to strengthen the reading of the moment as genuine 'corpsing', but what matters here is not what the answer is, but the strange undecideability of it, the fact that there is no way of knowing.[4] The question of this strange undecideability is very like the confusion between sign and thing, acting and matrixed behaviour discussed in relation to the various non-human performers in Chapter Three.

In the description of Cathy Naden's laugh I have used the word 'corpsing' to refer to the unintended laughter of a performer during their performance. This appears to be the standard usage of the term, at least in contemporary British conversation and, tellingly, since this is where it is most likely to occur in print, in the anecdotes of an actor's biography. 'Corpsing' can either be transitive, in a situation where one actor deliberately 'corpses' another, making them laugh, or intransitive, in which an actor starts to laugh of his or her own accord, sometimes inexplicably. It is also notoriously infectious, destroying rehearsals by making a particular moment in a scene the unavoidable occasion for collective giggling. Although this is the widely accepted usage of the term, definitions appearing in both standard and slang dictionaries sow some interesting confusion about what it means. To begin with the emphasis appears to be placed on error, disruption and absence, rather than on the fact of laughter as such. The *Oxford English Dictionary* offers:

To confuse or "put out" (an actor) in the performance of his part; to spoil (a scene or piece of acting) by some blunder.[5]

Here we understand that the actor is 'put out', removed from the rehearsed sequence of actions and words, and that it is this, and the confusion attendant upon it, the deviation from what is prescribed, that constitutes the spoiling of the scene. It is also something that is done to another. The verb is transitive. This is close to the definition offered in Partridge:

> To blunder (whether unintentionally or not), and thus confuse other actors or spoil a scene; the blunderer is said to be "corpsed".[6]

The verb is, or at least appears to be transitive again. One actor makes a mistake that 'puts' the others 'out'. One might presume from this logic that it would be the other actors, thus 'put out', who would be said to have been 'corpsed', but in fact it seems that it is the actor who committed the first blunder – 'the blunderer' – who is 'corpsed'. This definition allows the possibility that 'the blunderer' commits the 'blunder' on purpose, in its use of the truly peculiar negative form 'unintentionally or not.' While this seems to permit an account of corpsing in which one actor deliberately seeks to make others laugh – 'corpse' – which is compatible with the standard understanding of the term I have suggested above, it creates further problems, not simply by begging the question of what might constitute an intentional blunder or deliberate mistake, but also by insisting that, even when the initial blunder is committed on purpose, it is still the blunderer, not those who are confused by the blunder, who is 'corpsed', whereas the logic of the OED definition would presumably make the 'blunderer' corpser rather than corpsed. In neither of these definitions is there any reference to laughter (is this a successful suppression of some kind?), but in both the use of the term 'blunder' suggests clumsy and catastrophic movement down the wrong path or track. The same core terms appear, with one interesting addition in *Slang and its Analogues Past and Present,* which offers the definition

> To confuse; to "queer"; to blunder and so "put out" one's fellows; to spoil a scene.[7]

This appears to derive from the OED definition, but adds, usefully, the verb to 'queer', presumably to suggest the action of guiding someone away from their proper route and down a deviant path. The idea that corpsing might 'queer' theatre is a suggestive one, particularly if the act of 'queering' is viewed as positive, a fulfilment of theatre's interest in transgression. 'Queer' laughter in the theatre might not so much spoil the scene as make it. A certain performance aesthetic appears to invite such queer laughter in the comic act of insisting that we pay serious attention to such trivia as the theatre puts before us. Whenever theatre lays claim to seriousness it lays itself open to queer laughter, in performers and audience alike. This theatricality is precisely the fate to which drama must always succumb, if we are to continue this association of camp with queer laughter. Susan Sontag, on the way to insisting that camp is antithetical to tragedy, notes that camp is 'the sensibility of failed seriousness, of the theatricalization of experience'.[8] What Sontag supposes is that to deliberately produce a laughable *King Lear* will inevitably be an act of camp in the moment the tragedy is erased. To laugh at *King Lear*'s seriousness would be to queer the play. The term corpsing, however, appears to be a special instance of queer laughter, enjoyed by performers alone.

Two definitions of the term that do not use the same core terms of 'blunder', 'confuse' and 'spoil' offer further understanding of the nature of the phenomenon, and its relationship to other aspects of theatrical practice. *The Dictionary of American Slang* suggests that to corpse is:

To embarrass (another actor) during a stage show by forgetting one's lines, thus depriving him of his cue.[9]

Here the actor who is victim of the error encounters an obstacle rather than a deviation from the proper path. It is an obstacle composed of an absence. Rather than an 'accumulation of driftwood' that blocks the river the actor is navigating, the river just dries up as the line of text from which he is to take his cue goes missing. The actor is cut adrift from the play. This is not far from the experience suggested by the term 'put out', if we think of being put out in terms of the actor being dislodged from the vehicle of the part or role, dumped out of the textual fabric of the play to appear as just himself, not the character he is trying to present. Seen in this light, it is perhaps inevitable that the experience should be one of embarrassment, in which one's failure to perform one's job is intimately linked to a moment of public self-exposure. That corpsing might have something to do with the unwanted irruption of the real amid the unreality of the stage fiction is suggested here. But nobody is laughing. Something is going wrong and no one is prepared to admit that they find it funny. Only the *Cassell Dictionary of Slang* will own up. Here, to corpse is

to cause (intentionally or not) a fellow performer to forget their lines and/or laugh on stage; thus to make him or her "die."[10]

Again the issue of intention is left open, although without the additional confusion of the supposedly intentional blunder, and two possible outcomes of the act of corpsing are entertained: the other actor forgetting their lines, as in the example above, or the other actor laughing on stage. Both laughter and forgetting are here associated, not without some strain, with the idea of death. It is not immediately clear what justifies the use of the word 'thus' here. Nor is it clear why the word 'die' appears in inverted commas. Clearly there is an attempt to explain why the term 'corpse' is used under such circumstances, which none of the other definitions offer, but it is not clear why laughing or forgetting one's lines should be viewed as 'dying'. The term 'dying' on stage is another piece of theatrical slang, used to describe an act that is obviously failing to have its intended effect on its audience. It is usually used in the context of comedians failing to produce laughter. So to die on stage is something rather different from corpsing, involving the unwanted absence of laughter rather than its unwanted presence. If the *Cassell Dictionary of Slang* is using the word in this sense, this explains the inverted commas, but leaves the question of the use of the word 'corpse' *qua* dead body unresolved, since it is simply connecting two (or rather three) kinds of theatrical failure with the metaphorical idea of an act that fails to live. What the definition seems to be trying to do is to reach beyond both slang usages and suggest why morbidity might be differently evoked in these two (or three) specific theatrical situations of failure, without quite making the connection work.

Two possible explanations might help to activate the connection. The actor who is 'put out' is also the actor who has, at least momentarily, come out of character. In that coming out, nothing is left behind. There is no character left on stage into which the actor can be put back. The moment of laughter annihilates the represented being, leaving the performer alone on stage, helpless, with nothing to fall back on, nothing to do, no one to be. The actor does not 'die' himself, but rather commits an act upon the illusionary character: 'corpsing' it. The thing you were offering up, showing, demonstrating, has turned to dust in your hands. Alternatively, Martin Hyder suggests that the term may have something to do with the facial expression of an actor trying to resist, contain or suppress the outburst of laughter.[11] Like the actor experiencing stage fright, the actor who is corpsed feels with their full rigour the demands of the script and mise en scène, and in his efforts to adhere to them, contorts his face into a fixity that he hopes will arrest the unwanted flickers and convulsions of impending laughter. The effect is a fixed grin, an immobilisation of the expressive features, a freezing of the face into a mask that might resemble death. This second explanation is particularly helpful in that it lends further support to the idea that corpsing is not so much the laughter itself as the covering up of the laughter. Or rather, corpsing is the laughter that covers itself up, the laughter that works against the actor and which the actor must work against. The laugher is laughed and tries to prevent himself from being laughed.

Corpsing, then, is something that both happens and is done, is intentional and unintentional, has to be connected with death, as well as with the irruption of the real and the suspension of proper order. It also seems to be involved in a cover-up about itself, hiding the uncomfortable truth that this breakdown takes the physical form of a giggle. The word acts big, pretends, theoretically, to be about death, but in practice is just about laughing. Corpsing is a kind of working against itself: in courting failure and enacting blunders it seems to have intentions or unintentions as deadly as Tennyson's Crimean commander, yet all it can actually accomplish is suppressed hilarity. As a form of failure, it is something of a failure. As a breakdown it falls short of catastrophe, as a rupture in the order of representation it is a bit of a damp squib. In its problematic meaning it re-enacts precisely the struggle between the trivial and the serious, the dramatic and the (merely) theatrical, that often provokes its appearance on the stage. The shift in register between commitment to the dramatic action (I am Hamlet and I don't know how to kill my evil uncle) and recognition of the theatrical reality (my evil uncle is actually my friend Michael in a wig) is a frequent source of the classic 'corpse', as it features in the autobiographical anecdote.

Typical of anecdotes featuring corpsing is the following from Kenneth Branagh's (early) autobiography of 1990, *Beginning*:

The only drama was the predictable one of being ticked off for corpsing. Rupert was quite as bad as me when it came to giggling and the tea-party scene which took place between Rupert, David Parfitt, Piers Flint-Shipman and I, was too much. David William, the one senior member of the cast, and an inveterate giggler himself, feigned rage and turned on us all. "Just STOP. This really is boring. Balls-achingly boring." Silence and stifled whimpers followed.[12]

Considered in the light of laughter's supposedly subversive power, this moment, in which the young Branagh, Rupert Graves, Parfitt and Flint-Shipman, all playing schoolboys in the West End première of Julian Mitchell's *Another Country*, is beautifully located within structures of authority both real and fictional. The 'corpsing' appears as such because it is effectively (un)authorised both by the status of the young actors relative to the 'senior' David William, by whom they are 'ticked off', and their roles in the play as schoolboys engaged in transgressive sexual activity, for which they might also expect, at the very least, to be 'ticked off'. Branagh's experience of corpsing during this production has more serious implications, however, implications that are highly suggestive in the context of the present work. It is worth noting that Branagh's use of the term is intransitive: corpsing is something he experiences as happening to him, rather than something that he does to others. Corpsing is suffered: it is a passion, not an action.

The hysterical corpsing was partly induced by the unusual demands of a long run on inexperienced actors. After three months I began to go a little stir crazy . . . my concentration wavered in performance until I dried desperately in the middle of one show and had to walk off while Rupert saved the day with an ad lib – "I think Judd must have a headache or something". This produced a terrible stage-fright for the next two weeks.[13]

The demands placed upon the young Branagh by this production – demands which those with longer experience of theatrical employment apparently, or so Branagh implies, handle more easily – lead directly, it seems, to several 'hysterical' formations: the corpsing itself, followed by stir-craziness, momentary amnesia, and finally 'a terrible stage-fright'. One might imagine, suddenly, that if stage fright is as foundational for modern realist acting as it is an obstacle (as suggested in Chapter One), then corpsing and amnesia too may be component parts of a more generalised psychological malfunctioning that may turn out to be essential to the continued production of theatre. The idea that corpsing, like stage fright, might be an essential part of the economy of theatrical representation, and intimately connected with specific conditions of theatrical employment is, for the moment, the most suggestive aspect of Branagh's experience.

Later in his career, but again, interestingly, in a situation where the young actor's status within his profession would seem to be acutely felt, Branagh experiences another fit of this occupational hysteria. Here is his account of corpsing during the filming of close-ups for a television production of Ibsen's *Ghosts*, in which he appeared with Michael Gambon, Natasha Richardson and Judi Dench.

"Action" was called, and we solemnly began our desultory improvised dialogue. Natasha began, leaning over Gambon. "Would the Pastor like some potatoes?" Gambon replied. "Yes, I'll have eleven please." The face remained impassive. Then as the camera passed him he bent double over his soup and when he looked up the tears were rolling down his face. Judi's close-up was next and although the shot revealed only head and shoulders I could see that her hands were white, gripping the table-cloth for dear life. Once the camera passed her she threw her hands up to her face and stuffed a serviette in her mouth. By the time the camera reached me I was watching two Titans of the English theatre in silent convulsions. I was helpless and it was too late. I could no more have produced a straight face than swim the Channel. They tried for several minutes drying my eyes and asking Judi and Michael to turn round. It was no use, every time the magic word "Action" was called I could hear the telltale whimpers from Dench and Gambon and then I was lost . . . We all met in the make-up room, Dench, Richardson, Gambon and me swathed in shame.[14]

The scene is exemplary. Ibsen's *Ghosts* has canonical status as the play which theatre history has established as the foundational moment for modernist realism (the standard by which 'serious drama' is conventionally measured) in Britain. The idea that actors, however lofty their reputation, somehow ought to find this warhorse of Scandinavian gloom and venereal disease a source of childlike amusement is typical of the British theatre's traditional suspicion of the serious and the intellectual. The best corpsing is always going to happen in the most portentously serious work: one expects anecdotes of actors giggling in the final scene of *King Lear*, but not during performances of *A Comedy of Errors*. The physical symptoms are similarly perfect: Gambon sheds tears, Dench clenches her hands as though in the throes of death, both these 'Titans' are brought low by 'convulsions', and Branagh himself is so 'helpless' that the mere sound of their 'whimpers' (such an animal noise) leaves him lost. To cap it all, their involuntary self-exposure, in the eyes of an internalised audience of serious drama connoisseurs, leads to all four actors being 'swathed in shame'. The mutually reinforcing relationships established here by Branagh between his inappropriate laughter, stage fright, amnesia, shame, animality and death might have served as effectively as Kleist's *Über das Marionettentheater* as the key text for the present study. From Branagh's experience, consciously fashioned here in the self-deprecating mode in which theatrical employment demands its workers discuss their work and their selves, one might reasonably assume that the business of theatre necessarily, even deliberately, provokes and exploits a psychological condition in which the actor experiences himself as forgetful, stupid, less-than-human, helpless, frightened, prone to unmotivated giggling, all of which induces in him an enduring shame, lived out under the gaze of a public constructed as an austere and unforgiving authority. The direction of the present study would seem to suggest that the sources of the antitheatrical prejudice, at least in its modern formations, might be located in this peculiar socio-psychological phenomenon. The name of this phenomenon may be masochism. Clearly the claim, made throughout this study, that the uncomfortable political affects experienced in the modern bourgeois theatre by both actor and audience alike, are sources and resources for pleasure, would support this idea. In this case, both the prejudice, and the modern theatre itself, are masochistic formations.

The phrase 'helpless laughter' is the key term here. Branagh and colleagues suffer helplessly from their mutual infection of giggling. 'I was helpless,' writes Branagh. It renders them incapable, infantile, vulnerable. Enter the term 'helpless laughter' into an internet search engine and you will soon find yourself directed to a particular niche of fetish erotica – the tickling video – in which the experience of the performers appears remarkably similar to that of the actor corpsed. Keeping in mind Kleist's sexual exploitation in the erotic scene and the conditions of employment that appear to underpin both stage fright and embarrassment, the language in which a typical tickling video is promoted seems unstrangely familiar:

For ten minutes each one is mercilessly tortured, tickled in all of their most vulnerable spots and driven into ticklish hysteria. By this point, each girl has been mapped out for ticklish spots, with no secrets left, and they are totally exploited, milked for their most helpless laughter.[15]

The women are – as so often in pornography – stripped of their adulthood and described as girls. Their response is – again somewhat typically – characterised in terms of hysteria (while in fact it is of course almost the reverse, in that it is a physiological response to a physiological stimulus rather than a psychological trauma). Like all our previous victims of various kinds of unwanted intimacy in public (Kleist's young man, Kostya, myself confronted by Samuel West) they suffer an excessive outing of their insides; they have 'no secrets left'. In their exploitation – an economic reality that pornography's advocates frequently deny, but which is here intrinsic to the mise en scène – they are reduced to an animal function, as they are 'milked'. The physical experience of laughter is of course at its most obvious in tickling where there is (little or) no humour involved, and where, instead, the relations of power between the cause of the laughter and the one who laughs appear in sharp relief. With the mediating factor of comedy or humour removed from the interaction, the one who does the laughing emerges as the one who is laughed, when we are dealing with the tickler and the tickled. In the case of corpsing, although something funny may trigger the outbreak, in the form of Michael Gambon's request for eleven potatoes, the contagion and persistence of the convulsions that follow are out of all proportion to the comedy value of the initial trigger. The corpsing that ensues has no more to do with the (intentionally) comic than does the giggling in *Courtney and Tovia's First Time*. One imagines that the tickling fetish aficionado will not laugh at the video, but derive instead some other sensual pleasures. The idea of the actor as a body that is laughed, that suffers laughter, appears with equal clarity in the corpse and the tickling video. That both may involve a dissolution or abandonment of self, comparable to a kind of death, is the main line of the argument that follows below. The view of laughter, its meaning and its value, developed below departs from the strongest tradition in the theorisation of laughter, which turns out, on inspection, to be an investigation of the comic, the humorous or the funny. Although Rabelais's laughter is unquestionably a bodily phenomenon, its theorisation by Bakhtin is in the interests of developing a theoretical account of the comic in popular literature and other cultural forms, rather than a physiological or phenomenological project. The predominantly philosophical authors whose thoughts on laughter are collected together in a recent anthology (from Aristotle, through Descartes, Kant, Kierkegaard to the inevitable Henri Bergson) all tend to address laughter in terms of its causes.[16] There are rare exceptions to this general approach in which the cause of laughter is always sought outside the person who does the laughing. V.K. Krishna Menon, for instance, suggests helpfully that when only one person laughs and not another,

we shall not be wrong in considering that the consequence has probably more to do with the person than with the situation – that the situation is more likely to be an *occasion* than the *cause* of laughter in the strict sense of the term. We are then justified in seeking for the cause in the person himself who laughs and not in the situation.[17]

As with the discussion of stage fright in Chapter One, the intention here is to stop short of the search for an interpretation, offered here in the form of the cause, on the grounds that the too-rapid leap to cause and interpretation omits much that is of significance in the phenomenon. Even when seeking to ground the work in an historically specific social and economic location, the aim is to offer occasions rather than deterministic causes for the phenomena discussed. One advantage of this approach, in this particular instance, is that it allows a focus on the great neglected theorist of laughter, the sixteenth century French court physician, Laurent Joubert.[18] Unwilling to leave behind for too long the masochistic scenario at which I have been gesturing over the preceding pages, I would like to introduce Joubert's work with his own conviction that it is not possible to die of laughter, except when caused by tickling. Joubert calls this kind of fatal laughter 'dog laughter'.[19] Tickling, corpsing, animals, death.

For Joubert, laughter is significant for what it produces. As a specialist on the urinary system, he emphasises what laughter expels from the body.

Everybody sees clearly that in laughter the face is moving, the mouth widens, the eyes sparkle and tear, the cheeks redden, the breast heaves, the voice becomes interrupted; and when it goes on for a long time the veins in the throat become enlarged, the arms shake, and the legs dance about, the belly pulls in and feels considerable pain; we cough, perspire piss and besmirch ourselves by dint of laughing, and sometimes we even faint away because of it.[20]

This is a vision that would seem to have a lot in common with the laughter of Rabelais, and indeed, Joubert and Rabelais were not merely contemporaries, but Rabelais studied at the Montpellier Medical School where Joubert taught. Bakhtin, for one, is certain that Joubert's treatise exercised a direct influence on Rabelais:

Although this treatise on the philosophy of laughter was published after Rabelais' death, it was a belated echo of the thoughts and discussions that were current in Montpellier when Rabelais attended this school and that determined his concept of the therapeutic power of laughter and of the "gay physician."[21]

The heaving breast, the interrupted voice, the shaking limbs, the feeling of constriction, the sweating, pissing, besmirching and the fainting away are all more or less the same symptoms displayed by Kostya when he experiences stage fright. Is there any possibility that the two phenomena might be more intimately related than they might appear? They seem to derive from remarkably similar 'occasions', and both seem to be occasions on which the self is experienced as imperilled, and the body threatens to dissolve distinctions between inside and outside. Corpsing might be considered, momentarily, as though it were, like stage fright, a symptom of the specific conditions in which the actor finds herself on the modern stage. Stage fright may be understood as a socio-somatic phenomenon. It is experienced by someone with a perception of the self (in modernity) as bounded, who also feels social and professional pressures towards acts of intimacy in public. They then experience disruptive contact with a non-self (audience) in terms that unsettle the stability of the bounded self. In that unsettling the body starts to attempt some kind of flow or merging, a dissolution by means of the expulsion of liquid, as though to create some indeterminate mixture of me and not-me in which the attack can somehow be evaded, the attackers lost, smothered or drowned. Corpsing seems to do something very similar: volition abandoned, the body becomes a helpless object, shaken and squeezed until it starts to burst all over, overflow, exceed its bounds, lose all coherence. Like stage fright, corpsing occurs on occasions where the self is operating with particular self-consciousness as the agent of a discourse of discipline or control. In stage fright it is the score of the play and the gaze of the audience that prohibit action that might rescue the actor from her symptoms. In corpsing the score and the audience are woven together in the same disciplinary structure, with the additional devastating twist of the insistent voice that forbids laughter thereby making its outbreak all the more inevitable. In both cases self-control is both alienated (maintained in the interests of external forces) and threatened (by aspects of the same external forces), in a double movement which issues in the combination of outburst and cover-up, falling apart and pulling yourself together.

While the physiological emphasis offered by Joubert suggests some affinities with the 'Relief Theory' of laughter which those influenced by nineteenth-century biology tended to offer, the relief from the crisis or tension hardly seems to be welcomed, nor does it seem to bring a satisfactory end to the crisis, threatening instead to escalate it or – and this might be what is really desired – bring the occasion itself crashing down. Both corpsing and stage fright seem to involve a loss of control that will either allow the actor to stumble on, in shame and embarrassment, until they can escape the stage (as Branagh does), or until the stage or the theatrical act itself collapses into some kind of oblivion. Unless the actor is removed from the occasion, or the occasion from the actor, there can be no return to the security of the bounded self, and stuff will continue to leak out from every orifice, including that organ that is all holes, the skin. Corpsing and stage fright both seem to be calling for the curtain to be brought down for ever. But because the audience-actor relationship is a mise en scène touched with more than a little sadism and masochism, the audience may instead wish to see the curtain remain up, to prolong the pleasurable spectacle of the terrified wreck or to indulge itself in the infection of the corpse, to feel the liquids overflow the stage and splash into the auditorium. There may be perverse pleasures for the actor in this kind of exposure too. Let me really feel it – my exploitation; my shame.

Stage fright would seem to be the more insistent that the occasion be terminated, that the ground should open up and swallow its helpless victim. Corpsing (the more genuinely masochistic behaviour) actually seems to work more actively towards its prolongation, even though the desire for an end is of course present. The end and the prolongation are in a sense the same thing, if we think of corpsing as an infection that might end the crisis of the imperfect management of inside and outside in a sort of commingling, across the proscenium, of actor and spectator in a pool of unmotivated hilarity. The logic of the corpse might seem to involve an act or instance of theatre coming to an end not because the lights go out and the curtain comes down, but because the lights stay on and a kind of Rousseau-esque festival of mutual enjoyment kicks in. Thus the logic of the corpse would seem to lead us back, unwillingly, to the laughter celebrated by Bakhtin, the laughter of carnival.

Self-dissolution in laughter is celebrated also by writers seeking alternatives to what they would regard as excessively rigid accounts of the self. A work typical of this mode of understanding laughter is D. Diane Davis's *Breaking Up [at] Totality: A Rhetoric of Laughter* which carries in its title one of several suggestive terms, frequently used to describe the experience of laughter that point to fragmentation: in addition to 'breaking up', and its counterpart 'cracking up' come all the intimations of mortality, 'I died laughing', 'you slay me', 'you're killing me', as well as the clinically precise 'she had hysterics', or the more general but equally deserving of professional help, 'they were in fits'.[22]

Davis's opening chapter, 'Physiological Laughter: The Subject Convulsed', starts from a childhood memory of being overcome with improper laughter in church, and a further recollection of uncontrollable laughter witnessed in the *Mary Tyler Moore Show*. In both cases she thinks of the subject as an object that is being laughed. In the first the experience is as follows:

My amusement [at the out of place bit of hair on the Minister], however, doesn't last long. In the very next instant, and quite without warning, *my* subjectivity, too, is called into question. My body feels overwhelmed, intoxicated by an inexplicable force; I feel weak, out of control. My whole being wants desperately *not* to laugh, and yet it's clear to me that my will is not in control; something else has hold of me – I wonder if it's God. Despite my willpower, despite my squirming and my clenched teeth, I hear mySelf beginning to *lose it*; "I" am beginning to "crack up," both literally (the stability of the "I" is challenged when it becomes the *object* of this laughter's force) and figuratively. I feel harsh eyes boring into me from all sides, and I fight desperately for control. But to no avail. My body has been *possessed* by the force of laughter: Despite my reason and my will, laughter bursts out. The battle is over: "I" have been conquered.[23]

The rhetoric of this passage is in a different register from Kenneth Branagh's *Ghosts* anecdote, but its theoretical orientation is more or less the same, or at least its heart is in the same place. Bad authority associated with the control of the superego is challenged by the irrepressible 'force' of 'possession'. Branagh's anecdote demonstrates that the great actor, far from being in thrall to the bearded patriarchy of serious modern drama, is actually 'game for a laugh', firmly on the side of the good old boys. Davis's anecdote shows that the churchgoing child is always already free from her own bearded patriarchy, that her 'ego' constructed in and by that order is actually fragile in the face of some far deeper life force. One might speculate that the form of the 'anecdote' exists for just such purposes; it is the 'bit' of narrative that claims to refuse the system (blind to its key role in a wider system: the system that secures the rights of the philistine and the bohemian alike, by making all seriousness politically and morally suspect). Davis articulates the political value of such laughter:

To engage in a laughter that has no stake in control is to set one's feet upon momentary lines of flight from the tyranny of meaning and from the violence of a community held together by that tyranny. The hope involved in this political-cum-ethical mode of Being-in-the-world is not about (finally and for good) getting out of the negative; it is about, in a flash, experiencing the flow, the excess beyond our control, beyond our (violent) grasp.[24]

More firmly within the socialist terms of Bakhtinian thought, Terry Eagleton identifies in laughter a comparable if not similar political value:

In a collectivizing movement, the individuated body is thrown wide open to its social surroundings, so that its orifices become spaces of erotic interchange with an 'outside' that is somehow always an 'inside' too. A vulgar, shameless materialism of the body – belly, buttocks, anus, genitals – rides rampant over ruling-class civilities; and the return of discourse to this sensuous root is nowhere more evident than in laughter itself, an enunciation that springs straight from the body's libidinal depths.[25]

The point is, however, with corpsing, that 'the battle' is never over. The final breaching of the dyke never happens. There is no interrupted flow from a spring deep in the body. The 'flow' never becomes an 'excess beyond our control' for, instead, the grin of rigor mortis sets in, and the festival is on hold. Corpsing might seem to promise a line of flight, but it always chokes. It is a bursting out and a holding together at the same time. Steven Connor offers an etymology of one of Davis's key terms – 'convulsion' – that makes just this point:

The word "convulsion" comes from *con-vellere*, meaning to tear apart, to pull into all directions. The prefix "con" works to add the sense of pulling together; convulsion is a way of pulling yourself together, as well as being torn apart. It is the enactment of a dismemberment, the body torn into tiny pieces, that is nevertheless held in one place. Convulsion is a held-together-coming-apart.[26]

No one can corpse without at the same time knowing the power of the injunction to 'pull yourself together'. It is in this tension, this movement in both directions, that corpsing offers its special interest and insists, once again, upon its distance from the Rabelaisian belch. The conflation of the modern laugh – in this case, the corpse – with the laughter of carnival, rests on an error that Bakhtin himself clearly sought to dispel. The error lies in the understanding of the 'body'. Not only does the 'body' often figure as about the most immaterial of textual functions available to the contemporary theorist (Eagleton is a regular critic of this tendency), it is also frequently ahistorical in a way that Bakhtin could never allow. As Eagleton notes, for Bakhtin, laughter is about a de-individuating and collectivising movement, and thus works directly against the forces of urban modernity. The body of Bakhtin's grotesque realism is not about to reappear under conditions of modernity, because it

> is not the body and its physiology in the modern sense of these words, because it is not individualized. The material bodily principle is contained not in the biological individual, not in the bourgeois ego, but in the people, a people who are continually growing and renewed.[27]

Once nineteenth-century biology and ego psychology have successfully established the modern bounded self, and the codes of theatrical naturalism have reinforced it in the theatre, fluid or infectious interchange between individual bodies is no longer possible, the movement towards one-ness, by means of mutual liquid interpenetration or human osmosis will always be interrupted. There are membranes everywhere and some of them, at least, are impermeable. The corpse, then, marks the point at which this suturing closed of the opening-unto-others comes under intense physical pressure but does not, quite, come undone. Although it marks the spot where once festival or carnival might have ensued, the aperture through which Dionysiac possession or the infection of plague might have worked their de-individualising force, it is just a mark, a trace, a minor instance. Never undone, but always undoing. Not dead, but dying. Dying, but staying alive.

Fiasco

Some of the attempts to explain the use of the word corpse for the performer's unwanted laughter focus on the idea that something or someone 'dies' when the performer laughs. In the context of this study, where it is proposed that it is the experience of co-presence that determines the nature of the theatrical encounter, the idea that it is the character that 'dies' in such moments, thus precipitating a perhaps unmediated experience of this encounter between actual people, is particularly resonant. It suggests a resemblance between moments such as the corpse and other ruptures in the representational operations of theatrical impersonation, such as the confusions over identity triggered by

Samuel West making eye contact discussed in Chapter Two. In the example given above, of Cathy Naden laughing at her own stupid performance in *Disco Relax*, there is actually very little character in play at all. This is presumably why it was so difficult to know whether the laughter was voluntary or involuntary, whether it was laughed by Cathy Naden or by some minimally distinct persona based on and inhabited by Cathy Naden. In instances such as this the corpsing causes minimal destruction to whatever minimal representation is going on, unlike the more obviously disruptive consequences described by Kenneth Branagh. The slippage from persona to person, as it were, is such a micro-event that it is barely legible within the experience of the performance (although one might wish to argue that it can be felt, as affect, even though there is no sign that marks the moment of its passage). For a corpse to be truly visible, both actor and character need to be clearly distinguishable one from another, so that in the moment of the corpse the shift from one to the other can be registered, the vanishing of a sign being the sign of that vanishing. The moment of the corpse is the moment in which we see the character crumple, and in the same moment, or just after, see the actor in effect standing over the dead body of the character, smoking gun in hand and silly grin on face.

To explore the significance or potential of such moments more fully might require us to imagine a performance in which this moment is extended, amplified, placed centre stage, and thus registers more readily on the perceptual apparatus. We might try to imagine circumstances in which a performer is always on stage in front of an audience, consistently failing to offer up anything other than themselves while ostensibly (but only ostensibly) committed to presenting or representing something else. Because of its undecideability as a moment, Cathy Naden's laughter in *Disco Relax* begins to approach such a condition, suggesting that it is not so much the rupturing of the representation as the ongoing condition of its failure that is the key issue. That is to say, the exception starts to appear to be the rule, the smear or stain the real picture, the unravelling the real action. But, because it is a flicker, it evades our grasp, only hinting, momentarily, that the real action has come into view.

For a more extended viewing of the real action, if that is what it is, we turn to the peculiar pleasures of fiasco, a term used in certain forms of improvisation to describe the collapse of the clown's attempts to entertain.[28] The term fiasco appears to derive from the Italian *far fiasco*, to make a bottle, and presumably enters the language via the influence of commedia dell'arte.[29] Quite how this should have come to signify the kind of ludicrous collapse described here is unclear, although comparisons with the colloquial English terms 'to bottle it' or 'bottling out' are suggestive. A rule set for an improvised performance I was once involved with stipulated that if you were on stage and all attempts to come up with performance to make the audience laugh failed, you performed 'the Angel of Death', a despairing gaze into the heavens from which physically to relaunch yourself against the wall of the audience's rejection. After several such Angels you would be rescued by the entrance of another performer. The most glorious moments of performance were those when the rescuer, entering to save the show, entered in a state of already full-blown fiasco, found herself on stage with nothing, laughing at the absence of anything to perform and pointing only at the fact that she had nothing to offer. The pleasure an audience takes in such moments is far from *schadenfreude*. Perhaps it is closer to the connoisseur's delight at seeing how the mechanism works at the moment of its breakdown. But it is more than just cognition; it is also affect. The pleasure is a mutual one, and is self reinforcing. Like the infection of the giggle it seems to feed off itself. As the performer acknowledges the audience's hilarious acknowledgement of the performer's inability to offer anything, and the continuing absence of anything to offer, the pleasure on both sides seems to intensify, with a giddying escalation that unsurprisingly carries with it something of the erotic charge that we have earlier associated with tickling. In this instance, however, there is at least the appearance of an absence of exploitation in the scenario, in that everyone involved seems to be convulsed by helpless laughter, and no one is in the role of the cool, detached tickler.

Adrian Heathfield identifies the work of comedian-magician Tommy Cooper as a locus classicus for this kind of experience, commenting on the way in which Cooper triggers laughter from the moment of his entrance and can sustain long periods of performance in which he does nothing other than laugh with delight at the audience that is laughing, senselessly, helplessly, at him.[30] Cooper's entire act is based upon failure: the failure of the magic tricks, the stumbling and aimless wandering, the irruption onto the scene of stage or floor managers and the barrage of incomplete, unfunny jokes and bungled punch lines. What is more, Cooper is always laughing (or being laughed), pre-empting his jokes by being unable to deliver them because he is already laughing at their imminence (or the memory of their previous appearances). Heathfield also suggests that Cooper here achieves what Darwin, among others, insists is impossible; namely tickling himself. The audience might reasonably be said to be doing the same. In performances in which fiasco is sustained in this way an affective relationship between audience and performer seems to be generated, in which both appear to be caught up in a cylindrical bubble of mutual convulsion and stupefaction, each party astonished at the other's (and their own) capacity to make so much out of nothing, dazzled by their own stupid complicity in this patently senseless and stupid performance. The circularity of this infection, its self-tickling aspect, might suggest that the relations of masochism, if they are present as in other tickling scenarios, are internalised on either side of, rather than played out across the metaphorical footlights of the laugh-encounter. Everyone is equally baffled amid the feedback loops.

I have already suggested that 'minorisation' could be a key to understanding such events. Not only are the giggle, the titter and the suppressed laugh (including of course, all forms of corpse) minor forms of laughter in relation to the grand Bakhtinian tradition, but embarrassment might lay claim to be a minorised shame, stage fright a minor form of abjection, and animals and children minor forms of human adult. The possibility that what is being offered here is a kind of 'minor' theatre first came to mind when I encountered Simon Bayly's discussion of fiasco,[31] elaborated in relation to an earlier version of material that now forms part of this chapter.[32] Bayly suggests that the sense, if not the meaning of the term fiasco, might come close to an idea of 'disaster as a minor event, as aberration or upset'.[33] He is particularly struck by a potentially related term – 'Bologna' – referring to seventeenth-century glass bottles that did not shatter when dropped onto a solid floor unless smaller objects were inserted into them:

With this phenomenological observation, fiasco acquires the sense of a breaking up that is a breaking out . . . a kind of built-in principle of autodisintegration.[34]

This kind of breaking, the outbreak, is of course structurally analogous to the somatic crises of inside and outside we have described in relation to corpsing and to stage fright, and the idea of 'autodisintegration' as a principle might be extended first towards the phenomenon of stage fright, where the central acting technique for modern realist theatre appears to be founded upon the experience of this self-collapse, and then, towards the apparatus of theatre itself. It is interesting to note, in reflecting again on the phenomenon of stage fright, that its earliest theorist, Adolph Kielblock, actually uses the term 'fiasco' in this connection, and in terms which emphasise the pressures experienced in connection with the employment status of the actor.[35]

Bayly's 'autodisintegration' sounds very much like the 'undoing' with which the present study is concerned. The image of the Bologna bottle fails only in that, once disintegrated, it remains disintegrated, undone, not undoing. The viability of this argument about theatre's undoing, however, derives not so much from the principle of structural analogy or homology, as from the appearance and persistence of affects, including intense pleasure, in the experiencing of the supposedly anomalous phenomena. It is not merely the fact of the undone, but the pleasures to be won from the undoing, that ground the claims advanced here.

In such moments as Cathy Naden's laugh or the performer in fiasco, Bayly suggests that

an affecting surplus arises out of the performer . . . such a surplus does not belong to the order of representation. Naden's laughter is literally senseless. It has no cause or object that would merit such an extended and exaggerated cultivation. It is anomalous, both in terms of its excess of studied intensity and of its placement within the context of the entire performance. Such a propensity for anomaly also extends to the company's work as a whole, which has made much out of prolonging the apparently pointless beyond the point of no return.[36]

As occasions that offer 'affecting surplus' such moments must always retain some appearance of the anomalous, but they are of course already starting to look as though they may be intrinsic to the system. One might suggest in fact that the system itself, the entire edifice of appearance and representation, is either an elaborate feint or decoy made in order to permit such moments to occur, or a huge machine designed expressly to break down – reverse-engineered, as it were, from these moments of failure, and the pleasures they occasion, which are its true aim. This hypothesis might derive some support from a further consideration, in this light, of the work of Forced Entertainment, a company whose relationship with the practice of theatre has rarely been less than vexed, but who, at the same time seem to maintain a rigorous fidelity to its basic assumptions.

Forced Entertainment

Almost from the beginning, the typical Forced Entertainment mise en scène suggests a theatrical system in the form of a remnant.[37] The stage takes the form of a low platform, often with some kind of frame. There is sometimes a curtain, or something that will pass for a curtain, and perhaps a backcloth, decorated, maybe, with sparkling stars, a backcloth that presents itself as a space of representation as well as a tired reminder of the gestures of glamorous illusion. In this frame – this space of representation – a regular troupe of performers appear and seem to try to present a show of some kind. The company's name itself suggests the conditions under which this attempt is being made. Everyone seems to be here, somehow against their will, but for some reason determined, nonetheless, to go through with it, to act out whatever needs to be acted out, to go through the motions thoroughly enough to make sure that the wheels and cogs of the machine at least rotate, even if the machine doesn't produce anything, or anything which by normal standards, might be considered enough, acceptable, appropriate or satisfying.

A routine from the twenty-four hour durational piece *Who Will Sing a Song to Unfrighten Me?* is exemplary of this desultory but absolute commitment to the practice of theatre and the operation of its representational machinery.[38] On a large stage, bare apart from a litter of discarded bits and pieces of theatrical stuff (props, costumes) the company are sitting around. There's a small makeshift wooden stage in the middle of the larger stage and in the depths of the space a back wall of stars. It's late already and this show has been grinding slowly on for hours, but many hours still remain to be filled. Someone stands up and holds up a tatty cloth, a blanket perhaps. Someone else stands between this makeshift curtain and the audience in the auditorium and shines a light onto it. Someone else again puts on a head to complete their incarceration in one of those animal outfits you can rent, the kind that get used by football clubs as mascots or, as Etchells suggests, appear 'in pantomimes, stag-nights and hen-nights, 21st birthdays, kids' parties, office piss-ups, school plays and fancy-dress parties': bears, pandas, gorillas, rabbits, etc.[39] The bear (or panda, or gorilla) steps behind the 'curtain', and as though hidden from view (which is hardly the case, so makeshift is the curtain) clambers out of the outfit, leaving it 'onstage' as they themselves crawl 'offstage', 'unseen' by the audience to this piece of theatrical magic. The 'curtain' is then pulled aside to reveal the crumpled bear suit on the floor. The other performers manage a weary round of routine applause. Another 'animal' steps up to perform their trick. And so on. Or, a similar routine from the same show, as described by company director Tim Etchells:

The ape ambles up, takes a seat on the crude little stage. Gisela takes a quick look at the beast, writes ALIVE on the blackboard. The ape sits still and thoughtful then slowly crumples, falling prone, lain dead on the ground. G erases the word alive, replacing it with DEAD. There is faint applause from the other performers as they wait, watch or change. Hard to tell if this is applause at the no-nonsense death or at the ontological marvel of alive/dead itself.[40]

Look, this system lets us make anything happen, anything at all, and we don't even really need to try, it just happens. So what is the point? And anything that happens can un-happen:

G wanders from the stage, takes a drink from a bottle back near the huge wall of chalk-drawn stars. As she drinks, the creature on the stage rises slowly from the floor, brushes dust from its black-furred knees and takes its seat again. A simian Lazarus in workaday mode.
Applause. Whistles. Cat-calls.
G returns and DEAD gets replaced by ALIVE.[41]

The machine creates and uncreates creatures, effortlessly, without the wheels and the cogs even having to be in gear. They don't even have to engage. They can spin, meaninglessly, and still the creatures keep coming. Etchells certainly sees this as a joke about representation. Of 'those who wait and look on in full costume apart from the heads',[42] he writes:

> They sit in the ruins of representing, in the joke of it, and if character acting was always hard to take – that one person could "be" another – then this animal stuff is really very very ridiculous. A fool's errand. I think we loved it for that.[43]

The machine of theatrical representation is made to point at itself, and in pointing at itself expose its risible inadequacy. It is pointing at the stupidity of the animals and ours for buying the animals, for seeking entertainment in the manifestly 'pointless'. This pointing is an amplified version of Cathy Naden's laughter in *Disco Relax*, which I earlier characterised as 'laughing at her own stupid performance'. While Cathy Naden laughing is only a micro-event away from not registering any ironic distance, the animals who appear and disappear, die and are resurrected, make the gap open up like the Grand Canyon. Corpse, uncorpse. Yet, at the same time, in pointing at itself in this way the machine also affirms its continuing capacity, despite all the self-annihilating irony of the project, to deliver the goods. For these moments do not produce in the real audience any sign of derision, but instead a sensation of pleasure at seeing the thing at work. Every time one 'animal' steps out of the frame, the audience is longing for the next one to step up. It could go on for ever, this recycling programme, for as long as there were an audience there to witness the machinery in action, to take pleasure in its action. Why else would the company have hit upon such routines as ways of keeping up interest through a twenty-four hour performance? While it is hard to imagine watching, say, an Ibsen play of similar duration, there somehow seems no obstacle to simply sitting and witnessing the machinery – the same machinery we use to produce Nora and Hedda and all those other beasts of the realist menagerie – do its stuff.

It is quite clear that this is not simply a matter of trashing the machinery from a standpoint of ironic superiority. 'I think we loved it for that', affirms Etchells. Their love is a love for the machine, for the 'very very ridiculous' business in which they find themselves engaged. The company have 'invested' lives in this shabby enterprise. Cathy Naden's laughter is an act of love, and the processing of all these animals is yet another, as is our pleasure in these things, and this love is not Platonic. It is not an intellectual satisfaction; the pleasure of seeing through the illusion, a love of knowledge. It is not grounded in the superior wisdom of the individual who, having been freed from the Cave, returns and understands how the shadows work. It is a libidinal pleasure, at which we wriggle and grin, stupidly erotic. Stripped down to the machinery alone, the system of theatrical representation seems capable of maintaining its lover in a state of constant arousal, never disappointing by delivering satisfaction. Might this suggest, then, that the purpose of the system is not so much what it succeeds in delivering in terms of satisfactory representations, but rather what we normally only recognise as a kind of side effect, namely the libidinous pleasures of the stupid act itself? The animals seem, perversely and stupidly, to amplify the range of erotic reference too. Looking again at Etchells's list of their usual occasions it suddenly seems significant that most of those that are not explicitly theatrical are thick with sexual opportunity: 'stag-nights and hen-nights . . . office piss-ups . . . fancy-dress parties'. The animal suits transform the adult humans into silly bumbling beasts of erotic fixation. If the adult human who dresses up as a panda in the hope of getting laid after the office party is using representation in pursuit of sexual pleasure, then it is perhaps not too stupid to suppose that in the theatre we make the feint of feeble pretence in order to get some erotic kicks, for the sake, that is, of the 'affecting surplus'.

Lyotard on theatre last 'blow-back'

In moments of theatrical encounter like those offered by corpsing and fiasco, in which the whole thing seems to have broken down, or where we are simply watching the cogs of the machinery spinning around, ungeared, without gaining any traction, where nothing seems to be happening except the enjoyment of that nothing, theatre seems to be moving towards a forgetting or a transcendence of its supposed imbrication in economies of representation. That theatre, at least used as a metaphor, enjoys a privileged position in certain philosophical attempts to explore the possibility of a move beyond representation is well enough known, mainly through the influence (deeply resisted as it is by many theatre specialists) of Derrida's essay on the Theatre of Cruelty. Much of the theorisation of performance in the wake of Derrida, of which Josette Féral's essay discussed in the Introduction above, is perhaps exemplary in this regard, is, as I have suggested already (see Introduction), inspired by the promise that performance might deliver us from the theatre of representation. However, while Derrida (and this is perhaps what rubs the theatre specialists up the wrong way) shows little interest in the specific quality of the theatrical experience, Jean-François Lyotard's work demonstrates an ongoing interest in at least certain kinds of theatre, including, intriguingly, the work of Richard Foreman.[44] In his 'livre maudit', Libidinal Economy,[45] Lyotard deploys the theatrical metaphor with such insistence, and for the development of an argument that is so interested in stressing the experience of affect, that one is tempted to do what theatre itself so often does, and take things literally. What would come of reading the opening chapter of this book, 'The Great Ephemeral Skin', in the belief that when Lyotard writes 'theatre' he actually means theatre?

Lyotard offers a fable in which there is first (and this is not, of course a chronological first, simply a logical first) a libidinal band. It is a skin without articulation, stretched out without top or bottom, disorganised, disarticulated, very like the 'body without organs'.[46] It is a Moebius strip, in which the surface is continuous, and as a surface, it has no depth. It is of interest, Lyotard says, 'because it is one-sided'.[47] It spins until in its spinning it somehow resolves itself into a bar. Now it has one side and another side. It is organised and articulated, and may be used to divide one thing from another. It becomes a kind of spacing device, which can be used to separate surface from depth, here from there, me from it and all the other separation upon which the regime of representation founds itself. Here, then, is a theatrical set-up, founded not on a desire that arises out of some originary lack, but a desire born of the separation of libidinal energies from each other.

So before the separation of stage from auditorium – the formation of the bar – there was libidinal energy distributed all over the surface of a skin, or, shall I say, a social body that is not yet either an audience or a theatre company. The formation of the bar puts one face opposite another, bringing the theatre into being. Before the bar the face-to-face encounter did not take place. It was as though both faces were the same faces, perhaps a little like one of those pre-cinematic illusions in which the faces of a hideous crone and a beautiful girl are made to succeed one another on a spinning disk. After the bar the faces are definitively separated from one another and the libidinal energy is distributed, organised and articulated on the principle of here and there, onstage and offstage. The purpose of this fable about the origins of the theatre seems to be to suggest that behind the orderly relations of representation, there lurks a violent libidinal force, without which the whole apparatus would never have come into being. The theatre is the result of work being carried out on the libidinal band, work that produces the space that is theatre. Before the theatre, there was

no density, intensities running here and there, setting up, escaping, without ever being imprisoned in the volume of the stage/auditorium. Theatricality and representation, far from having to be taken as libidinal givens, *a fortiori* metaphysical, result from a certain labour on the labyrinthine and Moebian band, a labour which prints these particular folds and twists, the effect of which is a box closed upon itself, filtering impulses and allowing only those to appear on the stage from what will come to be known as the exterior, satisfying the conditions of interiority.[48]

In trying to find something libidinal that precedes representation (conceived of as theatrical in structure), Lyotard proposes a rereading of Freud's idea of polymorphous perversity as an apprehension of an endless, pocketed and furrowed skin, without holes, over which desire or libido plays. Geoffrey Bennington suggests that Lyotard sees this differently from Deleuze and Guattari in *Anti-Oedipus* (which was published in the same year, 1968, as *Libidinal Economy*, and which seems to be addressing some of the same questions in a similarly ecstatic and violent rhetoric) because he thinks that their model of the machine implies processes that involve accumulation, and thus memory and time,[49] whereas,

When the whirls of the disjunctive segment in its libidinal journey, being singular, produce no memory, this segment only ever being where it is in an ungraspable time, *a tense*, and therefore what was "previously" journeyed through does not exist: acephalia, time of the unconscious.[50]

A literal reading of this would suggest that it would not be possible to find in the theatre any instances of events working with the logic of this sort of libidinal economy, in which nothing is remembered or represented, since the theatre itself stands as the place in which memory is staged and things are represented. But what seems to be possible to construe from this idea is the possibility that a breakdown of that system that allows the collapse of inside and outside, the fiasco of the representational system, a stupefaction of amnesia on both sides of the footlights, might involve a momentary reversion (except there is no chronology here) to the great ephemeral skin traversed by desire and generating affect. That is to say that in fiasco, there may indeed be an 'affecting surplus' of the event that does exceed representation, or rather, precede it, in the manner of a primary process. What such moments might signal, furthermore, is that because such primary processes only really operate in the libidinal economy prior to the transformation of the libidinal band into the disjunctive bar and the introduction of the distinction between this and not this, there and not there, that constitutes the theatre (of representation), we can only know about them because of the effects they have elsewhere, i.e., within the theatre itself. You cannot access this energy in itself, only by means of its representation in discursive forms, its effects within representation.

That is why, perhaps, it is precisely within the theatre itself – the place of doubleness redoubled, Plato's Cave of Shadows – that the desire for singularity makes itself felt with the greatest intensity. This is how performance's longing for the 'real' that exceeds representation comes into being as and where it does, as the antitheatrical within the theatre. This is the longing of 'the madman, lover of singularities', who wants 'a proper name, a divine name, for each intensity, and thus to die with each of them, to lose even his memory (river-bed and course), and certainly his own identity'.[51] What this madman normally has to make do with, of course, is the fleeting apprehension of such singularities as they show up in representation, through words, images and affects. The madman is condemned, as it were, always to be seeking the absent cause of such showings-up, knowing all the time that this question of causality, with its incessant desire for an origin, whether it be the pre-tragic theatre of the feminine, the animal and the infant, or the psychic cause of stage fright, is unanswerable. The libidinal band should not become an object of desire or nostalgia and the stage a space for figuring it in its absence. Instead (and according to Bennington, Lyotard is not always careful enough to maintain this crucial distinction) the libidinal band, the primary processes even, need to be seen as retrospectively imagined, that which cannot be represented,

> and cannot be a cause (in any traditional sense) insofar as it escapes the temporality constitutive of causality. The libidinal band is/was/will be never present, and can therefore never be re-presented.[52]

Maintaining a literal-minded (mad) focus on the theatrical as theatrical here, it becomes possible to imagine that Lyotard is arguing by implication for a new kind of theatrical criticism. In the most general terms it is probably fair to assert that theatrical and dramatic criticism started making a movement from word to image in the latter part of the twentieth century, but that the languages of the visual, including semiotics, still hold sway. But if the experience of affect is where we perhaps get a little closer to the drive that seems to be the basis of theatre and the occasion of some of its most intense pleasures and discomfort, then the development of a critical language to deal with this seems essential, not least because it offers, in place of a weak surrender to the unspeakable, an attempt to speak and make meaningful such affects, to create words and images that might communicate what such affects might be like. Lyotard takes us only part of the way, when he suggests that

> the crisis is now that of the first limit (1); stage + house/"outside." It is a selective limit, par excellence; sounds, lights, words, eyes, ears, postures (and therefore also in capitalism, the wallets) get sorted out so that what is a libidinal displacement may yield to the re-presentative replacement of performance. On the "outside", the toothache, on the "inside," its representation by the clenching of the fist. But the business of an energetic theatre is not to make allusion to the aching tooth when a clenched fist is the point, nor the reverse. Its business is neither to suggest that such and such means such and such, nor to say it, as Brecht wanted. Its business is to produce the highest intensity (by excess of lack of energy) of what there is, without intention.[53]

The challenge is to move beyond a slightly awestruck intoxication in the face of an 'intensity . . . without intention' which is now perhaps too firmly established in the theoretical repertoire as the post-modern sublime. One way of doing this might be to 'minorise' this sublime, to propose that it is not simply a matter of an affective encounter with that which exceeds our capacity to represent it in discourse, but also perhaps an encounter with that which sneaks under our willingness to apply labour in order to render it visible and meaningful. The post-modern sublime, at least as it appears in the kind of moments that have inspired the present investigation, takes a distinctly unheroic form: if it is a kind of abjection, it is a mild and shivery one, from which you recover nightly; or it is an embarrassment, an outbreak of silly giggling, a crappy animal costume or an accidental mouse. If these are what the 'madman' is after – unrepeatable singularities – it is also clearly the case that they only ever seem to appear escorted by those processes of representation that they were imagined to be exceeding. This is why what I offer here ends up being not so much a critique as an affirmation of theatre, discovering what it wants to value only amid that which it might wish to devalue (the bourgeois theatre of modernity), identifying unrepeatable singularities in the moment of their being inscribed in the repetitions of theatrical representation, singularities which, as Bennington suggests Lyotard recognises are 'only "present" in an almost indiscernible co-presence with what they threaten'.[54] Any moment, then, which aspires to the grace of 'pure, punctual presence', must also live by its entanglement with repetition.[55] The god and the puppet appear only in human form (as representations). The theatre of 'pure energetics' is to be found right here, in the theatre of representation, by way of the gracelessness that fails, or the sheer pleasure of watching the wheels spin. For Bennington, this is where Lyotard's project in *Libidinal Economy* fails:

Notwithstanding the subtlety and rigour of the attempt to account for theatricality and representation without reproducing them, despite the generalisation of "theatrics" which should undermine the oppositions on which the theatre depends, *Economie libidinale* does nonetheless rebuild the theatre, if only on the shifting ground of the libidinal band, which is no doubt still too ontological, still a *subject* despite all protestations to the contrary. Despite the insistence on the death-drive and on dissimulation, the libidinal band is still 'out there', transcendent, absence, Zero, inevitably proclaimed as 'good', as lost. The real problem of *Economie libidinale* is not that of its violence or its apparent break with theory, dialogue, the theatre, but the tenacity with which the theatre withstands such violence and even thrives on it.[56]

For me, that is its grace and its provocation. The theatre 'thrives' by keeping its machinery running, not just for the representations that it will produce, but – and perhaps this is the real purpose of the whole business – for the sake of the side *affects*.

Afterword

So there you are, then. And there they are, too, now. The machinery of representation has been switched off. The lights in the house have come up. You applaud and they acknowledge your applause. That's how it is. At last, we meet face to face, all the pretending has come to an end and we know who everyone is and where we are. We can forget about 'ontological queasiness' until the next time. We have just these closing responsibilities to discharge and we can all be on our way. If we happen to bump into one another on the train home we can do so as strangers, can we not?

At the end of one of the performances of Raffaello Sanzio's *Giulio Cesare* in London in 1999 the lights come back up on an uncertain situation. The audience is scattered. It does not add up to a collective presence. It is clearly divided, and cannot properly be spoken of as a single entity. Yet it has a collective responsibility to discharge. The actors stand together near the centre of the stage. They do not form a line across the stage. This is the first time all of them have appeared together, because the second half of the production is performed mainly by two women who did not appear in the first, accompanied, briefly, by only four of the six others who appeared in the first half. They appear most unlikely as a company. Two extremely thin women, a small albino man, a man who looks like Jesus, a man with the body of a sumo wrestler, a man with a small hole in his throat and two men, probably in their thirties who look, very distinctly, like themselves. The key point is that they do not look like a theatre company, and that there is something distinctive and uncomfortable in their presence on stage. They do not repel or reject the applause that is now delivered on behalf of the audience by the collection of individuals in the auditorium, but nor do they perform in return the conventional gestures of accept-ance: the bow and the modest smile. There is nothing hostile or even unfriendly in this way of being there in front of us, but nothing that quite satisfies our requirements of the encounter, either. This curtain call appears to be failing.

As Bert O. States reminds us,

The curtain call belongs most broadly to the tradition of the parting, the introduction of the speaker, the invocation and the recessional – in other words, to the whole realm of formal beginnings and endings whereby we punctuate the events of social life and rescue them from the indifferent drift of time.[1]

What it is usually assumed to do therefore, is to regulate rela-tions between audience and performers, perform an act of social lubrication which might permit us to speak to the performers afterwards, confident that they are who they are and not who they have just appeared as. In short, it is to clear up any residual confusion between sign and phenomenon that may have been generated and left by the performance. It puts us back in our place and concludes a market transaction. Or so it seems.

On closer examination, the picture is a little more compli-cated. In the first place, it is not at all clear that the machinery of representation has really been switched off. Perhaps it is just winding down, and still generating sparks of representation that contaminate what we were hoping for – a straight face-to-face encounter without anyone pretending to be someone else. As States notes, the actor playing Hamlet carries with him some-thing of Hamlet over into his appearance in the curtain call. It is not possible to see him as simply himself if you have only ever seen him as Hamlet.[2] In practice, this residue of the role is usually stiffened by costume: actors in curtain calls do not usually appear in their street clothes, even if they have had plenty of time since their last appearance on stage to change out of their costumes. Presumably this convention helps secure the sense that for the duration of the play all of the characters are continuously 'alive' even if we do not see them. For an actor to appear on stage in a curtain call wearing her own clothes rather than the costume that appeared as the clothes of the character would be to make it too obvious that her appearance as the character was part of a job. It would expose to the audience the whole backstage world of dressing rooms, make up remover and fast getaways from the stage door that is conventionally kept hidden in the architectural division of the theatre into work space and leisure space, backstage and front of house. Paradoxically, since the everyday clothes that an actor might wear to and from her place of employment – the theatre – might be construed as the signifier of her leisure, while her costume is part of her work, the appearance of the actor in her own clothes during a curtain call seems to make the fact of her work more visible. It is as though she has been dragged back from a period of non-work, to perform a final duty from which she visibly intends to depart as soon as possible.

This effect was very powerfully in operation during the curtain call at the end of Raffaello Sanzio's *Genesi: from the museum of sleep*. This piece was in three acts, and the third involved only three performers. This meant that there were at least four actors from Act One, and the six children who performed Act Two, who had been offstage for over an hour by the time of the curtain call. Nearly all of these, including all six children, appeared for the curtain call in their own clothes. This had a particularly striking effect in the case of the children, who had performed in Act Two wearing white costumes, in most cases including hoods over their heads, which tended to emphasise similarities rather than differences in their physical appearances. When they appeared 'as themselves' in the curtain call, running around, talking to other company members and waving to the audience, the suddenness with which six very distinct individuals appeared, behaving with blithe disregard for the conventions of the curtain call, gave the audience a very vivid sense of lives lived beyond the working environment of the stage. Rather than seeing the six larval figures we watched at work in Act Two, we came face to face with six wholly other people, the six brothers and sisters who had been doing whatever it was they were doing backstage for the duration of Act Three. This impression was perhaps intensified by the fact that the eldest of the six children took a very dignified bow, as though to indicate that she knew what she was supposed to be doing, even if her brothers and sisters did not quite know how to behave. What these curtain calls that 'fail' to perform their usual function make clear is just what is expected from the convention itself. In this particular case, the powerful illusion – if not the reality – of coming face to face with the actors as themselves, with all residue of character removed, makes it very clear that the convention of the curtain call does not in fact involve any such encounter. There is always something in the way, something left over from the representation.

My second initial assumption, that the curtain call and the applause which it acknowledges are the final signing-off on a market transaction between audience and actors is also problematic. The market transaction involved the purchase of a ticket in exchange for the performance. The audience's applause does not in practice indicate that the audience feels it has got its money's worth. In any case, the transaction itself does not depend upon the audience feeling this. A certain risk is involved for the audience, since, however lousy or objectionable the performance, there will be no money back. By the same token, the performers will be paid for their night's work whether anyone applauds or not. When a modern actor delivers one of those Shakespeare epilogues in which 'the help of your good hands' is requested as a form of acquittal, a false note is almost inevitably struck. The economics of this engagement were sorted out before the curtain even rose. Anything that happens now, after it has dropped for the last time, is in excess. It might be a matter of courtesy. After all, there is nothing strange when a purely economic transaction – buying a newspaper from someone you have never met before and will never meet again – is 'lubricated' with mutual thanks. You thank the seller for the newspaper and the seller thanks you for the money. But in the theatre this exchange of courtesies is handled somewhat differently, and although there is a kind of reciprocity in it, there is also an inequality. There is reciprocity in that the audience's applause is usually met with a particular kind of appearance, certain kinds of performance, even. The actor who has laboured all night on a major role might play up her exhaustion, tropes of self-deprecation and modesty may be deployed, smiles of pleasure, with maybe even the hint of a blush, might be bestowed upon the audience. But the moment the actors attempt an exchange of like for like, as happens in your encounter with the newspaper seller, things are felt to be going wrong. The unease, the sense that this is not quite right that arises when actors applaud the audience back is a powerful affective clue to

the real meaning of the curtain call. It is not simply that applauding back communicates a manifest lie – that the actors are
as appreciative of the work done by the audience as the audience
is of the work done by the actors (a liberal fiction perilously close
to the film or music star's assertion that without their fans they
are nothing) – it actually gets in the way of what the audience is
trying to do.

The audience is trying to figure itself as the recipient of a gift.
Its applause is a paradoxical return, because it wishes to establish a relationship in which excess is preserved, in which the
economics of exchange are somehow suspended. It wants to feel
something extra, garner some 'affecting surplus' from the encounter that has nothing to do with either the literal or the
figurative economies of representation that obtain in modern
theatre. By giving back only that which expresses appreciation
for what has already been acquired by means of exchange the
audience is trying to frame the encounter in such a way that its
own action cannot be reciprocated. For, as Marcel Mauss
writes, the ideal outcome 'would be to give a potlatch and not
have it returned'.[3] That is why applause is not the same as
thanks. Indeed, applause from an audience can be met with
the mouthing of the words 'Thank you' from the stage without
the imbalance being disturbed. That 'Thank you' is always
already built into the transaction (as in the case of buying the
newspaper) is further demonstrated by the pre-emptive use of
the term at the end of their 'acts' by singers, stand-up comedians, speech-makers and even recorded public service an-
nouncements. The thanks in such cases do not cancel out the
applause, rather they enact on behalf of both parties the formal-
ity of the transaction, under circumstances where the other
party is unable to speak. Thanks are part of the 'restrictive
economy'. Applause seems to have aspirations to carve out a
more 'general economy',[4] an economy of the gift. For actors to
applaud back frustrates this aspiration, rather like the recipient
of praise who feels compelled to respond with protestations of
inadequacy: 'No, really. . .' A further indication of the affective
force of the desire for this experience of the gift might be
adduced from the sense of disappointment felt by an audience
when actors do not take a curtain call at all. Applause that is
offered, but not, as it were, accepted, with good grace, fails to

satisfy, because it deprives an audience of the gain it has set out to win for itself through the gift of applause. This tends to happen mainly when the subject matter of the performance is thought to be too 'serious' for its presentation to be met with anything so trivial as an accession to theatrical convention, as a way of asserting that the material is far more important than the fact of its theatrical appearing. In moments such as these theatre appears to be trying to annexe to itself something of the solemnity of religious ritual, trying to establish itself as commensurate with those performances of sacred musical works in churches, where the convention persists that there should be no applause. In the theatre the repudiation of the curtain call tends to signify a conviction that both actors and audience share something in their reasons for attending that transcends the theatre, and with it the comparable triviality of the market economy. But in signalling its lack of concern for the market economy in this way, the theatre would paradoxically be depriving itself of the only pleasures for which money might not be exchanged. What this account of the curtain call is more generally designed to suggest is that in reality both parties are in attendance precisely because of the theatre, and that anything else, including 'serious' subject matter, can only be a pretext, by means of which the gain of pleasure might be obtained.

The curtain call might figure then as emblematic of the real state of play in the theatre. What if, for example, it is the curtain call itself that we came for, after all? After all the representation, all the pretending, the running around and the shouting, all the talk and the coming on and off, the living and, of course, the dying, this is what we really want. Them, up there; us down here. Face to face with each other in a situation that moves momentarily outside the economies of representation. Or rather, and this is an absolutely critical distinction, a situation in which we can pretend that this is the case; hope, that is, that it might be. For, as we have seen, whether it succeeds or it fails, the curtain call, for all its gestures beyond the machinery of representation, always takes place in the place of representation, in the mode of representation, and it can only operate at all within and after conditions in which representation has most decisively held sway. If the moment at the end of the show when they stand there and we like them, and they enjoy our liking of

them might somehow fleetingly offer a glimpse of some other
kind of relation than those determined by economies of exchange and substitution, then what we experience in such
moments is not so much the reality of such a relation, but its
unreality. The promise of such a relation is made in the language
that would deny any other relation. The theatrical relation is not
closed down in the curtain call, and the momentary flavour of
the gift comes just as the division of labour appears at its most
intense. The glimpse of the horizon in which 'non-productive
expenditure' might be valued is acquired at precisely the
moment that productive expenditure is formally acknowledged.[5] The theatre is, among other things, the place we go to
feel what we feel about work and the constraints it places upon
our freedom, and certainly not the place we go to experience
some ahistorical freedom from work, however much it might be
trying to kid us otherwise.

It is only through those curtain calls which fail, or which,
more properly, are designed in advance to fail – for there is no
doubt that the effects and affects of Raffaello Sanzio's curtain
calls are carefully calculated whatever their lack of calculation –
that the nature of their functioning fully appears.[6] The movement of this analysis through such acts of failure turns out to be
a reaffirmation, of a kind, of course. Such moments as the
curtain call, like the various collapses into stage fright, embarrassment, corpsing or fiasco that perhaps foreshadow this final
face to face, live, as Geoffrey Bennington's account of Lyotard
reminds us, 'in an almost indiscernible co-presence with what
they threaten'.[7]

Until now I have been suggesting, I think, that theatre shares
with psychoanalysis and certain theories of representation (such
as Lyotard's) a structure in which meaning and signification
only operate on the basis of a certain meaninglessness around
which they circulate, or out of which they fabricate themselves.
What I am now suggesting, more fully than before, and in
addition rather than in contradiction to this possibility, is that
theatre constructs its representational system in order to produce that which can then at least attempt to escape it. The work
of making meaning out of these attempts, these leakages from
the system, is the work that theatrical affect elicits from its

audience and which this present work attempts, in its 'reading' of such moments, to undertake.

Whatever 'affecting surplus' there might be in such moments cannot appear or be experienced without the structures in respect of which it stands as a surplus. Theatre is a machine that sets out to undo itself. It conceives itself as an apparatus for the production of affect by means of representation, in the expectation that the most powerful affects will be obtained at precisely those moments when the machinery appears to break down. This is not just, as we have seen, that the breaking down of the machinery is in itself the source of pleasure, although this can be the case, but that the machinery itself only truly appears in its moments of breakdown. Our pleasure is derived, that is to say, from the operation of the machinery (effective or failing), rather than whatever it is that it is producing. The affects that I earlier characterised as 'side affects' are in fact nothing of the kind. They are the real thing: all the stories and the characters and the dénouements merely the side effects of the affect-machine.

Notes

INTRODUCTION

1. Marcel Proust, *Remembrance of Things Past: Volume One*, translated by C. K. Scott Moncrieff and Terence Kilmartin (Harmondsworth: Penguin Books, 1983), p. 480.
2. The figure of 'Berma' was based by Proust on Sarah Bernhardt.
3. Proust, *Remembrance of Things Past*, p. 477.
4. Ibid., p. 478.
5. Ibid., p. 479.
6. Ibid., p. 482.
7. Ibid., p. 485.
8. Ibid., p. 486.
9. Ibid., p. 486.
10. Jonas Barish, *The Antitheatrical Prejudice* (Berkeley and Los Angeles: University of California Press, 1981), p. 3.
11. See Michael Fried, 'Art and Objecthood', *Artforum*, Summer 1967, reprinted in Michael Fried, *Art and Objecthood: Essays and Reviews* (Chicago and London: University of Chicago Press, 1998), pp. 148–172. Fried's article has been influential in the study of art history, where it stands as a definitive text in the understanding of the relations between modernism in its final 'high' American form, and post-modern developments, most particularly the 'minimalist' or 'literalist' art of Robert Morris, Donald Judd, Frank Stella et al. It is probably fair to say that in his use of the 'theatrical' as a pejorative term, Fried did not actually intend any commentary upon the theatre itself. However, his work has been taken up so widely in the discussion of performance, especially when viewed as a post-modern form, that its unintended consequences may even have exceeded its intended influence.
12. See, for instance, Schechner, *Performance Theory* (New York and London: Routledge, 1988).
13. These moments denote positions to which these names have become attached in the history of the discussions of which they

form part. All resemblance to persons living or dead is now largely conventional.

14. I am thinking here of performance's tradition of emphasising real bodily presences as exemplified in the work of, inter alia, Marina Abramovic, Carolee Schneemann, Chris Burden, Hermann Nitsch, Ron Athey, Orlan, Vito Acconci.

15. Walter Benjamin, 'Paris – The Capital of the Nineteenth Century', in *Charles Baudelaire*, translated by Harry Zohn (London and New York: Verso, 1997). This was a draft designed to introduce the whole of Benjamin's uncompleted *Arcades Project*.

16. Martin Puchner, *Stage Fright: Modernism, Antitheatricality and Drama* (Baltimore: Johns Hopkins University Press, 2002).

17. Robert Morris, cited in Fried, *Art and Objecthood: Essays and Reviews*, p. 154

18. Fried, *Art and Objecthood: Essays and Reviews*, p. 155.

19. Ibid.

20. Ibid.

21. Josette Féral, 'Performance and Theatricality: The Subject Demystified', translated by Therese Lyons, *Modern Drama*, 25:1 (1982), pp. 170–181, reprinted in *Mimesis, Masochism and Mime: The Politics of Theatricality in Contemporary French Thought*, edited by Timothy Murray (Ann Arbor: University of Michigan Press, 1997), pp. 289–300.

22. Jon McKenzie, *Perform or Else: From Discipline to Performance* (London and New York: Routledge, 2001), pp. 38–44.

23. Jacques Derrida, 'The Theatre of Cruelty and the Closure of Representation', in *Writing and Difference*, translated by Alan Bass (London and Henley: Routledge and Kegan Paul, 1978), pp. 232–250.

24. Féral, in Murray, *Mimesis, Masochism and Mime*, p. 294.

25. See, for example, Philip Auslander, 'Presence and Theatricality', in *From Acting to Performance: Essays in Modernism and Postmodernism* (New York and London: Routledge, 1997).

26. Féral, in Murray, *Mimesis, Masochism and Mime*, p. 295.

27. Ibid., p. 295.

28. Ibid., p. 295.

29. Ibid., p. 297.

30. Ibid., p. 297.

31. Ibid., p. 297

32. Elin Diamond, 'Introduction', in *Performance and Cultural Politics*, edited by Elin Diamond (London and New York: Routledge, 1996), p. 2. I am grateful to Jen Harvie for bringing this to my attention.

33. Translated as *The Puppet Theatre*, in Heinrich von Kleist, *Selected Writings*, edited and translated by David Constantine, (London:

J. M. Dent, 1997), pp. 411–416. In the text I shall refer to it throughout as *Über das Marionettentheater*.

34. Kleist, *Selected Writings*, p. 413.
35. Ibid., p. 416.
36. Paul de Man, 'Aesthetic Formalization in Kleist', in *The Rhetoric of Romanticism* (New York: Columbia University Press, 1984) p. 267.
37. In an interview with Nick Kaye, Abramovic says: '. . . theatre was an absolute enemy. It was something bad, it was something we should not deal with. It was artificial. All the qualities that performance had were unrehearsable. There was no repetition. It was new for me and the sense of reality was very strong. We refused the theatrical structure'. *Art into Theatre: Performance Interviews and Documents*, edited by Nick Kaye (Amsterdam: Harwood Academic Publishers, 1996), p. 181.
38. Jean-François Lyotard, 'The God and the Puppet', in *The Inhuman: Reflections on Time*, translated by Geoffrey Bennington and Rachel Bowlby (Cambridge: Polity Press, 1991), p. 156.
39. Ibid., p. 159.
40. Ibid., p. 156.
41. Ibid., p. 156.
42. Ibid., p. 163.
43. Ibid., p. 163.
44. de Man, *The Rhetoric of Romanticism*, p. 267.
45. Lyotard, *The Inhuman*, p. 164.
46. Lyotard's phrase could work well as a general heading under which to think through the work of body artists such as Abramovic, Franko B and Orlan, not simply as a way of referring to their engagement with physical pain, but in order to mark their struggle with the structures of representation within and against which they make their work.
47. de Man, *The Rhetoric of Romanticism*, p. 268.
48. Immanuel Kant, *Critique of Judgement*, translated, with an introduction, by Werner S. Pluhar (Indianapolis and Cambridge: Hackett, 1987).
49. G. W. F. Hegel, *Introductory Lectures on Aesthetics*, translated by Bernard Bosanquet (London: Penguin Books, 1993).
50. Andrzej Warminski 'Introduction: Allegories of Reference', in Paul de Man, *Aesthetic Ideology*, edited with an introduction by Andrzej Warminski (Minneapolis and London: University of Minnesota Press, 1996), p. 3.
51. Warminski, 'Introduction: Allegories of Reference', p. 4.
52. Paul de Man, 'Phenomenality and Materiality in Kant', in *Aesthetic Ideology*, p. 89.
53. Kleist, *Selected Writings*, p. 414.
54. Ibid., p. 414.

55. Ibid., p. 415.
56. Ibid., p. 415.
57. Ibid., p. 415.
58. Ibid., p. 415.
59. Ibid., p. 416.
60. Ibid., p. 416.
61. The term is Michael Kirby's. See 'On Acting and Not-Acting', in *Acting (Re)Considered: Theories and Practices*, edited by Phillip B. Zarrilli, (London and New York: Routledge, 1995), pp. 43–58.
62. Kleist, *Selected Writings*, p. 416.
63. Ibid., p. 416.
64. de Man, *The Rhetoric of Romanticism*, p. 269.
65. Ibid.
66. Helmut J. Schneider, 'Deconstruction of the Hermeneutical Body: Kleist and the Discourse of Classical Aesthetics', in *Body and Text in the Eighteenth Century*, edited by Veronica Kelly and Dorothea von Mücke (Stanford: Stanford University Press, 1994), p. 212.
67. Kleist, *Selected Writings*, p. 413.
68. Ibid.
69. My reading of this moment of performance is indebted to the account presented by Rebecca Schneider, in *The Explicit Body in Performance* (London and New York: Routledge, 1997).
70. See, in particular, Emmanuel Levinas, *Totality and Infinity*, translated by Alphonso Lingis (Pittsburgh: Duquesne University Press, 1969). For sympathetic developments of Levinas's thought towards an ethics of deconstruction, see Simon Critchley, *Ethics-Politics-Subjectivity: Essays on Derrida, Levinas and Contemporary French Thought* (London and New York: Verso, 1999), and for a more sceptical account, Steven Connor, *Theory and Cultural Value* (Oxford: Blackwell, 1992).
71. Simon Critchley, 'Post-Deconstructive Subjectivity?', in *Ethics-Politics-Subjectivity: Essays on Derrida, Levinas and Contemporary French Thought*, (London and New York: Verso, 1999), p. 63.
72. See Stanton B. Garner, Jr., *Bodied Spaces: Phenomenology and Performance in Contemporary Drama* (Ithaca and London: Cornell University Press, 1994).
73. Alan Read, *The Theatre and Everyday Life: An Ethics of Performance* (London and New York: Routledge, 1993), pp. 53–54.

1 STAGE FRIGHT: THE PREDICAMENT OF THE ACTOR

1. Constantin Stanislavski, *An Actor Prepares*, translated by Elizabeth Reynolds Hapgood (London: Methuen, 1988), p. 7.
2. Ibid., p. 7.
3. Ibid., p. 7.

4. Ibid., p. 7.
5. Ibid., p. 8.
6. Ibid., p. 8.
7. Ibid., p. 10.
8. Ibid., p. 10.
9. Ibid., p. 11.
10. Ibid., p. 11.
11. Ibid., p. 82.
12. Adolph Kielblock, *The Stage Fright, or How to Face an Audience* (Boston: Press of Geo. H. Ellis, 1891).
13. Georg Simmel, 'The Metropolis and Mental Life', in *Art in Theory 1900–1990: An Anthology of Changing Ideas*, edited by Charles Harrison and Paul Wood (Oxford: Blackwell, 1992), pp. 133–134.
14. *Twentieth Century Actor Training*, edited by Alison Hodge (London and New York: Routledge, 2000), pp. 1–2.
15. Ibid., p. 2.
16. Ibid., p. 2.
17. Simmel, in Harrison and Wood, *Art in Theory 1900–1990*, p. 131.
18. Ibid.
19. Henry James, *The Tragic Muse* (New York: Charles Scribner's Sons, 1936), pp. 66–67.
20. Simmel, in Harrison and Wood, *Art in Theory 1900–1990*, p. 132.
21. Ibid., p. 132.
22. Ibid., p. 133.
23. Ibid., p. 133.
24. Fredric Jameson, *The Political Unconscious: Narrative as a Socially Symbolic Act* (London: Routledge, 1996), p. 62.
25. Jameson, p. 66.
26. Richard Sennett, *The Fall of Public Man* (New York and London: Norton, 1992), p. 37.
27. Ibid., p. 27.
28. Emile Zola, 'Naturalism', in *Modern Theories of Drama*, edited by George W. Brandt (Oxford: Clarendon Press, 1988), p. 87.
29. Ibid., p. 88.
30. See Joseph Roach, *The Player's Passion: Studies in the Science of Acting* (Ann Arbor: University of Michigan Press, 1993).
31. See Colin Counsell, *Signs of Performance: An Introduction to Twentieth Century Theatre* (London: Routledge, 1996), pp. 28–30 and p. 47.
32. Jean Chothia, *André Antoine* (Cambridge: Cambridge University Press, 1991), p. 64.
33. Donald C. Mullin, *The Development of the Playhouse* (Berkeley and Los Angeles: University of California Press, 1970), p. 30.
34. Wolfgang Schivelbusch, *Disenchanted Night: The Industrialisation of Light in the Nineteenth Century* (Berkeley and Los Angeles: University of California Press, 1995), p. 206.

35. Ibid., p. 210.

36. Ibid., p. 207.

37. Mullin, *The Development of the Playhouse*, pp. 133–134.

38. See Schivelbusch, *Disenchanted Night*, p. 212.

39. Kato Havas, *Stage Fright: its causes and cures, with special reference to violin playing* (London: Bosworth, 1973).

40. Glen O. Gabbard, 'Stage Fright', *International Journal of Psychoanalysis*, 60 (1979), pp. 383–392 (p. 383).

41. Havas, *Stage Fright*, p. 2.

42. W. Ritchie, *Nervousness and Stage Fright: A Never-failing Remedy* (45, Radnor Drive, Liscard, Cheshire: W. Ritchie, 1915.

43. Kielblock, *The Stage Fright*, p. 35.

44. Ibid., p. 5.

45. Ibid., p. 8.

46. H. Ernest Hunt, *Nerve Control: The Cure of Nervousness and Stage Fright* (London: William Richer and Son Ltd., 1915), p. 71.

47. Joe Kelleher, 'Writer's Block', in *Psychoanalysis and Performance*, edited by Patrick Campbell and Adrian Kear (London and New York: Routledge, 2000), p. 133.

48. Gabbard, 'Stage Fright', p. 383.

49. Donald M. Kaplan, 'On Stage Fright', *TDR* 14:1 (1969), pp. 60–83.

50. Stephen Aaron, *Stage Fright: Its Role in Acting* (Chicago and London: University of Chicago Press, 1986), p. 80.

51. Ibid., p. 83.

52. Glen O. Gabbard, 'Further contributions to the understanding of stage fright: Narcissistic issues', *Journal of the American Psychoanalytic Association*, 31 (1983), pp. 423–441 (p. 440).

53. Ibid., p. 440.

54. Kaplan, 'On Stage Fright', p. 64.

55. Ibid.

56. Ibid.

57. Nicholas Ridout, 'Who Does Cathy Naden Think She Is?', unpublished paper given at the American Society for Theatre Research Annual Conference, CUNY Graduate Center, New York, November 2000.

58. Gabbard, 'Stage Fright', p. 390.

59. Ibid., p. 389.

60. Ibid., p. 389.

61. Sandor Ferenczi, 'Stage Fright and Narcissistic Self-Observation', in Sandor Ferenczi, *Further Contributions to the Theory and Technique of Psychoanalysis* (New York: Basic Books, 1952), pp. 421–422.

62. Stanislavski, *An Actor Prepares*, p. 10.

63. Julia Kristeva, *Powers of Horror: An Essay in Abjection* (New York: Columbia University Press, 1982), p. 31.

64. Ibid., p. 1.
65. Ibid., p. 1.
66. Ibid., p. 2.
67. Ibid., p. 3.
68. Ibid., p. 4.
69. Ibid., p. 10.
70. Ibid., p. 4.
71. Ibid., p. 4.
72. Ibid., p. 16.
73. Aaron, *Stage Fright*, p. 120.

2   EMBARRASSMENT: THE PREDICAMENT OF THE AUDIENCE

1. Production directed by Steven Pimlott, for the Royal Shakespeare Company, first at The Swan Theatre, Stratford, 2000, and subsequently at The Pit Theatre, The Barbican Centre, London, 2001.
2. Bridget Escolme offers a detailed and persuasive account of this production and its performative effects in *Talking to the Audience: Shakespeare, Performance, Self* (London and New York: Routledge, 2005). I am indebted to her both for her detailed observations and for ongoing discussion of the production that has informed the writing of much of this chapter.
3. Harry Berger, Jr., *Imaginary Audition: Shakespeare on Stage and Page* (Berkeley and Los Angeles: University of California Press, 1989).
4. Ibid., p. 45.
5. Stanton B. Garner, *Bodied Spaces: Phenomenology and Performance in Contemporary Drama* (Ithaca and London: Cornell University Press, 1994). He is referring to Geertz's essay 'Thick Description: Toward an Interpretive Theory of Culture', in *The Interpretation of Cultures* (New York: Basic Books, 1973).
6. Berger, *Imaginary Audition*, p. 99.
7. W. B. Worthen, *Shakespeare and the Authority of Performance*, (Cambridge: Cambridge University Press, 1987), p. 178.
8. Garner, *Bodied Spaces*, p. 49.
9. Ibid., pp. 50–51.
10. Helene Keyssar, 'I Love You. Who Are You? The Strategy of Drama in Recognition Scenes', *PMLA* 92 (1977), pp. 297–306 (p. 297).
11. Ibid., p. 301.
12. Richard Sennett, *The Fall of Public Man* (New York and London: W. W. Norton, 1992), p. 37.
13. Richard Sennett, keynote address given at Civic Centre: Reclaiming the Right to Performance, London School of Economics, April

12, 2002. Sennett also discusses the *stoa* in *Flesh and Stone: The Body and the City in Western Civilization* (London: Penguin Books, 2002), pp. 50–55.

14. Keyssar, 'I Love You. Who Are You?', p. 303.

15. These and subsequent citations of definitions in this chapter are from the *Oxford English Dictionary*, 2nd edition (Oxford: Clarendon Press, 1989).

16. Christopher Ricks, *Keats and Embarrassment* (Oxford: Clarendon Press, 1974).

17. Erving Goffman, 'Embarrassment and Social Organization', in *Interaction Ritual: Essays in Face to Face Behaviour* (London: Allen Lane, 1972), pp. 97–112.

18. Ruth Benedict, *The Chrysanthemum and the Sword: Patterns of Japanese Culture* (London: Routledge and Kegan Paul, 1977).

19. Léon Wurmser, *The Masks of Shame* (Northvale, NJ: James Aronson Inc., 1994), p. 17.

20. Ibid., p. 51.

21. Helen Merrell Lynd, *Shame and the Search for Identity* (London: Routledge and Kegan Paul, 1958), p. 38n.

22. Silvan Tomkins, *Affect, Imagery, Consciousness, Volume 2, The Negative Affects* (New York: Springer, 1963), p. 119.

23. Ibid., p. 123.

24. Ibid., p. 134.

25. Ibid., p. 133.

26. Ibid., p. 136.

27. See Goffman, 'Embarrassment and Social Organization'.

28. Robert Antelme, *The Human Race*, cited in Giorgio Agamben, *Remnants of Auschwitz: The Witness and the Archive*, translated by Daniel Heller-Roazen (New York: Zone Books, 1999), p. 103.

29. Agamben, *Remnants of Auschwitz*, p. 104.

30. Ibid. Agamben may describe Levinas's account as exemplary on the basis that its terms are typical of the way in which shame and the self are discussed elsewhere, including and perhaps in particular, by Jean-Paul Sartre. See Jean-Paul Sartre, *Being and Nothingness: An Essay of Phenomenological Ontology*, translated by Hazel E. Barnes (London: Routledge, 1989), p. 290.

31. Emmanuel Levinas, *De l'évasion* (Paris: Fata Morgana, 1982), cited in Agamben, *Remnants of Auschwitz*, p. 105.

32. Agamben, *Remnants of Auschwitz*, pp. 105–106.

33. The term is now widely associated with Agamben, and its meaning for him is developed in full in Giorgio Agamben, *Homo Sacer: Sovereign Power and Bare Life*, translated by Daniel Heller-Roazen (Stanford: Stanford University Press, 1998).

34. Agamben, *Remnants of Auschwitz*, p. 107.

35. Giorgio Agamben, 'The Face', in *Means without End: Notes on Politics*, translated by Vincenzo Binetti and Cesare Casarino (Minneapolis and London: University of Minnesota Press, 2000), pp. 93–94.
36. Berger, *Imaginary Audition*, p. 99.
37. Bert O. States, *Great Reckonings in Little Rooms: The Phenomenology of Theatre* (Berkeley and Los Angeles: University of California Press, 1985), p. 32.
38. Herbert Blau, 'Universals of Performance; or amortizing play', in *By Means of Performance: Intercultural studies of theatre and ritual*, edited by Richard Schechner and Willa Appel (Cambridge: Cambridge University Press, 1990), pp. 258–259.

3 THE ANIMAL ON STAGE

1. Harold Pinter, *The Caretaker*, directed by Patrick Marber, at the Comedy Theatre, London, November 2000.
2. For an analysis of the *Mini-Pops* controversy in the British media, see Valerie Walkerdine, *Daddy's Girl: Young Girls and Popular Culture* (Cambridge MA: Harvard University Press, 1997).
3. *Genesi: from the museum of sleep*, Societas Raffaello Sanzio, directed by Romeo Castellucci, seen as part of the London International Festival of Theatre, at the Sadler's Wells Theatre, London, 2001.
4. *Giulio Cesare*, Societas Raffaello Sanzio, directed by Romeo Castellucci, first seen as part of the London International Festival at the Queen Elizabeth Hall, London, 1999.
5. Peter Conrad, 'Shakespeare Made Sick', *The Observer*, June 6, 1999.
6. Michael Billington, 'Bleak Russians at the Purcell Room', *The Guardian*, January 15, 2001. The 'freakshow' reference here is a slightly gratuitous throwaway in the context of a negative review of a Russian performance which Billington guesses admirers of *Giulio Cesare* might enjoy.
7. In conversation with the author.
8. Michael Peterson, 'Stubborn as a Mule: Non-Human Performers and the Limits of Semiotics', unpublished paper given at the American Society for Theatre Research Annual Conference, CUNY Graduate Center, New York, November 2000.
9. The distinctive 'presence' of the animal on stage is a widely noted phenomenon, discussed perhaps most fully by Bert O. States, in *Great Reckonings in Little Rooms: The Phenomenology of Theatre* (Berkeley and Los Angeles: University of California Press, 1985), pp. 32–37. One of the virtues of States's account is the way in which he accommodates both a semiotic and a phenomenological

view of the animal on stage, in which it is both animal thing and meaningful image, depending on the mode in which it is viewed, thus introducing a kind of self-parodic comment on theatre's own play between these two registers of perception.

10. Peterson, 'Stubborn as a Mule', p. 1.
11. Ibid., p. 1.
12. Ibid., p. 1.
13. Ibid., p. 6.
14. Robert Bresson, *Notes on the Cinematographer*, translated by Jonathan Griffin (London: Quartet Encounters, 1986), p. 53.
15. Peterson, 'Stubborn as a Mule', p. 6.
16. Ibid., p. 6.
17. Shakespeare, *Julius Caesar*, 1.320–22 and 26–28.
18. *Julius Caesar*, 1.3.29.
19. *Julius Caesar*, 1.3.34–35.
20. Peterson, 'Stubborn as a Mule', p. 6.
21. *The Mute Who Was Dreamed*, written and directed by Attila Posselyani, presented by Theatre Bazi at the Riverside Studios, London, 2002.
22. I am grateful to Judie Christie of the Centre for Performance Research, who organised Theatre Bazi's UK visit, for this information.
23. *L.#09*, presented by the London International Festival of Theatre at the Laban Centre, London, May 2004. I am grateful to Gilda Biasini for information about both the elephant and the cats.
24. *Swan Lake*, Royal Ballet of Flanders, directed by Jan Fabre, at The Playhouse Theatre, Edinburgh, 2002.
25. Joseph Roach, *The Player's Passion: Studies in the Science of Acting* (Ann Arbor: The University of Michigan Press, 1993), p. 165.
26. See for example, *Performance Research 5:2: On Animals* (2000), edited by Alan Read and including David Williams, 'The Right Horse, the Animal Eye – Bartabas and Theatre Zingaro', pp. 29–40. See also Steve Baker, *The Postmodern Animal* (London: Reaktion Books, 2000).
27. Romeo Castellucci, 'Il pellegrino della materia', in Claudia Castellucci, Romeo Castellucci and Chiara Guidi, *Epopea delle polvere* (Milan: Societas Raffaello Sanzio and Ubulibri, 2001), p. 271.
28. Romeo Castellucci, 'Il pellegrino della materia', p. 271, author's translation.
29. Romeo Castellucci, 'The Animal Being on Stage', translated by Carolina Melis, Valentina Valentini and Ric Allsopp, *Performance Research 5:2: On Animals* (2000), pp. 23–28 (p. 24).
30. This interview forms the basis for the video-document *Le Pèlerin de la matière*. It also appears, in French, in *Les Pèlerins de la matière: théorie et praxis du théatre. Écrits de la Societas Raffaello Sanzio,*

translated by Karin Espinosa (Besançon: Les Solitaires Intempestifs, 2001). In the published French version, translator Karin Espinosa does not attempt to clarify Castellucci's meaning but offers instead a direct translation of his words.

31. The passage cited continues as follows: 'Esiste una tradizione completamente dimenticata, cancellata, rimossa del teatro occidentale che è quella del teatro pretragico. Ed è rimossa perché è un teatro appunto legato alla materia e allo sgomento della materia. È legato piuttosto a una presenza o a una potenza di tipo femminile, senza dubbio.' Castellucci, C., Castellucci, R. and Guidi, *Epopea delle polvere*, p. 271. 'There exists in the Western theatre a completely forgotten, cancelled and erased tradition, which is that of the pre-tragic theatre. It is erased because it is a theatre linked to matter and the disturbance of matter. Or rather, it is linked to a presence or a power of a feminine type, undoubtedly.' Author's translation.

32. See Aeschylus, *Oresteia: The Eumenides*, translated by Richmond Lattimore (Chicago: University of Chicago Press, 1953), pp. 154–163.

33. That the broad outlines of this argument correspond with Castellucci's own understanding was confirmed in a conversation with the author (Paris, November 2004). Castellucci identified the work of Johann Jakob Bachofen as his source for the idea that this male assertion of power, contemporary with Attic tragedy, brings to an end a now-forgotten history of female power. See Johann Jakob Bachofen, *Mutterrecht. English. Selections, An English Translation of Bachofen's Mutterrecht (Mother Right) (1861): a study of the religious and juridical aspects of gynecocracy in the ancient world*, translated and abridged by Edward Partenheimer (Lewiston, NY: Edwin Mellen Press, 2003).

34. Karl Marx and Friedrich Engels, *The German Ideology* (London: Lawrence and Wishart, 1982), p. 42.

35. Plato, *Protagoras*, revised edition, translated with notes by C. C. W. Taylor (Oxford: Oxford University Press, 1981), p. 14. See also T. Cole, *Democritus and the Sources of Greek Anthropology* (Ann Arbor: Michigan University Press, 1967) and Aristotle, *The Politics of Aristotle*, translated with notes by Ernest Baker (Oxford: Clarendon Press, 1948), 1256 b23.

36. Marx and Engels, *The German Ideology*, p. 51.

37. Ibid.

38. Ibid.

39. Aristotle clearly equates war between humans and animals and war between humans and sees both as the exercise of political skills. '[If it is evident that there is thus a natural provision for food at birth, and during growth,] it is equally evident that we must believe that

similar provision is also made for adults. Plants exist to give sustenance to animals, and animals to give it to men. Animals, when
they are domesticated, serve for use as well as for food; wild
animals too, in most cases if not in all, serve to furnish man not
only with food, but also with other comforts, such as the provision
of clothing and similar aids to life. Accordingly, as nature makes
nothing purposeless or in vain, all animals must have been made by
nature for the sake of men. It also follows that the art of war is in
some sense [that is to say, so far as it is directed to gaining the
means of subsistence from animals] a natural mode of acquisition.
Hunting is a part of that art; and hunting ought to be practised, not
only against wild animals, but also against human beings who are
intended by nature to be ruled by others and refuse to obey that
intention – because war of this order is naturally just.' Aristotle,
The Politics of Aristotle, pp. 25–26.

40. Marx and Engels, *The German Ideology*, pp. 51–52.
41. Jean-Pierre Vernant, 'Tensions and Ambiguities in Greek Tra-
    gedy', in Jean-Pierre Vernant and Pierre Vidal-Nacquet, *Myth
    and Tragedy in Ancient Greece*, translated by Janet Lloyd, (New
    York: Zone Books, 1990), p. 33. See also Vernant's 'The Historical
    Moment of Tragedy in Greece' in the same volume, where tragedy
    is seen as engaging a conflict between 'values, social practices,
    forms of religion, and types of human behaviour [that] represent
    for the city-state the very things that it has had to condemn and
    reject and against which it has had to fight in order to establish
    itself. At the same time, however, they are what it developed from
    and it remains integrally linked with them.' Vernant, in Vernant
    and Vidal-Nacquet, p. 27.
42. Jean-Pierre Vernant, 'The Tragic Subject: Historicity and Trans-
    historicity', in Jean-Pierre Vernant and Pierre Vidal-Nacquet, *Myth
    and Tragedy in Ancient Greece*, p. 238. Perhaps the fact that Vernant
    and Vidal-Nacquet are themselves guided in their analysis by cat-
    egories and structures of thought derived from Marx should also be
    acknowledged at this point.
43. There is, of course, a significant body of literature testifying to
    attempts to divine the origins of tragedy itself, attempts which
    inevitably speculate as to the nature of the pre-tragic. The only
    consensus around which the major contributions to this literature
    (from Aristotle, through Nietzsche, to the Cambridge Ritualists
    and Richard Schechner) could possibly gather is that there is no
    adequate answer.
44. Aby Warburg, 'Images from the Region of the Pueblo Indians of
    North America', in *The Art of Art History: a critical anthology*, edited
    by Donald Preziosi (Oxford: Oxford University Press, 1998), pp.
    177–206.

45. See E. H. Gombrich, *Aby Warburg: an intellectual biography* (London: The Warburg Institute 1970), p. 216.
46. See Ibid., p. 91., n1.
47. Warburg, in Preziosi, *The Art of Art History*, p. 187.
48. Ibid., p. 192.
49. Ibid., p. 204.
50. In both *Giulio Cesare* and *Genesi: from the museum of sleep* the animals appear amid functioning technologies, of speech enhancement or distortion (artificial voice-box, helium canister), vision enhancement (endoscope) and, most pointedly, animatronics which variously make chairs walk across stage, stage floors rise and fall as if breathing, cats perform ironic comment and a robot humanoid applaud the end of the show. The co-presence of technologically mediated humans, free-standing technological devices and live animals seems designed to foreground the producedness of every thing as well as their possession of 'anima' and more generally, therefore, an effacement of generally accepted ontological distinctions between animal, human and machine.
51. The fates of the Ritualist hypothesis and subsequent efforts to make ritual in general and sacrifice in particular the direct precursor of tragic drama are judiciously summarised by Simon Goldhill, in his chapter 'Modern critical approaches to Greek tragedy', in *The Cambridge Companion to Greek Tragedy*, edited by P. E. Easterling (Cambridge: Cambridge University Press, 1997), pp. 331–336. See also Helene P. Foley, *Ritual Irony: poetry and sacrifice in Euripides* (Ithaca, NY: Cornell University Press, 1985), who additionally addresses the account of sacrifice offered by Georges Bataille.
52. Michael H. Jameson, 'The spectacular and the obscure in Athenian religion', in *Performance Culture and Athenian Democracy*, edited by Simon Goldhill and Robin Osborne (Cambridge: Cambridge University Press, 1999), p. 321.
53. Vidal-Nacquet, 'Hunting and Sacrifice in Aeschylus's *Oresteia*', in Vernant and Vidal-Nacquet, pp. 141–159.
54. Ibid., p. 152.
55. Marcel Detienne, 'Culinary Practices and the Spirit of Sacrifice', in *The Cuisine of Sacrifice Among the Greeks*, edited by Marcel Detienne and Jean-Pierre Vernant translated by Paula Wissing (Chicago and London: University of Chicago Press, 1989), p. 9.
56. Ibid., p. 9.
57. The figure of '. . .VSKIJ' refers to Stanislavski, who famously played the role of Brutus himself, and whose commitment to units and lines of action underpinned his acting technique, used here as a mocking comment on Brutus's 'uneasy caution'. It is the figure of '. . .VSKIJ' who appears at the start of the performance, and uses

the endoscope, displaying the inner self upon which, in Stanislavskian technique, the exterior show of the actor's character is based. An opening 'scandal of origins' which chimes perhaps with the revelation of theatre's own scandalous origins as elaborated in the discussion of sacrifice that follows below.

58. *Il Combattimento*, after Monteverdi's *Combattimento di Tancredi e Clorinda*, Socìetas Raffaello Sanzio, 2000.
59. Theodor Adorno and Max Horkheimer, *The Dialectic of Enlightenment*, translated by John Cumming (London: Verso, 1997), p. 10.
60. Bert O. States, *Great Reckonings in Little Rooms*, p. 37.
61. Simon Jarvis, *Adorno: a critical introduction* (Cambridge: Polity Press, 1998), p. 30.
62. *Orestea (una commedia organica?)*, in Castellucci C., Castellucci R. and Guidi, *Epopea della polvere*, p. 130. 'The body of the goat itself has started breathing again, albeit fictitiously.' Author's translation.
63. Ibid. 'exclaims, under her breath, King Agamemnon is alive.'
64. Jacques Derrida, 'The Animal that Therefore I Am (More to Follow)', translated by David Wills, *Critical Inquiry*, 28:2 (2002), pp. 369–418 (p. 372).
65. Ibid., p. 373.

4. MUTUAL PREDICAMENTS: CORPSING AND FIASCO

1. See, especially, Mikhail Bakhtin, *Rabelais and His World*, translated by Hélène Iswolsky (Bloomington and Indianapolis: Indiana University Press, 1984).
2. Howard Barker, '49 Asides for a Tragic Theatre', in *Arguments for a Theatre* (London: John Calder, 1989), p. 12, p. 11.
3. *Disco Relax*, directed by Tim Etchells, seen at Forced Entertainment's studio in Sheffield and again at Toynbee Hall, London, February and March 2000.
4. The origins and possible meanings of this term are discussed below.
5. *Oxford English Dictionary, Second Edition*, edited by J. A. Simpson and E. S. C. Weiner (Oxford: Clarendon Press, 1989).
6. *A Dictionary of Slang and Unconventional English* (London and New York: Routledge, 1994).
7. *Slang and its Analogues Past and Present* (New York: Routledge, 1965).
8. Susan Sontag, 'Notes on Camp', in *Against Interpretation* (London: Vintage, 1994), p. 287.
9. *A Dictionary of American Slang, Second Supplemented Edition* (New York: Thomas Y. Crowell, 1975).
10. *The Cassell Dictionary of Slang* (London: Cassell, 1998).
11. In conversation with the author.

12. Kenneth Branagh, *Beginning* (London: Pan Books, 1990), p. 94.
13. Ibid., pp. 100–101.
14. Ibid., pp. 168–169.
15. *Courtney and Tovia's First Time*, Magic Touch Productions, 1998.
16. *The Philosophy of Laughter and Humor* edited by John Morreal (Albany: State University of New York Press, 1987).
17. V. K. Krishna Menon, *A Theory of Laughter: with special relation to comedy and tragedy* (London: George Allen & Unwin Ltd., 1931), p. 17.
18. I am grateful to Simon Bayly for my encounter with Joubert's work.
19. Laurent Joubert, *Treatise on Laughter*, translated and annotated by Gregory David de Rocher (Auburn: The University of Alabama Press, 1980), p. 61, p. 76.
20. Ibid., p. 28.
21. Bakhtin, *Rabelais and His World*, p. 68.
22. D. Diane Davis, *Breaking Up [at] Totality: A Rhetoric of Laughter* (Carbondale and Edwardsville: Southern Illinois University Press, 2000).
23. Ibid., p. 22.
24. Ibid., p. 68.
25. Terry Eagleton, *Walter Benjamin or Towards a Revolutionary Criticism* (London: Verso, 1981), p. 150.
26. Steven Connor, 'The Shakes: Conditions of Tremor', http://www.bbk.ac.uk/english/skc/shakes.
27. Bakhtin, *Rabelais and His World*, p. 19.
28. The use of the term 'clown' here signals that the kind of improvisation discussed here is that which lies at the heart of the work of Jacques Lecoq and the many actors and companies who have made work under the influence of his teaching. In the UK, notable practitioners of such work include Theatre de Complicité, The Right Size and Told By an Idiot. The moment of fiasco described in this chapter was from a performance made in collaboration with founder members of Told By an Idiot in 1992. I am grateful in particular to Paul Hunter, Hayley Carmichael (of Told by an Idiot) and the performance's director Roxana Silbert, for the way in which their practice in this area has illuminated the present project, through many years of association and collaboration.
29. *Oxford English Dictionary*.
30. Adrian Heathfield, 'Last Laughs,' performance/paper, Queen Mary, University of London, February 2003.
31. In Simon Bayly, 'A Pathognomy of Performance: Theatre, Philosophy and the Ethics of interruption', Ph. D. dissertation, University of Surrey, 2002, pp. 25–26.
32. Nicholas Ridout, 'Who Does Cathy Naden Think She is?', unpublished paper given at the American Society for Theatre Research

Annual Conference, CUNY Graduate Centre, New York, November 2000.

33. Bayly, *A Pathognomy of perfomance*, p. 25.
34. Ibid.
35. 'He may not be able to prevent "the fright" creeping over him, but he can discipline himself so as to control it sufficiently to avoid a *fiasco*, and likewise to prevent his real condition being perceived, except perhaps, by the keenest observer. His duty is to give pleasure to the audience, not to make them uncomfortable.' Adolf Kielblock, *The Stage Fright, or How to Face an Audience* (Boston: Press of Geo. H. Ellis, 1891), p. 57.
36. Bayly, *A Pathognomy of Performance*, p. 44.
37. The company first made work together in 1984. The present analysis arises out of frequent encounters with the company's work, beginning in 1987 with the London run of *Let the Water Run Its Course (To The Sea Which Made The Promise)*. Work seen in this period therefore includes *200% and Bloody Thirsty, Emmanuelle Enchanted, Club of No Regrets, Hidden J, Showtime, Pleasure, Speak Bitterness, Quizoola, Dirty Work, Disco Relax, Who Will Sing a Song to Unfrighten Me?, First Night, The Travels* and *Bloody Mess*.
38. *Who Will Sing A Song to Unfrighten Me?*, Forced Entertainment at the Queen Elizabeth Hall, as part of the London International Festival of Theatre, 1999.
39. Tim Etchells, 'On the Skids: Some Years of Acting Animals', *Performance Research 5:2: On Animals* (2000), pp. 55–60, (p. 58).
40. Ibid., p. 58.
41. Ibid., p. 58.
42. Ibid., p. 58.
43. Ibid., p. 58.
44. See, for example, 'Speech Snapshot', in *The Inhuman*, pp. 129–134.
45. Jean-François Lyotard, *Libidinal Economy*, translated by Ian Hamilton Grant (London: Athlone, 1993).
46. A term that originates with Antonin Artaud and which is used by Deleuze and Guattari, principally in *A Thousand Plateaus: Capitalism and Schizophrenia*, translated by Brian Massumi (London: Athlone, 1988), pp. 149–166.
47. Lyotard, *Libidinal Economy*, p. 2.
48. Ibid., p. 3.
49. Geoffrey Bennington, *Lyotard: Writing the Event* (Manchester: Manchester University Press, 1988).
50. Lyotard, *Libidinal Economy*, p. 16.
51. Ibid., p. 26.
52. Bennington, *Lyotard: Writing the Event*, p. 27.
53. Jean-François Lyotard, 'The Tooth, the Palm', translated by Anne Knab and Michel Benamou, in *Mimesis, Masochism and Mime: The*

Politics of Theatricality in Contemporary French Thought, edited by Timothy Murray (Ann Arbor: University of Michigan Press, 1997).

54. Bennington, *Lyotard: Writing the Event*, p. 28.
55. Jean-François Lyotard, 'The God and the Puppet', in *The Inhuman*, p. 156.
56. Bennington, *Lyotard: Writing the Event*, p. 46.

AFTERWORD

1. Bert O. States, *Great Reckonings in Little Rooms: The Phenomenology of Theatre* (Berkeley and Los Angeles: University of California Press, 1985), pp. 197–198.
2. States, p. 202.
3. Marcel Mauss, *The Gift: The Form and Reason for Exchange in Archaic Societies*, translated by W. D. Halls (London: Routledge, 1990), 201n., p. 41.
4. These terms are Bataille's. See Georges Bataille, *The Accursed Share, Volume I*, translated by Robert Hurley (New York: Zone Books, 1988).
5. See George Bataille, 'The Notion of Expenditure', in *A Bataille Reader*, edited by Fred Botting and Scott Wilson (Oxford: Blackwell, 1997), p. 168.
6. That the company maintain a tense relationship with applause is evident at almost every performance, with applause seeming to emerge from the audience only after the passage of a few moments of uncertainty or disquiet. That this is the result of deliberation on the company's part might reasonably be assumed from the fate of the acephalous robot in *Genesi*, which bangs its metal hands together at the end of Act One, only to suffer the indignity of rubble being dumped on its non-existent head.
7. Geoffrey Bennington, *Lyotard: Writing the Event* (Manchester: Manchester University Press, 1998), p. 28.

Bibliography

Aaron, Stephen, *Stage Fright: Its Role in Acting* (Chicago and London: University of Chicago Press, 1986).

Adorno, Theodor and Max Horkheimer, *The Dialectic of Enlightenment*, trans. John Cumming (London: Verso, 1997).

Aeschylus, *Oresteia: The Eumenides*, trans. Richmond Lattimore (Chicago: University of Chicago Press, 1953).

Agamben, Giorgio, *Homo Sacer: Sovereign Power and Bare Life*, trans. Daniel Heller-Roazen (Stanford: Stanford University Press, 1998).

Remnants of Auschwitz: The Witness and the Archive, trans. Daniel Heller-Roazen (New York: Zone Books, 1999).

Means Without End: Notes on Politics, trans. Vincenzo Binetti and Cesare Casarino (Minneapolis and London: University of Minnesota Press, 2000).

L'aperto: l'uomo e l'animale (Torino: Bollati Boringhieri, 2002).

Archer, William, *Masks or Faces? A study in the psychology of acting* (London: Longman, 1888).

Aristotle, *The Politics*, trans. Ernest Baker (Oxford: Clarendon Press, 1948).

The Poetics, trans. Malcolm Heath (Harmondsworth: Penguin Books, 1996).

Auslander, Philip, *From Acting to Performance: Essays in Modernism and Postmodernism* (New York and London: Routledge, 1997).

Artaud, Antonin, *The Theatre and Its Double*, trans. Victor Corti (Montreuil, London, New York: Calder, 1993).

Bachofen, Johann Jakob, *Mutterrecht. English. Selections, An English Translation of Bachofen's Mutterrecht (Mother Right) (1861): a study of the religious and juridical aspects of gynecocracy in the ancient world*, trans. Edward Partenheimer (Lewiston, NY: Edwin Mellen Press, 2003).

Baker, Steve, *The Postmodern Animal* (London: Reaktion Books, 2000).

Bakhtin, Mikhail, *Rabelais and His World*, trans. Hélène Iswolsky (Bloomington and Indianapolis: Indiana University Press, 1984).

Banes, Sally, *Terpsichore in Sneakers: Postmodern Dance* (Middletown, CT: Wesleyan University Press, 1987).

Writing Dancing in the Age of Postmodernism (Hanover, NH: Wesleyan University Press/University Press of New England, 1994).

Barber, Stephen, *Antonin Artaud: Blows and Bombs* (London: Faber and Faber, 1993).

Barish, Jonas, *The Antitheatrical Prejudice* (Berkeley and Los Angeles: University of California Press, 1981).

Barker, Howard, *Arguments for a Theatre* (London: Calder, 1989).

Barthes, Roland, *Critical Essays*, trans. Richard Howard (Evanston: Northwestern University Press, 1972).

The Rustle of Language, trans. Richard Howard (Berkeley and Los Angeles: University of California Press, 1989).

Bataille, Georges, *The Accursed Share, Volume I*, trans. Robert Hurley (New York: Zone Books, 1988).

A Bataille Reader, eds. Fred Botting and Scott Wilson (Oxford: Blackwell, 1997).

Bayly, Simon, 'A Pathognomy of Performance: Theatre, Philosophy and the Ethics of Interruption', Ph.D. dissertation, University of Surrey, 2002.

Benedetti, Jean, ed. *The Moscow Art Theatre Letters* (London: Methuen, 1991).

Benedict, Ruth, *The Chrysanthemum and the Sword: Patterns of Japanese Culture* (London: Routledge and Kegan Paul, 1977).

Benjamin, Walter, *Illuminations*, trans. Harry Zohn (London: Fontana, 1973).

Charles Baudelaire, trans. Harry Zohn (London and New York: Verso, 1997).

The Origin of German Tragic Drama, trans. John Osborne (London and New York: Verso, 1998).

Understanding Brecht, trans. Anna Bostock (London and New York: Verso, 1998).

Bennett, Susan, *Theatre Audiences: A Theory of Production and Reception* (London and New York: Routledge, 1997).

Bennington, Geoffrey, *Lyotard: Writing the Event* (Manchester: Manchester University Press, 1988).

Berger, Harry, Jr., *Imaginary Audition: Shakespeare on Stage and Page* (Berkeley and Los Angeles: University of California Press, 1989).

Bergson, Henri, *Laughter: An Essay on The Meaning of the Comic*, trans. Cloudesley Brereton and Fred Rothwell (New York: Macmillan, 1911).

Berman, Marshall, *All That Is Solid Melts Into Air: The Experience of Modernity* (London and New York: Verso, 1983).

Bernasconi, Robert and Critchley, Simon, eds. *Re-reading Levinas* (London: Athlone, 1991).

Billington, Michael, 'Bleak Russians at the Purcell Room', *The Guardian*, January 15, 2001.

Blau, Herbert, *The Audience* (Baltimore and London: The Johns Hopkins University Press, 1990).

Branagh, Kenneth, *Beginning* (London: Pan Books, 1990).

Brandt, George, ed. *Modern Theories of Drama* (Oxford: Clarendon Press, 1988).

Brecht, Bertolt, *Brecht on Theatre: The Development of an Aesthetic*, trans. John Willett (London: Methuen, 1964).

Bresson, Robert, *Notes on the Cinematographer*, trans. Jonathan Griffin (London: Quartet Encounters, 1986).

Buck-Morss, Susan, *The Dialectics of Seeing: Walter Benjamin and the Arcades Project* (Cambridge, MA: MIT Press, 1989).

Campbell, Patrick and Adrian Kear, *Psychoanalysis and Performance* (London and New York: Routledge, 2000).

Carlson, Marvin, *Places of Performance* (Ithaca: Cornell University Press, 1989).

Performance: a critical introduction (London and New York: Routledge, 1996).

Castellucci, Claudia and Romeo Castellucci, *Les pèlerins de la matière: théorie et praxis du théâtre. Écrits de la Socìetas Raffaello Sanzio*, trans. Karin Espinosa (Besançon: Les Solitaires Intempestifs, 2001).

Castellucci, Romeo, 'The Animal Being on Stage', trans. Carolina Melis, Valentina Valentini and Ric Allsopp, in *Performance Research 5:2 On Animals* (2000), 23–28.

Castellucci, Claudia, Romeo, Castellucci and Chiara Guidi, *Epopea delle polvere* (Milan: Socìetas Raffaello Sanzio/Ubulibri, 2001).

Ching, James, *Performer and Audience: An Investigation into the psychological causes of Anxiety and Nervousness in Playing, Singing or Speaking Before an Audience* (Oxford: Hall the Publisher Ltd., 1947).

Chothia, Jean, *André Antoine* (Cambridge: Cambridge University Press, 1991).

Cole, T., *Democritus and the Sources of Greek Anthropology* (Ann Arbor: Michigan University Press, 1967).

Connor, Steven, *Theory and Cultural Value* (Oxford: Blackwell, 1992).

Postmodernist Culture (Oxford: Blackwell, 1997).

'The Shakes: Conditions of Tremor', www.bbk.ac.uk/eh/eng/skc/shakes

Conrad, Peter, 'Shakespeare Made Sick', *The Observer*, June 6, 1999.

Counsell, Colin, *Signs of Performance: An Introduction to Twentieth Century Theatre* (London: Routledge, 1996).

Critchley, Simon, *Ethics-Politics-Subjectivity: Essays on Derrida, Levinas and Contemporary French Thought* (London and New York: Verso, 1999).

Darwin, Charles, *The Expression of Emotion in Man and Animals*, ed. Paul Ekman (London: HarperCollins, 1998).

Davis, D. Diane, *Breaking Up [at] Totality: A Rhetoric of Laughter* (Carbondale and Edwardsville: Southern Illinois University Press, 2000).

Deleuze, Gilles, *Cinema 1: The Movement-Image*, trans. Hugh Tomlinson and Barbara Habberjam (London: Athlone, 1986).

Cinema 2: The Time-Image, trans. Hugh Tomlinson and Robert Galeta (London: Athlone, 1989).

Deleuze, Gilles and Félix Guattari, *Anti-Oedipus: Capitalism and Schizophrenia*, trans. Robert Hurley, Mark Seem and Helen R. Lane (London: Athlone, 1984).

Kafka: Toward a Minor Literature, trans. Dana Polan (Minneapolis and London: University of Minnesota Press, 1986).

A Thousand Plateaus: Capitalism and Schizophrenia, trans. Brian Massumi (London: Athlone, 1988).

De Man, Paul, *The Rhetoric of Romanticism* (New York: Columbia University Press, 1984).

Aesthetic Ideology (Minneapolis and London: University of Minnesota Press, 1996).

Derrida, Jacques, *Writing and Difference*, trans. Alan Bass (London and Henley: Routledge and Kegan Paul, 1978).

'The Animal That Therefore I Am (More to Follow)', trans. David Wills, *Critical Inquiry* 28:2 (2002), 369–418.

Detienne, Marcel and Jean-Pierre Vernant, eds. *The Cuisine of Sacrifice Among the Greeks*, trans. Paula Wissing (Chicago and London: University of Chicago Press, 1989).

Diamond, Elin, ed. *Performance and Cultural Politics* (London and New York: Routledge, 1996).

Diderot, Denis de, *Selected Writings on Art and Literature*, trans. Geofrrey Bremner (Harmondsworth: Penguin Books, 2001).

Eagleton, Terry, *Walter Benjamin or Towards a Revolutionary Criticism* (London: Verso, 1981).

The Ideology of the Aesthetic (Oxford: Blackwell, 1990).

Sweet Violence: The Idea of the Tragic (Oxford: Blackwell, 2003).

Easterling, P. E., ed. *The Cambridge Companion to Greek Tragedy* (Cambridge: Cambridge University Press, 1997).

Ekman, Paul, *Emotion in the Human Face* (Cambridge: Cambridge University Press, 1982).

Escolme, Bridget, *Talking to the Audience: Shakespeare, Performance, Self* (London and New York: Routledge, 2005).

Etchells, Tim, 'On the Skids: Some Years of Acting Animals', *Performance Research 5:2: On Animals* (2000), pp. 55–60.

Farmer, John S. and William Ernest Henley, *Slang and Its Analogues Past and Present*, New York: Kraus Reprint Corporation, 1965.

Ferenczi, Sandor, *Further Contributions to the Theory and Technique of Psychoanalysis* (New York: Basic Books, 1952).

Foley, Helene, P., *Ritual Irony: poetry and sacrifice in Euripides* (Ithaca: Cornell University Press, 1985).

Foreman, Richard, *Unbalancing Acts: Foundations for a Theater* (New York: Theatre Communications Group, 1992).

Freud, Sigmund, *On Metapsychology: The Theory of Psychoanalysis*, trans. James Strachey et al., (Harmondsworth: Penguin, 1984).

Pre-Psycho-Analytic Publications and Unpublished Drafts, trans. James Strachey et al. (London: Vintage, 2001).

Fried, Michael, *Art and Objecthood: Essays and Reviews* (Chicago and London: University of Chicago Press, 1998).

Gabbard, Glen O., 'Stage Fright', *International Journal of Psychoanalysis*, 60 (1979), 383–392.

'Further contributions to the understanding of stage fright: Narcissistic issues', *Journal of the American Pyschoanalytic Association*, 31 (1983), 423–441.

Garner, Jr., Stanton, B., *Bodied Spaces: Phenomenology and Performance in Contemporary Drama* (Ithaca and London: Cornell Univesity Press, 1994).

Geertz, Clifford, *The Interpretation of Culture* (New York: Basic Books, 1973).

Works and Lives: The Anthropologist and Author (Cambridge: Polity Press, 1989).

Goffman, Erving, *Interaction Ritual: Essays in Face-to-face Behaviour* (London: Allen Lane, 1972).

Goldhill, Simon and Robin Osborne, eds. *Performance Culture and Athenian Democracy* (Cambridge: Cambridge University Press, 1999).

Gombrich, E. H., *Aby Warburg: an intellectual biography* (London: The Warburg Institute, 1970).

Gurr, Andrew, *The Shakespearean Stage 1574–1642* (Cambridge: Cambridge University Press, 1992).

Harrison, Charles and Paul Wood, *Art in Theory: An Anthology of Changing Ideas, 1900–1990* (Oxford: Blackwell, 1992).

Harvey, David, *The Condition of Postmodernity* (Oxford: Blackwell, 1990).

Havas, Kato, *Stage Fright: its causes and cures, with special reference to violin playing* (London: Bosworth, 1973).

Heathfield, Adrian, 'Last Laughs', performance/paper, Queen Mary University of London, February 2003.

Hegel, G. W. F., *Introductory Lectures on Aesthetics*, trans. Bernard Bosanquet (Harmondsworth: Penguin Books, 1993).

Heidergger, Martin, *The Fundamental Concepts of Metaphysics*, trans. William McNeill and Nicholas Walker (Bloomington and Indianapolis: Indiana University Press, 1995).

Hodge, Alison, ed. *Twentieth Century Actor Training* (London and New York: Routledge, 2000).

Hunt, H. Ernest, *Nerve Control: The Cure of Nervousness and Stage Fright* (London: William Richer and Son Ltd., 1915).

Ibsen, Henrik, *Ghosts*, trans. Michael Meyer (London: Eyre Methuen, 1973).

Jackson, Shannon, 'Professing Performance: Disciplinary Genealogies', *TDR* 45:1 (2001), 84–95.

James, Henry, *The Tragic Muse* (New York: Charles Scribner's Sons, 1936).

Jameson, Fredric, *The Political Unconcious: Narrative as a Socially Symbolic Act* (London: Routledge, 1996).

Jarvis, Simon, *Adorno: a critical introduction* (Cambridge: Polity Press, 1998).

Joubert, Laurent, *Treatise on Laughter*, trans. Gregory David de Rocher (Auburn: The University of Alabama Press, 1980).

Kant, Immanuel, *Critique of Judgement*, trans. Werner S. Pluhar (Indianapolis and Cambridge: Hackett, 1987).

Kaplan, Donald, 'On Stage Fright', *TDR* 14:1 (1969), 60–83.

Kaye Nick, *Postmodernism and Performance* (Basingstoke and London: Macmillan, 1994).

Kaye, Nick, ed. *Art Into Theatre: Performance Interviews and Documents* (Amsterdam: Harwood Academic Publishers, 1996).

Kelly, Veronica and Dorothea von Mücke, eds. *Body and Text in the Eighteenth Century* (Stanford: Stanford University Press, 1994).

Kershaw, Baz, *The Radical in Performance: Between Brecht and Baudrillard* (Routledge: London and New York, 1999).

Keyssar, Helene, 'I Love You. Who Are You? The Strategy of Drama in Recognition Scenes', *PMLA* 92 (1977), 297–306.

Kielblock, Adolph, *The Stage Fright, or How to Face an Audience* (Boston: Press of Geo. H. Ellis, 1891).

Kleist, Heinrich von, *Selected Writings*, ed. and trans. David Constantine (London: J. M. Dent, 1997).

Konijn, Elly A., *Acting Emotions: Shaping Emotions on Stage* (Amsterdam: Amsterdam University Press, 2000).

Krauss, Rosalind, *The Originality of the Avant-Garde and Other Modernist Myths* (Cambridge, MA: MIT Press, 1986).

Kristeva, Julia, *Powers of Horror: An Essay in Abjection*, trans. Leon S. Roudiez (New York: Columbia University Press, 1982).

Leacroft, Richard, *The Development of the English Playhouse* (London and New York: Methuen, 1988).

Levinas, Emmanuel, *Totality and Infinity*, trans. Alphonso Lingis (Pittsburgh: Duquesne University Press, 1969).

De l'évasion (Paris: Fata Morgana, 1982).

Lynd, Helen Merrell, *Shame and the Search for Identity* (London: Routledge and Kegan Paul, 1958).

Lyotard, Jean-François, *The Inhuman: Reflections on Time*, trans. Geoffrey Bennington and Rachel Bowlby (Cambridge: Polity Press, 1991).

Libidinal Economy, trans. Ian Hamilton Grant (London: Athlone, 1993).

Marx, Karl and Friedrich Engels, *The German Ideology* (London: Lawrence and Wishart, 1982).

Mauss, Marcel, *The Gift: The Form and Reason for Exchange in Archaic Societies*, trans. W. D. Halls (London: Routledge, 1990).

McKenzie, Jon, *Perform or Else: From Discipline to Performance* (London and New York: Routledge, 2001).

Menon, V. K. Krishna, *A Theory of Laughter with special relation to Comedy and Tragedy* (London: George Allen and Unwin Ltd., 1931).

Morreal, John, ed. *The Philosophy of Laughter and Humor* (Albany: State University of New York Press, 1987).

Mullin, Donald C., *The Development of the Playhouse* (Berkeley and Los Angeles: University of California Press, 1970).

Murray, Timothy, ed. *Mimesis, Masochism and Mime: The Politics of Theatricality in Contemporary French Thought* (Ann Arbor: University of Michigan Press, 1997).

Nietzsche, Friedrich, *The Birth of Tragedy from the Spirit of Music*, trans. Francis Golffing (Garden City: Doubleday, 1956).

Partridge, Eric, *A Dictionary of Slang and Unconventional English*, ed. Paul Beale (London and New York: Routledge, 1994).

Pearson, Keith Ansell, *Germinal Life: the difference and repetition of Deleuze* (London: Routledge, 1999).

Peterson, Michael, 'Stubborn as a Mule: Non-Human Performers and the Limits of Semiotics', unpublished paper given at the American Society for Theatre Research Annual Conference, CUNY Graduate Center, New York, November 2000.

Penzel, Frederick, *Stage Lighting Before Electricity* (Middleton, CT: Wesleyan University Press, 1978).

Phelan, Peggy, *Unmarked: the politics of performance* (London and New York: Routledge 1993).

Phelan, Peggy and Jill Lane, *The Ends of Performance* (New York and London: New York University Press, 1998).

Plato, *Protagoras*, trans. C. C. W. Taylor (Oxford: Oxford University Press, 1981).

The Republic, trans. Desmond Lee (Harmondsworth: Penguin Books, 1987).

Pontbriand, Chantal, 'The eye finds no fixed point on which to rest . . .', trans. C. R. Parsons, *Modern Drama* 25:1 (1982), 154–162.

Preziosi, Donald, ed. *The Art of Art History: a critical anthology* (Oxford: Oxford University Press, 1998).

Proust, Marcel, *Remembrance of Things Past, Volume I*, trans. C. K. Scott Moncrieff and Terence Kilmartin (Harmondsworth: Penguin Books, 1983).

Puchner, Martin, *Stage Fright: Modernism, Antitheatricality and Drama* (Baltimore: Johns Hopkins University Press, 2002).

Read, Alan, *The Theatre and Everyday Life: An Ethics of Performance* (London and New York: Routledge, 1993).

'Prodigious Performance: Infants, Animals and Other Anomalies', Inaugural Lecture, Roehampton, University of Surrey, 2002.

Rees, Terence, *Theatre Lighting in the Age of Gas* (London: The Society for Theatre Research, 1978).

Ricks, Christopher, *Keats and Embarrassment* (Oxford: Clarendon Press, 1974).

Ritchie, W., *Nervousness and Stage Fright: A Never-failing Remedy* (45, Radnor Drive, Liscard, Cheshire: W. Ritchie 1915).

Ridout, Nicholas, 'Who Does Cathy Naden Think She Is?', unpublished paper given at the American Society for Theatre Research Annual Conference, CUNY Graduate Center, New York, November 2000.

Roach, Joseph, *The Player's Passion: Studies in the Science of Acting* (Ann Arbor: University of Michigan Press, 1993).

Sartre, Jean-Paul, *Being and Nothingness: An Essay of Phenomenological Ontology*, trans. Hazel E. Barnes (London: Routledge, 1989).

Sayre, Henry, *The Object of Performance: The American Avant-Garde since 1970* (Chicago: Chicago University Press, 1989).

Schechner, Richard, *Performance Theory* (New York and London: Routledge, 1988).

Performance Studies (New York and London: Routledge, 2002).

Schechner, Richard and Willa Appel, eds. *By Means of Performance: intercultural studies of theatre and ritual* (Cambridge: Cambridge University Press, 1990).

Schivelbusch, Wolfgang, *Disenchanted Night: The Industrialisation of Light in the Nineteenth Century* (Berkeley and Los Angeles: University of California Press, 1995).

Schneider, Rebecca, *The Explicit Body in Performance* (London and New York: Routledge, 1997).

Sennett, Richard, *The Fall of Public Man* (New York and London: W. W. Norton, 1992).

Flesh and Stone: The Body and the City in Western Civilization (Harmondsworth: Penguin Books, 2002).

Shakespeare, William, *The Complete Works* (New York: Viking, 1977).

Simpson, J. A. and E. S. C. Weiner, eds. *Oxford English Dictionary, Second Edition* (Oxford: Clarendon Press, 1989).

Smith, Anne-Marie, *Julia Kristeva: Speaking the Unspeakable* (London: Pluto, 1998).

Sontag, Susan, *Against Interpretation* (London: Vintage, 1994).

Stanislavski, Constantin, *An Actor Prepares*, trans. Elizabeth Reynolds Hapgood (London: Methuen, 1988).

States, Bert O., 'Phenomenology of the Curtain Call', *Hudson Review* 34 (1981), 371–380.

'The Dog on Stage: Theatre as Phenomenon', *New Literary History*, *XIV* (1983) 373–388.

Great Reckonings in Little Rooms: The Phenomenology of Theater (Berkeley and Los Angeles: University of California Press, 1985).

Tomkins, Silvan, *Affect, Imagery, Consciousness, Volume 2, The Negative Affects* (New York: Springer, 1963).

Turner, Victor, *From Ritual to Theatre: The Human Seriousness of Play* (New York: Performing Asts Journal Press, 1982).

The Anthropology of Performance (New York: PAJ Publications, 1986).

Vernant, Jean-Pierre and Pierre Vidal-Nacquet, *Myth and Tragedy in Ancient Greece*, trans. Janet Lloyd (New York: Zone Books, 1990).

Walkerdine, Valerie, *Daddy's Girl: Young Girls and Popular Culture* (Cambridge, MA: Harvard University Press, 1997).

Wentworth, Marold and Stuart Berg Flexner, eds. *A Dictionary of American Slang, Second Supplemented Edition* (New York: Thomas Y Crowell, 1975).

Williams, David, 'The Right Horse, the Animal Eye – Bartabas and Théâtre Zingaro', *Performance Research 5:2 On Animals* (2000), 29–40.

Worthen, W. B., *Shakespeare and the Authority of Performance* (Cambridge: Cambridge University Press, 1997).

Wurmser, Léon, *The Masks of Shame* (Northvale, NJ: James Aronson Inc., 1994).

Zarrilli, Phillip B., ed. *Acting (Re)Considered: Theories and Practices* (London and New York: Routledge, 1995).

Index

Lightning Source UK Ltd.
Milton Keynes UK
UKOW03f1804250914

239195UK00001B/34/P